Many Sides
Debate Across the Curriculum

Revised edition

Many Sides
Debate Across the Curriculum

Revised edition

Alfred Snider and Maxwell Schnurer

International Debate Education Association
New York · Amsterdam · Brussels

Published by
International Debate Education Association
400 West 59th Street
New York, NY 10019

Library of Congress Cataloging-in-Publication Data
Snider, Alfred.
 Many sides : debate across the curriculum / Alfred Snider & Maxwell
Schnurer.-- Rev. ed.
    p. cm.
 ISBN 1-932716-17-3
        978-1-932716-17-7
 1. Debates and debating. I. Schnurer, Maxwell. II. Title.
 PN4181.S66 2006
 808.5'3--dc22
                        2005036035

Printed in the United States of America

 **IDEBATE Press Books**

Contents

Foreword

The history of education reform shows a variety of movements that have met resistance from the expectations of the cultural status quo. The current trend toward instructional techniques that enfranchise a partnership between students and teachers to construct both learning environments and actual learning are no better embodied than in the Debate Across the Curriculum (DAC) method. This instructional tool employs the process of classroom debate to teach in virtually all of the intellectual disciplines in a school.

Alfred Snider and Maxwell Schnurer have written the first definitive book on the DAC process and application. Snider has been a powerful advocate of academic debate for more than 30 years. A nationally prominent intercollegiate debate coach, his experience in pioneering debate education for inner city students through the Urban Debate League national curricular reform movement has been applied to the international debate community. He has pioneered the use of the Internet to promote debating everywhere. He has personally helped to promote discussion and debate in the People's Republic of China, Chile, South Korea, Serbia, and many of the former Soviet Union satellite countries. Many of the concepts in this book were field tested at his internationally recognized World Debate Institute at the University of Vermont.

Maxwell Schnurer, a former student of Snider's, has developed his own reputation as a nationally ranked intercollegiate debate coach and pioneer in classroom applications of competitive debate. As an assistant coach at Wake Forest and the University of Pittsburgh, as the director of debate at Marist College, and now at Humboldt State University, Schnurer committed to working with novice and beginning debaters, emphasizing the transformative nature of the debate activity. In addition to being a top national judge and coach of policy debate competition in the United States, he has placed great emphasis on political activism, including animal rights, social justice, environmentalism, and gender issues. Schnurer has also been an innovator in the areas of public debate and debate outreach, staging numerous public debates and engaging in debate outreach programs in Pennsylvania, New York, California, and nationwide. He represented the United States on a debate tour of Japan, maintains international debate connections, and is always willing to explore debate in a new venue or space. He is a longtime faculty member at numerous debate institutes and has participated in extensive evaluation of the DAC process.

Academic tournament debate has a proven track record of teaching critical thinking at the middle school, high school, and college levels. Many have used debate in the non-speech classroom as an instructional tool that meets multiple educational objectives: interactive instruction, student-teacher partnership, democratic dialogue, student ownership of learning, experiential education, communication skills of listening and speaking, argument construction, cooperative learning, critical thinking, research (traditional and computer), strategic note taking, logical organization, critical reading, evaluation, and, not least, fun. Debate, both in and out of the classroom, is a profound example of cooperative learning that promotes critical thinking. A foundational tenet of debate is that competition supports intellectual achievement. Can cooperation also be possible in competition? On the competitive debate team, shared research allows students to participate in one another's successes, to be motivated to research harder following one another's defeats. On a highly functioning debate team, competition motivates individuals to cooperate for the good of the community as well as the individual. Snider and Schnurer demonstrate the power of that application in the classroom. Exploration of ideas and research gives rise to both individual and group ownership of learning. Teachers and students work together in ways that encourage partnerships for learning. Paulo Freire calls this collaboration the path to a liberating education, one that encourages democratic dialogue and critical thinking.

Democratic dialogue is a powerful antidote to traditional education's penchant for the development of authority dependence in students. Such dialogue has the capacity to open the student up to new ways of thinking and problem solving while encouraging the creativity of teachers. Snider and Schnurer illustrate this potential with unique format suggestions and creative methods of evaluation. The book is thorough in its approach to practical application in most academic disciplines while encouraging the synergy between student and teacher to invigorate the traditional roles of educational actors.

Over the last several years I had the privilege of using some of the curriculum materials from this work for a Providence Urban Debate League workshop for teachers at Brown University, a National Urban Debate League conference for teachers at Emory University, and to help train more than 400 teachers in schools serving students from all socioeconomic backgrounds in Atlanta, Miami, and Nashville. While the evaluations were exceptional, perhaps the most impressive result was the ease with which this material can be shared within a school, department by department. DAC has the possibility of creating genuine change in urban, suburban, and rural schools by engaging students and teachers in a rich conversation of mutual learning.

Melissa Maxcy Wade
Emory University

Preface

Debate changed my life because it taught me to listen. This may seem strange because most of us visualize debates as contests between strident advocates who are intent on pushing their points of view. For me, debate had the opposite effect. When I arrived at college I was already strident. A seasoned political activist, I was prone to polemic-laden political outbursts. Debate challenged me, and for the first time I was forced to examine my arguments with a critical lens.

Debaters were the first folks that I couldn't push around—they wanted to examine the evidence I was using to support my arguments, and they wanted me to explain myself. More important, my friends who were debaters often had good ideas of their own.

Curious about how students could develop these kinds of communication and critical thinking skills, I joined the Lawrence Debate Union at the University of Vermont. I quickly found myself addicted to debate. It was a method of learning that encouraged me to explore new ideas. I could mentally travel as fast as I wanted to—learning about new subjects and researching new areas of interest as my curiosity drove me. Debate stimulated and agitated my interested mind, driving me to ask more questions and to be reflective about the answers I had already decided. Debate was wonderful for me and helped mold me into the person that I am today.

The wonder and excitement that debate engendered within me can be experienced by anyone. Debates do not have to be formal events or even organized by schools. Debates are natural, exciting interactions between people who want to critically examine an issue. I believe that debate can be a format for community groups, activist organizations, social movements, political parties, friends, and businesses.

This perspective is not shared by all. Many believe that debate should be the special realm of political scientists, experts, "debaters," or communications departments. I fundamentally disagree. Debate should be in the hands of the people. Debate should be used in grade schools, in chemistry classes, and in as many places as there is interest. Debate should be everywhere.

This book represents a starting point for that vision. Encouraging the use of debate in classrooms is a reclaiming of the notion that debate is something sacred to be kept in a special place. Debate should never be cordoned off into special areas of academic inquiry. Instead, everyone should encounter it. I believe that the success of debate grows with familiarity, and I hope that debate will spread to have a contact with every person in the world. This book is for everyone who ever wanted to try debate. I hope that you will see the wonder.

I would like to sincerely thank my co-author and inspiration, Dr. A. C. "Tuna" Snider. You have been my mentor, guide, debate coach, and friend for many years. Your vision of debate for everyone is infectious, and I appreciate your energy and ideas. I would also like to thank Elena Cattaneo, who is a constant inspiration and my favorite mental sparring partner. Thanks to my mother Jai Holly for encouraging my activism and my frank dialogue. Thanks to all the activists who have kept me honest in a world worth fighting for! Thanks to Gordon Mitchell, a wonderful friend, whose spirit of open-mindedness and willingness to debate anywhere and with anyone permeates my writings in this book.

Thanks to all of my friends, debate coaches, colleagues, and debaters who have influenced me through the years.

Maxwell Schnurer
Humboldt State University

Preface

The first edition of this book looked to be the one and only when it was originally published. I anticipated a small niche audience among some teachers. Although certainly not a best-seller, the book turned out to be very popular in a variety of disciplines, at a variety of levels of the educational system, and in a variety of countries. It seems as if teachers, educators, students all over the world are searching for educational methods that are active, involve critical thinking, and ask students to integrate knowledge and improve communication skills. This is certainly one of those methods.

The appeal of debate in the classroom is that it deals with a skill set that students need for success in the 21st century. It is not the only way to teach these skills, but it is useful in that it bundles many of them together into one activity. "Debate" per se is not the palliative in our quest to better prepare students for personal and social success; it is the skill set that is useful. Debate is a way to engage students in that skill set.

I know more about how to use this technique than I did when the first edition was written. Although familiar with debating as well as teaching classes at the university level, I lacked a firm understanding of the classroom situation in high schools and middle schools in different settings. Many teachers and educators have helped me improve my understanding. Since the first edition was published, I have worked in many schools and in many countries to share my ideas and, most important to me, learn from others.

I want to thank some of these individuals. Kate Shuster of the Claremont Colleges Debate Outreach program has helped me modify and adjust my goals and means. Bojana Skrt of Slovenia has been a tireless advocate for debate across the curriculum and has been a powerful force for promoting this technique in the Slovenian national school system. Liana Miholic and Martina Domanjnko of Slovenia, dedicated teachers with a willingness to experiment, have been very instructive. All of the members of the panel on this subject at the 2004 International Debate Education Association conference in Istanbul helped me understand the intersection of theory and practice. Frank Duffin of the United States has provided me with very useful hard data on what the concept can actually mean to student achievement. I will always be indebted to the late Joan Smith for originally goading me to pursue this concept. Of course, my co-author Maxwell Schnurer has been a tireless innovator and effective critic in our work. I am not able to thank everyone I have worked with on this idea, but they know who they are and how grateful I am.

I want to thank Noel Selegzi of IDEA and Martin Greenwald of the Open Society Institute for their support of both volumes. Eleanora von Dehsen has been an excellent editor to work with.

I want to thank a location as well, my small house in Puertecitos, Baja California, Mexico, for providing a calm respite in which to write. It is easier to conceptualize while watching the tide go up and down, the pelicans fishing, and the fish jumping.

Finally, I want to thank Russell T. Davies for restoring hope to my world and a strong sense of savvy magic to the universe. I had faith, and he came through for me.

Now the task is to carry this idea forward, to improve implementation within school settings, and to assess and evaluate the outcomes of this technique. It will be a big task, but I know I will have a lot of help. My posse is huge and very able.

Alfred C. Snider
University of Vermont

Chapter One

~ ~ ~ ~

Introduction to Debate
as Educational Method

Alexander Meikeljohn, former president of Amherst College, said:

> I try to select from the long line of students, some one group
> which shall stand forth as intellectually the best—best in col-
> lege work and best in promise of future intellectual achieve-
> ment. Much as I would like to do so, I cannot draw the line
> around my favorite students in philosophy, nor the leaders in
> mathematics, nor those successful in biology; nor could I fairly
> award the palm to the Phi Beta Kappa [women and] men who
> have excelled in all their subjects. It seems to me that stronger
> than any group, tougher in intellectual fiber, keener in intel-
> lectual interest, better equipped to battle with coming prob-
> lems, are the college debaters—the [students] who, apart from
> their regular studies, band themselves together for intellectual
> controversy with each other and with their friends from other
> colleges. (Quoted in Willhoft, 9)

Malcolm X wrote:

> I've told how debating was a weekly event there, at the
> Norfolk prison colony. My reading had my mind like steam
> under pressure. Some way, I had to start telling the white man
> about himself to his face. I decided I could do this by putting
> my name down to debate ... Once my feet got wet, I was
> gone on debating. Whichever side of the selected subject was
> assigned to me, I'd track down and study everything I could
> find on it. (X, 98)

Both Meikeljohn and Malcolm X emphasize the power and capacity of
debate as a method of learning. Meikeljohn suggests that debate above
all other intellectual endeavors contains the potential for learning and

preparation for the future. Like Meikeljohn, Malcolm X emphasizes the emancipatory potential of debate—teaching new worlds, new skills, and new ideas. Debate is a way of creating ideas that empowers students and requires the application of critical learning skills.

This book is a resource for all teachers and educators who are interested in using debate as a classroom teaching technique. We believe that debate is an engaging, stimulating, and illuminating practice that can help educate students and encourage them to take responsibility for their education. This book will guide you through the practical needs to establish debates in a classroom. Using our almost 50 years of combined experience, we have provided tactical tools to help create classroom debates.

In this chapter we will review and discuss common ideas about debate and sketch out the essential elements of debating. We will review debating and debates as found in society and our everyday lives in order to understand the basic processes. We will clear up some of the misunderstandings some people have about the debate process. We will show that debating can be a useful classroom method in many different settings and provide the tools necessary for teachers to use debate in their classes.

Critical Advocacy for the Information Age

The nature of knowledge and information generation has become increasingly complex. The amount of information generated and the pace of change have accelerated; thus, educational methods must change to better fit the times. It is essential to teach students a lifelong method of learning.

Several developments influence our need to rethink our educational methods. First, more information than ever before is available. The sheer volume of data in existence is as distant from the Ptolomeic Great Library of Alexandria as a single book is to the number of volumes in the Library of Congress in the United States. Increasingly the mastery and use of information are the keys to success and positive social results.

Second, the pace of social change has quickened substantially and shows no sign of slowing. In previous generations, life would change little from one lifetime to another. Citizens were trained for specific tasks and roles with a fairly static kit of educational skills, and they achieved success with them. Vocations and lifestyles were passed down from one generation to another. In the 21st century, we have come to realize that we may well need several different careers in a lifetime. We cannot assume that we can confine "learning" to the "school years." And we cannot be sure that a job that we have trained for will be available to us in a corporate economy. Increasingly, we find it essential to teach our students methods they can apply to changing situations.

Third, the interrelationship between events heightens complexity. Previously, communities and nations existed in relative isolation from other communities and nations. Now, with global commerce, environmental stresses, and information exchange, each community is influenced in powerful ways by other parts of the globe. In addition, many technological changes (such as wireless communication, powerful portable computers, and rapid transportation) have system-wide effects, influencing all parts of society. Understanding global and systemic interrelationships is a challenge to every citizen.

Fourth, the effects of the above points have led to a domination of discourse and decision making by so-called experts. While our ancestors might have striven to be "Renaissance" persons, today specialized knowledge is prized. The result is that "talking heads" and "quoted experts" dominate most discussions. Increasingly, the role of average citizens is one of emotion, anger, and grief at the occurrence of social tragedies (police brutality, environmental poisoning, closing of locations of employment, injuries from a string of consumer product defects, etc.), while the deeper issues surrounding such incidents and the public policies directed at them are discussed all too often almost exclusively by such "experts" and often in defense of their vested interests. Debating calls for individuals to engage in independent thinking. Waldo Wilhoft made this clear back in 1929:

> The hardest business in the world is thinking. A student can go through an entire academic course without doing any original thinking. Learning what is in a book and what a teacher says is true is not thinking. Thinking consists in hewing out for oneself new lines of thought—new to the thinker, not necessarily new to the entire world. Debating requires thought, thought, and still more thought. The debater learns that thinking is not just a realignment of prejudices nor a justification of congenital bias. (10)

Like Malcolm X, Wilhoft points to the ability of debate to teach students to think new thoughts and explore new ideas. Many of the students we have worked with through the years have shared with us the transformative nature of debate to bring about wholesale changes by introducing new ideas.

Fifth, the communication landscape is increasingly illogical. One wonders at the difference between earlier advertisements, which focused on needs, uses, and features of products, and the current focus on images, associations, and often illogical connections that try to persuade citizens of a direct relationship between any number of commodities and basic sexual and social needs. Political communication is also increasingly symbolic, source-oriented, and characterized by slogans that are originated and disseminated by huge multimedia campaigns. Democracy has spread laterally to new countries, but everywhere it remains increasingly shallow in terms of real citizen awareness and participation. Increasingly the so-called marketplace of ideas rewards ideas that are stylish and hyped as opposed to logically valid. Debate trains students to combat this trend by using logic as the first tool of analysis. McBurney, O'Neill, and Mills argue that debate is uniquely suited to teach students to reject shallow reasoning and encourage critical thought coupled with the ability to communicate those ideas to others (266).

For each of these five ills, we believe that debate is a possible solution. Debate provides the potential for independent vigorous free thought and dialogue. Debate cannot easily be policed or controlled, and its process requires active thinking. Classrooms are increasingly important spaces to teach students intellectual survival skills.

We believe that using debate as a classroom technique is valuable in addressing these issues and how citizens deal with them. Debate teaches content as well as process and requires information acquisition and management. Different aspects of an issue must be investigated and understood by the debater. Debaters learn how to gather information and marshal that knowledge for their purposes. The process of debating is dynamic, fluid, and changing. Every day brings new ideas and new arguments. Every opponent uses some arguments that are expected and some that are not. Connections need to be made between the arguments in every debate as debaters search for ways to use what others have said against them. Debaters also learn to compete against others in the realm of ideas while cooperating with team and class members in their efforts. Debaters learn to cooperate in order to compete. Debaters must critically analyze and deconstruct ideas presented by their opponents in preparation for doing the same thing for the rest of their lives in all of their information transactions.

Debate calls to task simplistic public dialogue and foments a kind of global critical thinking. By encouraging participants to look carefully at the root causes and implications of controversies, and by teaching students that experts often have their own interests in mind when they produce facts and norms, debate can create a powerful resistance to many problems that seem to overwhelm us today. Most important, debate teaches a method of critical questioning and learning that can help anyone who seeks out new interpretations. Debates encourage students not only to debate about content but also about the frameworks of problems and how to solve them.

Debate heightens mental alertness by teaching students to quickly process and articulate ideas. Thinking on their feet, debaters are required to hear an idea and then provide a response. This pressure-laden scenario enhances the educational outcomes and spontaneity of debates.

This work is intended to help bring this exciting method to every classroom across the curriculum. We hope that this text will be useful to those who are interested in integrating this ancient, yet dynamic, learning method with the needs of today's students and citizens.

Definition of Debating

While many processes masquerade as "open debate," we feel it is important to define what we mean by debate in this text. A debate is an equitably structured communication event about some topic of interest, with opposing advocates alternating before a decision-making body.

This definition implies a number of principles for a debate. A debate should be equitably designed. All designated "sides" should be given an equal opportunity to present their views. A debate should be structured, with established communication periods and patterns with a beginning and an end. This structure allows for preparation and strategy.

A debate is a communication event where the mode of operation is oral or written communication (a text debate) and serves as performance as well as a method of transmitting ideas and arguments. Every debate has a topic, allowing the debate process to be more directed than a normal conversation. The topic itself should be of some importance and interest to the participants and any audience that may observe the debate. A debate is often composed of two or more sides of an issue where the advocacy positions are identified in advance.

For example, a debate might be held on the issue of the creating a national death penalty for certain crimes, one side is in favor of the death penalty (thus they may be called "pro," "affirmative," "proposition," or "government"; in this text we favor affirmative) and one side will be against the death penalty (thus they may be called "con," "negative," or "opposition"; we favor negative). This sense of "opposing sides" is critical to the probing analysis of the topic to be debated because debaters will bring the strongest arguments to back their side and be prepared to challenge the ideas of the other side. Presentations in a debate should alternate between the sides, creating a pulse of critical communication in opposition to previous and subsequent pulses. During the debate the advocates will be asking other participants and observers to agree with their point of view and, at the end, call for a "decision" by those present, either publicly or privately. These decisions are valid in the present, and, of course, they may change over time and in the presence of new information.

Debate in Society

While an infinite number of forms of debate may exist in any society, the common public examples of debate help us understand the dynamics of the debate process. Looking at the popular conceptions of debate can help us model our classroom debates. We'll discuss government debates, court proceedings, debates between candidates, and debates in the media as examples of debates in society.

The most obvious debates are those connected with governance. Legislative bodies debate over pieces of legislation, regulations, and appropriations. Equal time is allowed and all sides are heard. The specific measure under discussion serves as the topic. At the conclusion, a decision is made by a vote of the legislators. These debates are wonderful models for classroom debates; often teachers can draw a debate topic right from the front-page reports of a government policy debate.

Court proceedings are also examples of debates, but they follow a specific set of long-established legal rules. There is a topic under consideration, advocates alternate, and a judge or jury makes a decision at the conclusion.

Perhaps the most common example is a debate between political candidates. While not a part of governance, these events are a precursor to governance, and their subjects are usually politics and policy. Candidate debates have varying formats, some meeting our definition of a debate and others barely recognizable as a format for the discussion of ideas. The power of the debate process is shown by the vigor with which candidates try to influence and design the debate event to meet their needs. The debate between candidates is fraught with danger for the participants, such as a mistaken statement, a show of ignorance, a projection of an unflattering image, and a potential loss of composure. Most often, in our experience, candidates prefer to avoid direct interaction with their opponent(s), choosing to take questions from a panel of journalists or audience members instead of making alternating speeches. In fact, most debates between candidates are actually grand press conferences where the opponents answer some of the same questions but avoid the confrontation and clash of a true debate. A real formal debate offers deep insight into people and their ideas—no wonder candidates approach them with such caution and some refuse to participate at all.

The media provide countless examples of debates, although many are fairly watered down. News programs and talk shows often have segments where individuals who disagree speak about an issue briefly. Panel discussions often feature various points of view. These programs can be revealing and informative, but rarely achieve the enlightening potential of a true debate. They generally are too short to be very illuminating and allow only very brief presentations from speakers even though they often deal with very complex subjects. Listeners receive the impression that issues have been "debated," but such events rarely provide the necessary detail for a decision by those hearing them. The short attention span of television and television viewers (which is created by the availability of such shallow events) and the dominance of so-called experts make these events far from optimal. Models of these kinds of talk shows can be interesting as debate formats, where students represent different positions—the talk show format requires a strong moderator, however.

While these are valuable models for teachers to draw on for debating and debate topics, genuine public debates, forums, and other events often provide a better setting for meaningful debate. The many public debates and events we have held show that citizens are willing to watch and listen to an extended debate on an important issues, are willing to engage in questions and short speeches, and often come away quite impressed and excited by the event and in a better position to make decisions for themselves. Our experience demonstrates that a public debate event is more successful when it more closely approximates the suggestions we have offered for constructive debate. This is the model that most inspires us to suggest classroom debating as a technique for teachers.

Debate in Everyday Life

Although far less formal, many of the components of a debate are found in our everyday lives. We are constantly engaged in persuasive attempts to influence the decisions of others. It is the very nature of human existence to call for change in some manner. It may seem banal that the roots of this book are these regular day-to-day interactions, but we believe that a vigorous sense of debate can only improve our world. More important, it is in these small persuasive moments that our lives are most powerfully affected.

Teaching students to become more skilled both in persuasion and resisting persuasion is valuable. Consider some of the following examples.

A job interview is a one-sided debate over whether someone should be hired. You present your reasons through communication, the interviewer poses questions and issues that you must respond to, the interview situation is structured, and a decision emerges at the end.

A meeting with a teacher to gain a deadline extension on an assignment is a similar situation. You make your arguments, the topic of the discussion is your persuasive appeal for the extension, and in the end a decision is made.

Attempting to make a sale in a retail situation, asking parents for use of a car or an increase in special privileges, discussing government policy with friends, evaluating various books and movies—all of these have the components of a debate, although they are far less formal. In all of these examples, and in many parts of everyday life, people present opposing ideas and a decision is called for during and after the discussion.

Debate is a natural process, something with which we all have experience. Realizing that debate is an inherent part of our lives should help to reduce the fears and anxieties about the process. Students should realize that this is not a totally alien practice, but simply a more formal type of discourse that they engage in regularly. The debate skills learned through the practice of debating will serve students well in their persuasive encounters for the rest of their lives.

Misunderstandings Surrounding Debate

We urge teachers to aggressively challenge students who don't think they can debate. Debate is for everyone and everyone can debate. In this section we take a few minutes to debunk these ideas and provide some support for teachers selling a class on the idea of debate.

One common belief is that "Debating is for the experts, not for me." The thought is that you need to know everything before you can speak about it, neglecting the long tradition that discussion and debate about a subject is how one learns about it in an interactive way. We tell students that no one knows everything and that each of us knows different things, so the sharing of our ideas is crucial to the advancement of mutual understanding and knowledge. Besides, so-called experts still represent a point of view, and often it is a point of view and a set of interests that do not match those of the individual citizen. The individual citizen—prepared to be a critical advocate (a debater)—is in the best position to defend his or her interests, and thus participation is vital. Freedom withers when citizens accept the lie that the voice of the people is inferior to that of the experts.

Another common misunderstanding is that students do not have the "necessary skills to engage in a debate." We often tell students that they engage in debate processes in all areas of their lives—they attempt to influence through communication, they make arguments to support a certain point of view, they are critical of ideas of which they do not approve, and they ask people to make decisions in their favor. They have succeeded enough in these efforts to reach the class-room, so obviously they have demonstrated these skills that only need to be enhanced. The major difference for those holding this untruth is the structure and setting of a debate, but their role is one with which they are already familiar.

Finally, many students fear that the audiences will give a bad evalu-ation of their presentation. It is natural to fear that the audience will not pay attention or disagree with the message. Remind your students that the clash of ideas is one of the goals of the debate, and that they need not worry about intellectual disagreement. The classroom situ-ation, in fact, is a uniquely supportive one. Every class member will have to debate; so feared behavior will be moderated. Students will not assertively "mock" a debater because the same fate awaits them when they are in the spotlight. In our experience, students become supportive and helpful toward each other as they all grapple with a uniform experience of a new setting and structure for the kinds of influence attempts they engage in every day.

Conceptual Components of a Debate

While we have discussed the structural components of a debate, it is useful to understand the conceptual processes involved in a debate: development, clash, extension, and perspective. These elements describe a prescriptive approach to what a "good" debate should involve. Robert Branham, one of America's leading debate proponents, outlined this distinction in 1991:

> If debate is "the process by which opinions are advanced, supported, disputed, and defended," the fulfillment of these actions in turn requires that the arguments of the disputants possess certain attributes. Thus, true debate depends on the presence of four characteristics of argument:
>
> 1. Development, through which arguments are advanced and supported;
> 2. Clash, through which arguments are properly disputed;
> 3. Extension, through which arguments are defended against refutation; and
> 4. Perspective, through which individual arguments are related to the larger question at hand. (22)

In a debate ideas and positions are developed. This development involves description, explanation, and demonstration. In a debate about universal health coverage, the debater does not simply state that it is a good idea, there is also an obligation to explain why we need this policy, what that policy will be, and how it will operate successfully. Some specificity is always called for in a debate as advocates outline what it is they are in favor of and what it is they are opposed to. This kind of idea development increases research skills and builds student confidence.

In a debate, ideas are refuted: in debate jargon, this is the concept of *clash*. Those ideas presented by opposing advocates need to be examined with a critical eye, locating weaknesses, faults, and inconsistencies in these ideas. We call this "clash" because opposing advocates must not just disagree, but must demonstrate the specific reason why they reject the specific ideas of opponents. In a useful debate, the ideas of the other side cannot be ignored but must be critiqued.

In a debate ideas are defended. In debate jargon, this is the process of *extension*. When an opponent has criticized an advocate's ideas, these criticisms should be answered. This process creates a cycle of critical analysis, where ideas are presented, refuted, defended, refuted again, and then defended again until the debate has concluded. Extension creates a rich interchange of ideas that audiences and participants find to be some of the most intellectually stimulating experiences of debates.

Finally, each debate should call for a decision. This is the process of perspective. The decision is the sum of the arguments and ideas presented. Some ideas are more important than others, and ideas in a debate can relate in complex ways. Debaters should assist the audience in weighing the ideas and issues so that a logical decision can be made. While many other kinds of discussions urge people to "consider further," a debate calls for a decision at the end, either about the issue at hand or about who did the better job of presenting or defending the issue. The decision phase allows for closure and forces participants to stand in advocacy with some intellectual commitment.

Not every debate contains all of these elements, but we believe that these are the vital characteristics of debating. These are the conceptual components that the classroom debate should try to encourage. They are, in our view, the essence of how human beings learn from each other and grow through communication.

Debate Techniques to Improve the Educational Experience

We undertook this work because we believe that debate can be a highly useful educational method in the classroom. Teachers and students react very positively to debate as a way to study a wide array of subjects. Debate activities can increase student involvement in the educational process and with the subject matter, encourage independent and critical thinking, and are quite often enjoyable for students and teachers. These ideas will be further explored in Chapter 3. However, some examples might illustrate this point.

A German language class has students debate the topic, "Vienna is a culturally German city." The experience has been very positive, with students going beyond simple conversation using an exchange of memorized sayings by making points and using the language to build ideas. Students integrate their study of the language with some knowledge of German culture and its existence outside of Germany itself.

A literature class has students debate the topic, "Shakespeare's character Hamlet acts in an immoral fashion." This topic has been staged either as a debate between two teams of students or as a trial, complete with prosecution, defense, judge, witnesses (students playing the role of characters), and the rest of the class as jury. Students are encouraged to become a part of the play, to imagine themselves in it, and to make it more relevant to their lives.

A current events class has students debate the topic, "Palestinians should have a permanent homeland." Students can either represent themselves or one side can represent the state of Israel and the other side the Palestinians. As students learn the basic arguments and justifications used by each side, they begin to understand the roots of this conflict, and they personalize the experience through their involvement. This class debate has had the almost universal effect of helping students understand why this continuing conflict has not been resolved.

A teacher-training class has students debate the topic, "Standard grading practices in high schools should be replaced by portfolio evaluation of long-term student work." Students become more aware of alternatives to standard grading, they reflect on the meaning and uses of teacher evaluation, they explore issues such as student and teacher motivation, and they learn about issues of educational accountability. Once again, the issue is made real through personal involvement.

A history class has students debate the topic, "The United States should not have dropped the atomic bomb on Japan during World War II." Students explore the value issues inherent in this question (innocent victims vs. saved lives of soldiers, ethics in war, etc.), political realities at the time in Japan and the United States, as well as the military situation and the difficulties of mounting an invasion of Japan. What has long been a controversial decision becomes a very real issue once subjected to the scrutiny inherent in a debate.

Participants often develop strong opinions after such a debate, but it is always a more informed and considered opinion. These and countless other examples show how easily and productively debate can be used as a learning tool in almost any classroom. A dean at a major university mentioned that some faculty had not wanted to use debate in the classroom because "all of our major issues have been decided." Her response was that if this were the case, then their program should be cut or canceled, because it was obviously a "dead" subject that needed no further exploration. Debate in the classroom illustrates that learning is a process of growth and individual development through communication and interaction, not the simple memorization and internalization of discrete bits of data.

Austin Freeley, America's most popular debate textbook author, summarized the intellectual power of debate for students this way:

> Debate is distinctive because of its unique dialectical form, providing the opportunity for intellectual clash in the testing of ideas. The creation of an argument is one of the most complex cognitive acts a student can engage in. To create an argument, a student is required to research issues (which requires knowledge of how to use libraries and databases), organize data, analyze the data, synthesize different kinds of data, and evaluate information with respect to the quality of conclusions it may point to. To form an argument after this process, a student must understand how to reason, must be able to recognize and critique different methods of reasoning, and must have an understanding of the logic of decision making. The successful communication of arguments to audiences reflects another

cognitive skill: the ability to communicate complex ideas clearly with words. Finally, the argumentative interaction of students in a debate reflects an even more complex cognitive ability—the ability to process the arguments of others quickly and to reformulate or adapt or defend previous positions. (30)

How to Use This Book

This book is structured to be useful to the busy educator. The first 10 chapters offer a simple "how-to" approach to classroom debating. Our experience shows that although many educators attempting to integrate debate into the classroom are able to handle most of the planning and implementation with very little assistance, most find one or more areas, such as format design or topic creation or evaluation, difficult.

This book attempts to outline the major steps needed to stage classroom debates. Feel free to consult the chapters that cover the areas about which you have questions. Our organizational schema is functional and our style attempts to be straightforward. We provide examples because they are useful for illustrating abstract concepts.

Chapter 11 provides suggestions and guidance for specific subject areas. Teachers should feel free to turn to the appropriate section of this chapter and discover some basic approaches for using debate to further the educational goals they have in their specific subject.

Finally, we provide references for support information that might be useful for both teachers and students. These readily available materials facilitate many of the basic skills needed for a student to engage in a debate.

As educators we shape the future. Every time we expand the critical advocacy skills of our students while at the same time involving them in a more serious consideration of the subject matter at hand, we make a positive contribution to that future. Our advocacy of debate as a method recognizes that the knowledge and information landscape of the 21st century calls for new critical methods and a new approach to education. We do not believe debate is the only way to approach this daunting challenge, but we strongly believe it is a powerful tool for creating a better world.

Chapter Two

Basic Debate Processes

This chapter provides teachers with the basic information they will need to teach students how to debate. If you have ever thought that you might be interested in having a debate in your classroom but you were not sure how to go about making a debate work for your students, then this chapter will provide you the tools you need.

Investigation and Issue Discovery

Debate is a stimulating way to explore new ideas. It can help push teachers and students toward exciting new areas of literature and thinking that they might never otherwise encounter. Through the research required to prepare for debate, students can find a world of new ideas. A well-crafted classroom debate creates a climate for interactive learning where students apply ideas and have to explain their thoughts.

The first consideration in creating a strong debate is determining a debate topic. As the topic is the foundation for all the arguments that follow, an exciting debate topic will intrigue your students and get them enthused about the debate process. Much of the success of the entire project of a debate can come down to how you sell the issue and format of the debate. If students are hooked by the ideas of a debate, then they will be interested enough to make the whole process succeed. So spend some time working out the core issues of the debate with your students to make the process appealing.

For example, you might want to use debate to teach students the Aristotelian ideas of proof: ethos (speaker credibility), pathos (emotion), and logos (logical argument). If you propose to students that they debate which type of proof is most effective, students might express discomfort because they can't imagine how to win such a debate. But if you create a public forum in class where students are asked to use each kind of proof to argue a single topic, then they can see how to articulate different arguments on the same topics. Put students into groups of three with each group assigned a shared topic such as "The Earth is doomed" and then ask them to compare the different rhetorical approaches of ethos, pathos, and logos—they almost certainly will be able to use these concepts. Debates offer a chance for students to discover on their own terms, but planning the topic and the setup are vital for success.

One easy way to develop debate topics is to allow the class to participate in generating and selecting them. You will get a lot of mileage out of the debates when you use your students' ideas. This does not mean abandoning classroom topics, for you can guide the students to focus their topics on class-related issues. You might give students a homework assignment to write down three classroom subject areas they would like to learn more about or pursue in depth. You might have a brainstorming session where your class spends a set amount of time tossing out ideas and then select exciting ideas out of that process. We suggest that you encourage your students to seek out areas with which they are not familiar—push them to take chances and learn new things rather than rework familiar material. Getting students involved by having them drive the areas of interest will ensure their involvement and make your job of instructing them easier. Chapter 5 discusses these ideas in greater depth.

Once the topic is established, guide your students through the subject matter with some analysis of the themes that you expect will emerge in the debate. Teachers can help students to discover elements of an issue that they might otherwise miss. You will want to introduce the concepts and major thinkers who write about this particular controversy. If students are to represent a particular perspective, ask them to read a newspaper from another state or country. You might want to talk about terms with which the students might not be familiar. One of the easiest ways to do this is to provide the class or the debaters with a basic article that outlines what is at stake in any debate. This also offers you an opportunity to guide the debate toward your classroom topics.

An interesting and relevant lesson plan will always help students learn. Positioning students as decision makers in the world can help to create new understandings. If students feel involved and excited about the debate topic, they will reward you with powerful outputs of their own intellectual growth, sparking a dialectic relationship—launching the learning experience beyond your lesson plans and into something else (Giroux 1988, 197). Thus you must not only provide them with information, but also allow them to share their perspectives and views with the class. This process of discovery is vital to the success of your debates.

Research

Many students have done research projects, but research preparation for a debate will be a new experience for them. The most obvious difference is that, unlike traditional research projects, where students seek to build an argument and gather information that supports their argument and avoids contrary evidence, the debate research process encourages a kind of holistic approach, where students need to pay attention to the critics of their argument because they will have to respond to those attacks. Combine this with the usual trepidation about research and you will often find students are more worried about the research process than the debate. This section offers ways you can reassure them and guide their research efforts.

One exciting way to focus the time spent on research and help students become confident with the debate format and research is to have a debate with a limited research pool. In this format, teachers provide students with a restricted number of sources that they can use. You might, for instance, provide your students with a short bibliography and explain that this is the extent of the research you expect; or you might give each student a single article to read and prepare for a debate the next day. Limited research pools help students who have never debated before practice the holistic reading necessary to draw out ideas needed for a debate. It also can help you guide the topics that will be discussed and fit a research-based debate into a short amount of class time.

When you discuss the debate topic, you should provide an explanation of how to research it and what kinds of information students can expect to find. Research can be as simple as using the ideas already presented in a textbook or reading, or as complex as using the library to research a subject extensively. Clearly articulating the type and extent of research you require is necessary because of the rapidly increasing amount of information readily available to 21st-century students. With the rise of the Internet, the research process can seem daunting, and the tremendous amount of data available makes focused research agendas essential. If you provide a breakdown of the steps for successful research, then students can learn a system for exploring ideas that they can use throughout their lives. Here are our suggested steps for successful research:

- Make a keyword list. A keyword is an identifying word or phrase that can be used when searching databases to find information on certain topics. A keyword list is an important part of any research process because it enables your students to find information efficiently in libraries and particularly in electronic media.
- When looking something up in a library or typing a search request into a computer search engine, you are using keywords that are shared by those who organize information. Librarians, database administrators, and information scientists all share a format for organizing information based on a standardized keyword list. For example, if you were searching for information about the Inuit, the native tribe that lives in Alaska, many libraries categorize that information by the keywords *Inuit, indigenous—Alaska, Native Americans—Alaska.* If researchers only

searched under the term *Inuit*, they might miss some important ideas.

- Keywords are the tools necessary to unlock the mysteries of research, thus keeping a good list of keywords for a research project is vital. The keyword list should be updated and adapted as new information is found. One of the easiest ways to add to a keyword list is by looking at the end of journal articles; often there is a list of the keywords that librarians should use to file the articles. If you discover these keywords, then you should have access to other articles that are filed using the same keywords.

Find a Basic Article or Two About the Subject

Remind students that they are not expected to know about their topic before they research, so they should not be surprised when they encounter new concepts and unexpected terms. Sometimes the initial forays into research can make the subject seem overwhelming. This is not a permanent state! After some preparatory reading and some cross-researching to understand the terms that experts use, anyone can use even advanced literature on a topic. Some kinds of research require more terminology (hard sciences) and others might require background ideas (philosophy), but all of them can be understood if a student commits to thinking through the ideas presented.

The easiest way to begin this process is by looking for introductory articles. The first artifact that you should look for when researching in an area that is new to you is a basic article outlining the ideas and background of the subject. This will allow you to make an educated decision about what direction you want your research to take. Where you find these articles depends on the debate topic. You might learn about a current events topic from in-depth newspaper research, while you would have to go to the library to understand a topic on philosophical values.

Imagine a young student is researching the issue of the North Atlantic Treaty Organization (NATO) expansion so that she can oppose it in a debate. Her initial computer search generates only articles that are complex discussions about Eastern European nations joining NATO. She keeps searching until she finds an article that provides background, and she starts keeping a list of questions about her reading. As she proceeds through the articles she has collected, she comes to understand the basic terms and themes of the controversy over NATO expansion.

Begin Holistic Reading

Holistic reading is careful, active reading that draws out important arguments regardless of which side of the debate it helps. When engaging in holistic reading, debaters should look for all the major arguments and begin thinking of them in terms of the topic being debated. As they encounter quotes, statistics, metaphors, and examples that can help to build an argument, he should consider how these ideas would play out in a debate and take note of those ideas.

Holistic reading allows students to reflect on the debate topic and how the research concepts interact with their emerging understanding of it. Our student debating NATO expansion begins to note the ideas she finds and starts to develop her arguments and opinions. Is there a strong argument for the other side? If so, she will want to make sure to find answers to that argument.

Holistic reading turns information on a page into evidence that a debater can use—translating information into ideas. While engaging in holistic reading, students should be revising and adding to their keyword list and beginning to identify lines of argument that they might want to pursue. Students should also be taking notes through this entire process. It is in this process that debaters start thinking about how they plan to create their debate arguments. Students should plan what their major arguments are going to be and start looking for research holes that need to be filled.

Imagine that a young student is researching the issue of the North Atlantic Treaty Organization (NATO) expansion to Eastern European nations. Having been assigned to debate against the topic, she needs to find a basic article discussing the problems of NATO expansion. She crafts her search to include terms like "critical," "crisis," and "problems." She quickly finds an article outlining the basic controversy and providing three strong arguments against expansion.

She then researches each argument in depth to discover other good reasons for opposition. With this information she can organize her debate notes and craft a good speech.

Use the Bibliography and Footnotes

While engaged in holistic reading, a student might come across a particularly exciting article or essay. Through research, he might also find a single great paragraph or exceptional quote. In these cases, the student should follow the lines of research back to the sources that each author used. Using the bibliography, the student can often find lists of books and essays that mesh with the ideas he is developing. Using footnotes is a fantastic way to get deeper into a particular argument when a wonderful quote or passage has been found. Following the research paths that other authors have used to make their arguments is extremely valuable because students will come upon new ideas and encounter lots of new types of literature (sometimes older and more diverse). This is one of the best ways to fill missing spaces on a research outline.

Evaluate Sources

Prospective debaters must evaluate the sources that they intend to use for the debate. Watch for bias, arguments that are out of date, and sources that lack credibility. When evaluating credibility, examine even the most respected sources critically because all sources have biases, and every source makes errors. Students must learn to be critical about every issue they research, relentlessly pursuing the ideas in the debate. In the world of competitive national news, even the most powerful and widely respected news sources are often blind to their own biases. Make sure to emphasize the importance of critical analysis of even "respected" sources.

Related to the simplistic notion that some sources are good and others are fundamentally flawed is the bias against Internet-based sources—that they are inferior to hard-copy sources. The sheer size of the Internet requires some skills in navigating information, but just because a source is only available on the Internet does not necessarily mean that it is a bad source. Yes, some Internet resources are simplistic propaganda from obviously biased individuals, but this is certainly not unique to the Internet. In fact, you can find newsletters and pamphlets published (many of which are widely circulated) that are low-quality propaganda. Many of the sources that can be found on the Internet are high quality. Many academics publish papers on their Web pages; many journals publish online copies of their work. The Internet makes many sources available to people who lack easy access to a major research library.

Learning to evaluate research is a skill that comes with experience. Initially, students should focus on the arguments that authors present and the evidentiary support within those arguments. Students should be aware of the author's qualifications, paying close attention to those that are relevant to the debate (an art history professor's opinion about political redistricting might not carry much weight). Timeliness is also an issue: More recent research is more valuable. Most important, when evaluating research, students should focus on the ideas presented.

Follow Up Research Trails

After students have created their notes and organized them, they may have some peripherally connected arguments that seem interesting. Have your students follow up the research trails to discover new ideas. Most arguments in the public sphere tend to mimic and recreate the perspectives of experts. This is a rare opportunity to break out of that pattern and develop new ideas. Your students may need to do extra research, but no other forum offers this opportunity to explore ideas in such depth.

Do Not Feel Trapped by Research

Students may have a concept of what should be done that comes from their own experience and then discover that no one has written about this perspective. The students should feel free to make their argument and defend its merits. Their own ideas and experiences should be valued in the debate process. Search for alternative kinds of evidence. Historical examples, narratives, poetry, and music all represent very powerful kinds of evidence that should be used in debates. Debaters should use their hearts and brains to follow up valuable kinds of support for their arguments.

Organizing Debate Notes

Once debaters have a good idea of what they want to argue and how they want to position their ideas, they should organize their notes. There are two excellent ways to do this. The first involves taking notes on index cards. Put a single argument with supporting evidence and ideas on a card. Once this is done, debaters can organize the cards in a logical sequence. The second method of note taking is to put arguments with big-issue labels on the tops of pages and then include all the information and arguments about that issue on each page. For example, in a debate about food choices, a debater might have a page for arguments about taste, another for arguments about cost, and still another for arguments about ethics. The first method is useful for debaters who are not sure what their final arguments will be. The second is more useful for students who have determined their major arguments.

Students should organize notes to maximize their usefulness. Encourage your students to seek out the information that they need for their arguments. Sometimes they will have to refine their notes between the research phase and the time they use them in the debate. But if students practice taking notes with speaking in mind, they can translate their research notes into snippets of arguments ready for inclusion in a speech.

Students should outline their arguments to get an idea of how they want to persuade an audience with special focus on the arguments of their opponents. In the case of the NATO expansion debater, she would put the notes associated with the value of NATO expansion first and then prepare the responses to the contrary arguments. The opposition argument that NATO expansion puts a nation's security at risk by drawing member nations into unnecessary conflicts seems like a strong, central argument and a good one to start with when preparing to debate this issue. Argument notes should be organized to help the debaters understand and argue their positions.

Making an Argument

Creating good arguments is the central part of any debate because arguments are the central tool of persuasion. To make good arguments, students have to get used to moving beyond their traditional concept of arguments. Arguments are not simply statements that make a claim. "Cats are good companions" is not an argument because it does not include a reason why that statement might be true or any evidence to support the argument.

We suggest that you use the ARE format for teaching students to make strong arguments. ARE is an acronym that stands for Assertion, Reasoning, and Evidence—the three vital parts of making an argument.

Assertion is the central claim of an argument.

Reasoning is the warrant or reason that the statement is true.

Evidence is some kind of support for the assertion and reasoning.

Two brief examples of the ARE format in action:

Assertion: Cats are good companions.

Reason: Cats provide psychological support and friendship to those they trust.

Evidence: My aunt Geeba has lived with a cat for 10 years and she considers the cat to be her best friend.

Assertion: NATO should extend membership to the Baltic States.

Reason: NATO provides stability through alliance building that will prevent any Eastern European nation from attacking any other.

Evidence: The long-standing respect that all of the current NATO members have for one another suggests that the organization provides stability.

Using the ARE format does not guarantee that your arguments will be strong, but it discourages many mistakes that beginning debaters make in framing their arguments by simply making claims or presenting evidence without any explanation of how the ideas interact. If students get used to the ARE format, they will have a template not only for building arguments, but also for attacking other people's arguments. Recognizing the value of these sections of arguments illuminates the flaws in other arguments.

In the first example above, a student could clash with the reason that cats provide psychological support by arguing that many people are allergic to cats and that their very proximity can cause increased psychological stress. Knowing the value that undergirds each argument enables students to more clearly clash with presented arguments.

In the second example, a debater could clash with the evidence presented about the respect that many NATO states have for one another by pointing out that France has left NATO in anger and many others chafe under the alliance system. A debater could also argue against the reason presented by stating that the extension of NATO to the Baltic States will only anger Russia and increase the likelihood of tension in the area. The value of the ARE format is not just that it helps students to develop and understand arguments (it certainly does), but that it also provides a framework for people to comprehend arguments.

Building a Case

Teams advocating the affirmative side should conceptualize and organize their research into the format of the case. The case is a cohesive set of arguments that justify the side of the topic that they have been assigned. More important, the case allows debaters to choose the ground that they would like to defend. The debate case allows debaters to focus on the arguments they think are important and how to interpret the topic to defend these arguments. The case is important because it sets up the framework for the rest of the debate. Making a debate case depends in large part on the kind of resolution being presented. Participants in a debate must focus their ideas on the central topic to be debated.

For a **policy-based resolution** or when calling for a change or advocating some transformation, the problem solution format works best. In this type of debate, participants want to outline the problem that calls upon us to make a change, then indicate their specific advocacy (what should be done) and the reasons their solution will solve the problem. Students may also want to be aware of the reasons why the solution is yet undone (ignorance, lack of political will) and be aware of any additional benefits that might stem from their advocacy.

An example is a debate on the topic "Educational reform is justified." An affirmative side might want to argue that the educational system should support same-sex educational institutions. If this were their case, then the affirmative team might want to outline the harms of a coeducational system, particularly outlining the damage done to women. Then they might propose that the government provide funding for women-only educational institutions. Then they would want to present arguments that prove that their proposed solution would solve the problem they outlined. In this case, that single-sex educational institutions would be better for women.

For a **value resolution**, it is generally accepted to have a criteria-based case. Here, you would want to provide a way to evaluate the values in the debate. Because debates of value are extremely subjective, it is important to establish a way for everyone to think about the arguments in the debate. This means providing criteria for judgment, perhaps something as simple as suggesting that the debate round be judged on a particular value.

Consider a debate on the topic "The body is sacred." An affirmative team might want to use this topic to argue against recreational tattooing and piercing of the body and frame the debate using the criterion of bodily integrity. They would build their case by defining bodily integrity as the highest value in the debate round. They would talk about religious traditions that hold the body to be a gift from a higher power and the practical dangers (infection or disease) associated with piercing and tattooing. A negative team could present a counter-criterion that clashes with the affirmative's chosen criterion. In this example, a negative team might want to argue in favor of personal freedom as being the higher value. After asserting and supporting the importance of personal freedom, they would then analyze the debate about tattooing and piercing through this lens.

For a **resolution of fact**, debaters should organize their ideas to support their position. Because resolutions of fact contest our perceptions of truth, these debates are most easily conceptualized through a case—a coherent series of examples—that proves the resolution. Within this framework, debaters might want to organize their arguments chronologically or based on the topic being debated.

Understanding the type of debate and then building a case that fits that type of topic is essential in persuading your audience. Building a case helps students focus their advocacy on the goals of the topic and the class.

Critical Analysis of Opposing Viewpoints

Each team *must* be prepared to respond to the arguments made by the other side. The easiest way for students to do this is to brainstorm the best arguments on both sides and then, during the research phase, use holistic reading to keep track of these ideas. Students should make a list of all the arguments they would use if they were on the other side of the debate and then prepare to defeat them.

Rather than simply attacking their opponents' ideas, debaters should examine them critically. Debate is a unique opportunity to hammer out the strengths and weaknesses of big ideas. Teachers should encourage students to focus on the most significant parts of debates and not to shrink from strong arguments presented by the other side.

Debaters should put each opposing argument at the top of an index card or a piece of paper and then think of responses to each one. Doing this will let them discover points of logic that are flawed, evidence that is missing, or weak points in the ARE format. One good way of finding these weaknesses is to search the literature for criticism of a particular advocate. Almost every advocate has a critic most willing to point out her mistakes; the disagreements of two experienced advocates can help outline many debate arguments. Much of this work happens when students become familiar with the topics through research. Discovery, analysis, and preparing to defeat opponents' arguments are fundamental parts of debate.

Decision Making

Debaters need to learn decision-making skills because these will help them make choices throughout their lives. Debate is a wonderful opportunity for students to weigh difficult decisions affecting their world. In debate, students are asked to examine a controversy and then decide how to approach a complex question.

Learning how to make decisions during a debate can be a difficult skill to master, but it is vital because it can determine the outcome of the debate. If a student chooses to emphasize a certain line of argument and the other side has excellent counter-arguments, then the debater is in trouble.

The most important and difficult decisions that debaters will make are how to spend their time during their speeches. Coach your students to look for the weakest points of their opponents' arguments and make sure to beat them. If a debater can point out substantial flaws in her opponents' arguments, the opponents lose credibility and she can defeat some of their arguments. This strategy can be risky because sometimes one side of the debate will be careful not to make any obvious logical mistakes, or their mistakes will be so minor that a debater who fixates on those arguments could lose out because of the time spent focusing on a trivial part of his opponents' arguments. This approach also risks moving the focus of the debate away from the central concerns and losing the audience.

Debaters should focus on the most important arguments—those that provide the foundation for the other side's claims. These arguments represent the best that opponents have to offer, and if a debater can defeat these arguments, then she can usually win the debate. At the same time, a debater must constantly reinforce her own points. Strong debaters usually extend their own arguments and also focus on defeating the strongest arguments presented against them.

The decision-making skills that debaters develop are some of the most important life lessons that students can take from debate. Debate scholar Austin Freeley argues that "many problems in human affairs result from a tendency to see complex issues in black-and-white terms." Freeley believes that the decision making in debate, where students look at many different perspectives from a position of respect, engenders strong critical learning skills. "As they debate both sides of a proposition, they learn not only that most problems of contemporary affairs have more than one side but also that even one side of a proposition embodies a considerable range of values" (28).

Much of the decision making in debate occurs when debaters have to emphasize distinct arguments in order to win. These decisions can make a significant impact on the outcome of the debate. Decision-making skills emerge with practice and experience. As students become more comfortable with their arguments and ideas, they are better able to recognize the turning points in debates and make important decisions quickly and effectively.

Oral Communication Skills

Regardless of the format of the debate, these skills are vital. Clarity of idea and speech are the hallmarks of a great debater. You can teach students the basics of these concepts even if you do not have a background in communication. The fundamentals of oral communication skills rest in common sense. Students should carefully prepare and organize their arguments so that they make sense on first listening. They should employ a good tempo and tone in their arguments.

Their arguments should neither be all opinion nor all fact, but a strong mixture of the two.

We teach our students to use the extemporaneous style of delivery—neither reading directly from a prepared speech nor speaking with no notes. Memorizing speeches is a time-consuming and risky proposition because a mistake when memorizing can result in a student forgetting what comes next and a complete breakdown of a speech. It is much better to have an outline of basic notes and to speak from that outline, using it only to remind the speaker of where he is in his speech. The extemporaneous style is also good because it encourages debaters to maintain eye contact with the audience and allows them to adapt their speeches if things are going poorly.

Imagine a team that prepares a series of arguments made irrelevant by the arguments of the opposing side. If the speech was memorized, then the team would be making those arguments because they were part of a memorized speech. However, with an extemporaneous style of delivery, students can swap parts of the speech for other parts, provided they are prepared to do so.

Fitting into the time limits provided for the speech is a fundamental part of oral communication. Audiences expect debaters to give their speech within the time provided. Students should be encouraged to practice their speech so that they won't come up short or speak for too long. Being aware of the audience is a fundamental part of communication skills.

Practice is the common element in all of these skills. A good student can remedy almost all of the common fears about debate simply by practicing arguments orally a couple of times. Eye contact will improve, confidence in speaking will increase, and phrases that seem awkward when spoken aloud will resolve themselves with practice. Practicing will also help students understand their ideas and make sure that they are communicating their ideas clearly.

Debate involvement naturally produces improved public speaking skills. Austin Freeley notes: "Since composition and delivery of the debate speech are among the factors that determine the effectiveness of arguments, debaters are encouraged to select, arrange, and present their materials in keeping with the best principles of public speaking" (28). Freeley points out that many debaters are called upon to debate in different contexts (classrooms, on the radio) and that each different audience requires that students vary up their debate skills and public speaking: "Constant adaptation to the audience and to the speech situation develops flexibility and facility in thinking and speaking" (28).

Listening

Debate is one of the best ways to teach students listening skills, because their motivation to listen carefully is high. In debate, the success of their performance hinges on their ability to listen closely.

Debate students should be encouraged to pay attention to the central ideas in the debate, focusing on the turning points of arguments. Learning to listen and take notes at the same time takes practice; you might need to practice with the whole class. One good exercise is simply reading a newspaper article aloud and then asking the class what they heard.

Encouraging students to be active listeners when they are in the audience is difficult. When students are watching classmates in a debate, they may be tempted to zone out and ignore what is going on in the classroom. Alternatively, they might want to get ready for their own upcoming debate. Regardless, you must set the class up to be active listeners. Remind them that the class acts as a community and that support for one another is fundamental to the success of the debates. Remind them that each debate has been a heavily researched synthesis of some complex ideas—a great chance to learn. Every student in the class is working in a new medium, and many are worried about how they will do in the debates. Remind them that they will also be speaking to the class and that they should be the kind of audience that they would like to face. Having students in the audience decide a winner or providing a question-and-answer session about the subject of the debate for the rest of the class can encourage students to pay attention to their debates.

Many students have a difficulty learning to listen. One of the most important parts of debating is active listening. Students need to improve their listening skills if they are to succeed, and debating can provide a method to achieve this goal. Scholars like Freeley have pointed out that humans use only 25 percent of our listening capacity. In the debate context, if we allow our attention to wander while an opponent speaks, our reply will be ineffective and "off the mark." And if we miss 75 percent of our opponents' arguments, the debate will be terrible.

Debaters soon learn to listen to their opponents with sharply focused critical attention, taking careful notes so that their own responses may be precisely to the point as they adapt the very words of their opponents, turning the subtleties and limitations heard to their own advantage. The ability to listen critically is widely recognized as an important attribute of the educated person.

Two easy ways to foster active listening are to require students to take notes during the debate and to require a student ballot. Taking notes encourages students to listen carefully to the arguments being presented and to envision how ideas are interacting in the debate. Try to get your students to imagine what they would argue after each speech. Get them to think about the debate as though they were participants.

Student balloting forces students to make a decision about which side they believe won the debate, encourages careful consideration of arguments, and gets them thinking about judgment. For more on student balloting, see Chapter 4.

Conclusion

Debate teaches vital skills—confidence in ideas as well as effective research, preparation, and communication skills. These are all concepts that build on one another and create a foundation that will serve students for the rest of their lives. Involving students in a debate does much more than get them excited about the subject; it also provides them with the tools they need to succeed in many different areas.

Chapter Three

~ ~ ~ ~

Goals of Classroom Debating

Despite an interest in debating, many instructors still wonder if they should take time from their busy classroom schedules to use for debate. We believe that debate is not only useful to help you get your students involved in your subject, it also has independent educational benefits. In this chapter we will explore the goals and advantages of integrating debate into your classroom curriculum.

Engage Students in the Subject Matter

Debate provides a great opportunity to get students excited about the subjects they are studying. Educational traditions are often established in a formulaic top-down method, with instructors providing information and students simply receiving the knowledge. This educational format often is coupled with a heavy focus on examinations in an effort to test students' knowledge. While this method of education has a long tradition, many education experts question the value of this approach (Giroux, 128; Whang and Waters, 198).

Arguing that students engage with material only long enough to memorize it and then move on, experts have identified this kind of learning as passive learning that often fails to stick with students. We have certainly seen this to be true at the postsecondary level in the United States. Many students arrive in our college classrooms prepared to memorize information and regurgitate it during examinations but unable (and often uninterested) in getting involved in the subject.

This kind of educational process is a learned one; students do not simply become uninterested. They are taught that their job is merely to absorb knowledge like sponges; as a result they become numb to the exciting potential of knowledge. This learned behavior can be challenged with the introduction of new kinds of teaching. Active, exciting educational methods get students involved in the subjects we are teaching and encourage them to be excellent students, not because they are preparing for a test but because they want to learn.

This idea is probably not new to you. If you have taught for a long time, you know that students respond to activities and opportunities that bend the traditional parameters of the classroom format. The difficulty teachers have is how to do these exciting kinds of activities and still impart information to the students. Debate as an educational method helps in both areas. Debate calls upon students simultaneously to know the subject and to be able to speak articulately and persuasively about it.

Students must do more than just listen—they must be involved in active learning. They must engage in higher-order thinking involving analysis, synthesis, and evaluation. Strategies promoting active learning have students both doing and thinking about what they are doing. As educators Charles Bonwell and James Eison conclude, "Use of these techniques in the classroom is vital because of their powerful impact upon students' learning. For example, several studies have shown that students prefer strategies promoting active learning to traditional lectures. Other research studies evaluating students' achievement have demonstrated that many strategies promoting active learning are comparable to lectures in promoting the mastery of content but superior to lectures in promoting the development of students' skills in thinking and writing"(2).

These dual motivations work to encourage students to want to be informed. Usually only one debate where a student feels ignorant is needed to create the intense desire to understand the subject and be prepared the next time. Participating in a debate will often pull students to not simply be aware of information, but to process it in a way that they can then use it in the debate. Debate fundamentally encourages students to become their own educational activists, seek out knowledge and ideas, and then become engaged with those ideas so that they can use that knowledge in a clash of dialogue.

The necessity of taking a public stand in a debate is key to this process. In a normal situation we use grades to evaluate students; in a debate students stand up and personally represent ideas. They propose them and defend them. This public commitment is very important, and students take such situations quite seriously. They make the connection between themselves and their ideas because they have made this public declaration (Cialdini, 78). The debaters will not necessarily retain the beliefs they advocated, but because they formed a personal attachment to their ideas these beliefs will be important. We all know that when we say to ourselves that something is important it is meaningful, but it is far more meaningful when we make a public declaration because we are social creatures and feel obligated to stand by what we have said to others.

Debate fosters new visions of old problems. Because students become responsible not simply for a one-to-one transmission of knowledge (on an examination), but instead for a presentation to a larger group of people (the rest of the class), debate fosters a desire to understand the roots of issues. Debate encourages the asking of the monumental question, "Why?" This change of perception from someone whose interest in a subject matter is cursory to a person who is responsible for defending an idea requires that a debater know what he or she is talking about. As students prepare for debates, their approach to the subject of scholarship is radically transformed from a passive approach to an active one.

In *Everything's an Argument*, Andrea Lunsford and John Ruszkiewicz explained the forces that encourage students to pursue arguments to a greater depth when they are responsible for defending them: "When people write arguments themselves, they are also aware of options and choices. Typically, they begin an argument knowing approximately where they stand. But they also realize they'll need evidence strong enough to convince both themselves and others more completely that their position makes sense. And often they surprise themselves by changing their views when they learn more about their subject" (19–20). Debate calls upon students to follow this line of questioning—not to be satisfied with the cursory level of knowledge, but instead to pursue arguments to their depths.

Debate helps teachers to resolve the problem of uninterest—because in many ways the responsibility of comprehension lies on the shoulders of the students. It also creates a kind of self-interest that encourages exploration of the foundations of problems and issues. Regardless of your approach to education, when debates are integrated with your curriculum, they can excite and stimulate your students.

Operationalize the Issues of the Subject Matter

One of the chief benefits of debate is the transformation of knowledge into a useful form that students can operationalize. This simply means that through debate students become adept at the application of the knowledge gained in your classroom.

Most educational requirements call upon students to be familiar with a topic and able to use it in a fairly simplistic manner. Consider the subject of art history, for example. Most art history classes require students to memorize a large number of paintings and be able to provide the date it was created and artist. The purpose of this approach is to develop a sense of history and to show how changes in art affect other artists. The application of this knowledge usually comes through reports or examinations where students apply what they have learned and usually in the same patterns that they learned it.

Debate challenges this kind of education because students must not only learn the knowledge, they must also turn it into parcels they can manipulate into creative arguments and responses. This process requires that students not only memorize vital concepts in art history, but also reorganize that information into a pattern they can use to make a particular argument. This "learning by doing" is an effective educational tool and models the natural way people learn in their daily lives (Schank and Cleary, chapter 6).

Consider a debate on the topic "Advances in art are sudden and shocking." To support this topic, a student would have to draw connections between various artists and periods of art. Rather than talking about the Cubists and recounting the important Cubist artists, spaces, and paintings, debate requires a student to make new connections with information. In this instance, a student might draw examples from Chinese artists, early Impressionists, Andy Warhol, and Chris Ofali in order to make the point that art changes only when radical artists push for new space.

Some might respond that these kinds of connections could be just as easily made in a research paper. In debates, however, the application of knowledge is significantly different because students must defend their ideas. In a research paper on this same subject, a student might have to plunder his or her brain to create these kinds of connections; in a debate the student not only has to make such connections but also has to defend them. The student supporting the affirmative side of this resolution not only has to create these arguments, but also has to be prepared to respond to the argument that the Impressionists contributed a particularly mild and complacent form of artistic change and did not push the boundaries of art at the time.

In addition, because debate provides for a live performance in the defense of ideas, students learn to organize and utilize information during an intense interaction. This interaction results in a kind of utilization of knowledge that cannot be easily replicated in a classroom. Because students plan and organize their information and then implement those plans when challenged, they become aware of their arguments (and the subjects of the debates) at a level that is extremely complex. This operationalization of knowledge creates new patterns of understanding in subject matters and can contribute significantly to classroom learning.

Create Advocacy-Oriented Education

When we examine traditional education instructional methods, we can see that the stakes for the students are fairly minor. Information is provided to students and they have the opportunity to accept the invitation to knowledge and become participants by memorizing or familiarizing themselves with that knowledge. This process often results in halfhearted attempts to understand ideas or pursue concepts, particularly if they are confusing, in large part because there is no real need or justification for such effort. This educational model is too often a disaster because it continues with students for the rest of their lives, and they come to believe that it is the approach to learning anything.

We can identify this approach to learning as a "consumer" approach, where students peruse the possible educational options and then casually invest their money (or time) into learning something with the expectation that someone else will provide them with the things they need to know. Particularly dangerous is the acceptance of the parameters of educational frameworks—where students come to expect that simply fulfilling the class requirements will result in receiving knowledge (or a positive grade). The implication of this kind of consumer approach to thinking is that the drive to pursue knowledge falls behind an expectation that someone else will provide it.

The German philosopher Friedrich Nietzsche described the perils of this approach to education in his 1874 essay, "On the uses and disadvantages of history for life," where he laments the current state of education that does not seek out the complex causes of historical problems and is content to explore surface level effects.

> Individuality has withdrawn within: from without it has become invisible; a fact that leads one to ask whether indeed there could be causes without effects. Or is a race of eunuchs needed to watch over the great historical world-harem? Pure objectivity would certainly characterize such a race. For it almost seems that the task is to stand guard over history to see that nothing comes out of it except more history and certainly no real events!—to take care that history does not make any personality 'free', that is to say truthful towards itself, truthful towards others, in both word and deed. It is only through such

truthfulness that the distress, the inner misery, of modern man will come to light, and that, in place of that anxious concealment through convention and masquerade, art and religion, true ancillaries, will be able to combine to implant a culture which corresponds to real needs and does not, as present-day universal education teaches it to do, deceive itself as to those needs and thereby become a walking lie. (85)

Nietzsche positions education as a vital opportunity to ask critical questions and to avoid a consumer approach. Education can be important because it helps us to become more informed participants in public life. Such education can help us to understand what things are valuable and good, it helps us to understand when leaders make bad (and even dangerous) arguments, and it helps us to speak up when necessary. Unfortunately, the consumer approach to education hinders all of this by encouraging simplistic approaches to learning. Debate, on the other hand, nurtures a kind of education that centers on advocacy and critical thinking.

Advocacy is vital, because active, engaged citizens are the most powerful advocates for social change. These kinds of change advocates are increasingly important in our world. Young people especially need to learn how to become advocates for themselves and what they care about, as Dawson explains, "By empowering your teenager to self-advocate, you'll help him develop skills necessary for success in learning and life" (1). Henry Giroux, the sociologist and critic, has argued that the status of American society was perilous because of the loss of informed democratic advocates—"Coupled with the general public's increasing loss of faith in public government, public institutions, and the democratic process, the only form of agency or civil participation offered to the American people is consumerism as opposed to substantive forms of citizenship" (3). The solution to Giroux's frustrating perspective on American political reality is to teach students to be active advocates, not necessarily by informing them of their opinions, but by teaching them how to research and critically reflect on public controversies and then teaching them how to persuade others that their opinions are valuable. This is the fundamental project of debate.

Choosing debate as a method of analysis has broad implications for the kinds of advocacy and analysis it urges on students. Douglas Ehninger and Wayne Brockriede suggest several mental experiments to draw the distinctions between debate and other types of communications.

> To understand the full significance of the choice one makes in selecting debate as his method, perform five mental experiments: (a) Inquire, "Do fanatics and rigid sectarians appeal for arbitration or for unqualified belief and unthinking acceptance?" (b) Contrast the patient examination of evidence in a court of law with the impulsive, emotionally charged decision of a mob fired by its leader. (c) Recall how frequently a certain type of candidate for political office refuses to meet his opponent in public debate. (d) Ask, "Does the advertiser contract for equal time or space for his closest competitor, and request that buyers delay their decision until both sides have been heard?" (e) Most revealing of all, perhaps, listen to an hour of earnest debating in a courtroom. Then compare it with an hour's run of radio or television commercials. (18)

Debate teaches students how to argue for and defend ideas. This lesson is central to the success of our public life. Debate is valuable because it provides a counter to the traditional consumer mentality of education. Debate helps to teach skilled, critical advocates for change. Debate is fundamentally about researching, thinking, organizing, and advocating, skills that are fantastic primers for public advocacy.

Teaching Persuasion Skills

This method allows students to be better able to persuade and teaches them the responsibility associated with that skill. The very conception of debate is premised around the idea of persuading an audience to respond positively to arguments. The performance elements of debate require that students not only be aware of the vital arguments and logic of their side, but also of the subtle techniques associated with persuasion.

One of the most impressive persuasive techniques that debate teaches is confidence. Advocates who are confident about their arguments and ideas offer up a very positive ethos to their audience. This is a vital element of preparation—students who are familiar with their arguments and ready to debate will appear confident. But debate confers another level of confidence: the courage to remain calm when things seem to have fallen apart. Because debates have at least two sides to them, opponents often shock each other with an argument to which they were not prepared to respond. Debate teaches the quick thinking skills needed to be prepared for the unexpected. The ability to respond quickly often comes naturally to a person who has experienced a few debates.

Along with confidence, debate teaches a host of other persuasive skills, including powerful use of language, speaking tactics, organization, and audience analysis. Students who debate become aware of these persuasive skills through the natural process of discovery. Even in a class where the instructor might not feel comfortable talking about the persuasive nature of language choices, the students will evolve their own sense of what works. Debate fosters these kinds of realizations because of the nature of the activity, not necessarily because of the classroom subject. Whatever persuasive techniques a teacher might desire to include in the introduction to the debate will certainly be valuable for the students. In a language class, the power of particular kinds of phrasing might be emphasized. In a class about politics, an examination of persuasive historical speakers might be the focus. Teachers need not include any formal instruction in persuasion, students will learn by debating and understanding the outcomes of the debates they are in. This is one reason why we encourage students not directly involved in the debate to act as judges and at times provide written comments in the form of ballots to student debaters. The judgment of their peers is very important to students, and the feedback they gather from other students about their debate performances will provide fertile ground for learning about the process of persuasion.

By understanding more about persuasion, students can also learn to resist undesirable attempts to influence their attitudes. These attempts manipulate factors associated with the communicator, the audience, the message itself, and the channels through which it is delivered to try to increase a message's persuasive power (Marlin, 95). Debate would seem to be a particularly useful laboratory for such learning.

Regardless of the subject matter or approach, debate teaches students about persuasion. In addition, it teaches students about the responsibility associated with their newfound persuasive skills. Students may quickly recognize a debater whose preparation was deep in language choices and persuasive tactics while shallow in research about the topic. Debaters become aware that many politicians and leaders try to disguise their arguments in a show of flowery words. Debaters become inoculated against the use of persuasive techniques in exchange for good arguments because they are aware of the tactics that persuaders use to win the minds of their audiences. More important, debate encourages students to see the ethical relationship between a speaker and his or her audience. While students learn to persuade, it is not at any cost and often the sense of responsibility of the persuasive act is even clearer after someone has been participating in debate for a while.

The skills of persuasion that come from being involved in debating are natural ones that flow from the performance and the preparation for the performance. The skills of persuasion that come from practicing debate are extremely valuable and cannot be overstated. Along with these skills emerge defenses against being persuaded and an ethical understanding of the possible negative elements of persuasion. These methods can have negative effects and thus the debater may gain a realization that "cheap" avenues of persuasion should be avoided.

Teaching Critical Thinking

Debate is one of the most effective methods of teaching critical thinking. Because debate requires active learning and calls upon students to be prepared to defend their arguments, debate preparation and actual debating encourage critical thinking. While traditional educational methods teach students content and concepts, debate takes that knowledge and encourages students to use it as the beginning of a journey of self-exploration.

Because students are responsible for their own claims in the debate, debaters are quick to explore the roots of their claims. Rather than being satisfied with what they are told about a subject, debate encourages students to seek out their own understanding, and often to challenge ideas by researching and critiquing the foundation of arguments. This process is fundamental to critical thinking.

Critical thinking is the active skill of applying knowledge to new problems and controversies. Critical thinking does not just mean thinking hard about a problem; it means applying ideas and concepts in new ways. Critical thinking happens when students take a concept they have learned and apply it to a new encounter—applying their knowledge in a situation that they previously had not been prepared to analyze. Consider what a student learns about the historical roots of agricultural globalization, including the "green revolution" that encouraged majority world (or so-called Third World) countries to use high-yield seed and pesticides with a focus on export rather than home consumption. That student becomes aware of the devastating impact this approach has had on most countries—draining the quality of soil and often poisoning drinking water supplies. This research is not critical thinking, it is the first step in critical thought—seeking out the roots of an idea. Critical thinking occurs when that same student encounters an article advocating the forgiveness of the debt of majority world countries. When that student combines these pieces of knowledge and makes the connections between these two seemingly unconnected pieces of information, then he or she is engaged in critical thinking.

Empirical research seems to support the relationship between debating and critical thinking. While more tightly controlled and larger studies are needed, what evidence we have is encouraging (Shuster, 2). Austin Freeley notes:

> A number of studies that have investigated whether college courses in argumentation and debate improved critical thinking scores on standardized tests have found that argumentation students out gained the control students by a statistically significant amount. Kent R. Colbert found that, after a year's participation in either CEDA or NDT debate, the debaters

significantly outscored the nondebaters on critical thinking tests. (270)

Critical thinking doesn't simply emerge in students by teaching them skills and content; instead, it develops in participants who learn the ability to make these connections—largely by simply thinking through the relationships between ideas. One of the best activities to teach these critical thinking skills is debate. Because the research for debate is focused on making precisely these kinds of connections, it is extremely valuable.

Paul and Elder explain the problem surrounding a lack of critical thinking:

> Everyone thinks; it is our nature to do so. But much of our thinking, left to itself, is biased, distorted, partial, uninformed or downright prejudiced. Yet the quality of our life and that of what we produce, make or build depends precisely on the quality of our thought. Shoddy thinking is costly, both in money and in quality of life. Excellence in thought, however, must be systematically cultivated. (1)

When we combine this critical research skill with the necessity to stand up and speak for your position, we come up with a great educational combination to foster these kinds of critical thinking skills.

Create Positive Classroom Atmosphere

One of the benefits of using debates in your classroom is that they engender a more exciting classroom. Students are up and moving around, they are excited about the subjects, they are bringing their own ideas and research to share with the rest of the class, they are actively working with partners, and the classroom positively hums with energy. This is the kind of classroom that we all dream of having, where students are excited to be there and they take away ideas and experiences that will serve them well for the rest of their lives.

Debate helps to create this kind of atmosphere in the classroom by getting students involved and rewarding their interest with the public debate performances. Because students are responsible for their own performances, they become more involved in the educational process.

What many instructors don't realize is that this excitement will carry over to many other areas of the class. Students who are excited and stimulated will be eager to learn more from a teacher because the knowledge that they receive has an outlet, a place where they can use that information. Debate answers the question of how students use their classroom knowledge by allowing them to actualize their information into arguments. After a debate, students are more interested and some are even excited to be involved in the class.

Create New Patterns of Knowledge

Debate encourages students (and teachers) to think new thoughts. The very nature of debate as an activity creates new cognitive spaces for all involved. Debates are living dialogues between informed advocates; we cannot predict what ideas a debate will reveal. Debates emerge between participants with a flow back and forth—with students making claims and counterclaims. It is in this space that new ideas emerge—through the critical application of knowledge.

Even the preparation for debates creates new knowledge in participants. Students who are assigned to defend an argument that they do not know very much about (or that they disagree with) will benefit from the research process where they get the opportunity to learn about new concepts that they may have never considered.

It is in the actual debates that students create new patterns of knowledge. Starting with a student being at the front of the room speaking while the instructor and the rest of the class are listening, debate is a transformative experience. The traditional structures of power in a classroom can be exposed and explored during a debate. Because the student is at the center of the educational nexus, the nature of the education is formally changed.

Henry Giroux calls for teachers to become involved in political education—what he means is intense critical exploration. Although Giroux doesn't explicitly advocate debate, his justifications for this kind of education resonate extremely well with using debates in the classroom.

Political education also means teaching students to take risks, ask questions, challenge those with power, honor critical traditions, and be reflexive about how authority is used in the classroom and other pedagogical sites. A political education provides the opportunity for students not merely to express themselves critically, but to alter the structure of participation and the horizon of debate through which their identities, values, and desires are shaped. A political education constructs pedagogical conditions in order to enable students to understand how power works on them, through them, and for them in the service of constructing and expanding their roles as critical citizens. Central to such a discourse is the recognition that citizenship is not an outcome of technical efficiency but is instead a result of pedagogical struggles that link knowing, imagination, and resistance. (139)

Giroux expresses a vision for what education should be. His goal encourages imagination, critical thinking, and political thought, and explores the power relations in the classroom. Debate as a method of pedagogy does all of these things. Debate can bring students to a place where their own confidence and excitement can drive them to discover new ideas and concepts. Through debates in the classroom, students can make new connections and blaze new pathways of intellectual growth.

Because debating is inherently interdisciplinary, it can enhance the ability of students to engage in interdisciplinary efforts. Debates about science often involve questions of ethics, debates about ethics must examine the new possibilities revealed by science, debates about economics require considerations of human psychology and sociology, and debates about international relations require considerations of history and political science. Debating allows students to burst the constraints of discipline-based curriculums and view the world in its true complexity.

Have Fun

Debates are enjoyable and exciting events to watch and participate in. Debates can bring your classes to a new level of pleasure. Despite the very serious benefits that debate can provide to your classroom, it can also help make your classroom fun both for you and your students.

Teaching is too often difficult, stressful, and unrewarding. Debate represents an opportunity to share the work of teaching with students. Rather than teaching from the front of the classroom, you can help guide students who are teaching other students through their debates. It can be enjoyable for you because you get to see an actualization of the knowledge that you help to share. It is often hard to know how much of an effect you are having on your students. Students whom you might perceive as lazy may surprise you by representing arguments that you taught the class months before. The shy student who had significant trepidation about the entire debate process may blossom when called upon to get up and speak.

Roger Schank and Chip Cleary in *Engines for Education* remark that few students describe school as enjoyable, yet the "fun" instances are what students remember and are often what are the most important. They write:

> But it is quite clear that for most people their one-word description of their lives as students would probably be something quite different than "fun." One cannot read a description of any writer's time in school without hearing quite painful (and often funny) tales. For most people, school was an annoying, stressful, and sometimes painful experience. The tales that people tell when they look back fondly at school rarely have anything to do with school itself but are instead about making friends or playing on teams. When people do tell tales of school-related success, the stories are usually about cramming for the big exam, or working hard to get a grade. They are almost never about learning. Why not?
>
> It is clear that the interesting action, the stuff that comprises a child's mental life in school, is about interaction with other children in one form or another. School is not about learning. It is about jobs, it is about winning the competition; it is about money, it is about getting other kids to like you, and it is about getting the teacher to like you. None of these things are inherently bad. Most of the things that school is really about are a normal part of life, and there is no reason why kids shouldn't deal with them in school, too. But the kids should also be learning.

Mostly, they should be learning that learning is fun. They should be learning that expanding one's horizons is fun, that learning you were wrong about something is not so painful, and that taking an educational risk is worth doing. They should be learning that school is a good place to do these things. The children of today dread going back to school in September, dread exams, dread receiving their grades, and are generally fearful. No wonder school is stressful. But there is no reason children cannot have intellectual fun, cannot be excited by ideas, and cannot be challenged to acquire new knowledge. Natural learning is a basically enjoyable thing to do. (epilogue)

Students love debates because they are lively and fun. The education in the classroom emerges as students strive to make better arguments or, in the case of role-playing debates, settle themselves more deeply into their assumed identities. Debates are enjoyable for students because they are in charge of their own learning and get to follow their interests. When they discover something new, they can share that knowledge and receive the praise of the community of their peers.

Conclusion

This chapter brought the goals and benefits of debate to the forefront. Our hope was to encourage you to explore debates in your classrooms and to experience some of these benefits yourself. Not every classroom debate will be flawless and you will have moments of doubt. But when you find the right formats to fit your class and make debates a part of your curriculum, and have had a few practice debates to get the kinks worked out, we believe that debate will serve you and your students well.

Chapter Four

Formats for Classroom Debating

Classroom debates can be completely flexible to fit teachers' needs and lesson plans. If this book has one overarching theme, it is this: There is no right or wrong way to have a debate. Where there is space to think critically and argue about ideas, good things will happen. Beyond the basic goals of the debate (to have fun, to learn, to experience speaking in public), the only constraints are the amount of time and the interest of the teacher. One of the greatest fears that teachers have about debating in the classroom is that they are not sure how to set up the debates—they might not have any experience with formal debates. This chapter provides you with all the information you need to pick a format for your class.

This chapter will explore the wide variety of formats that can help fulfill your goals for your classroom. The purpose of this chapter is to bring you basic information about the setup and framework of various styles of debates. You should not feel constrained by the suggestions in this chapter; this is merely a beginning.

Choosing a Debate Format

Deciding what format of debate is right for your situation requires you to do some preparation. You need to determine what your goals are for the classroom, what kind of constraints you might have that would limit the kinds of activities you can do, and what kinds of debate formats will fit in with your educational goals. Navigating these questions can provide you with the best kinds of debates for your class.

The most important factor when preparing to do a debate in class is to keep in mind your teaching goals. If you wanted to use a debate to warm up a classroom, you would want to have a format that ensured that everyone had an opportunity or was required to speak. If you wanted to use a debate as a final project where students were required to prove their mastery of a subject in a clash of ideas, then a formal debate whose ground rules were clearly established would give the participants enough time and opportunity to prepare. Be assured that there is a debate format that can supplement your educational goals and provide a way to involve and excite students.

You should also keep in mind any classroom-based constraints that you might have when selecting a format for your debate. These might include the amount of time that you (and your students) have available, the number of students in your class, awareness of the issues to be debated, language difficulties, and space considerations. These small elements can add up to make simple debate projects seem overwhelming if not considered before the debate begins.

Introductory Formats

We will profile a number of different formats for debates. Each format has its value and place in the classroom. For each format, we will look at the educational possibilities and limitations. We will also outline the preparation requirements for each debate and the practical setup steps of each format. Further discussions of this subject can be found in Chapter 7.

Roundtable Discussion

One format that is relatively easy for beginners is the roundtable discussion. It can directly involve a large number of students in a single class. The format is just as it sounds, a discussion by students sitting together at a table.

Roundtable Discussion

Student	Activity	Time
Chair	Introduces topic and asks for panel to participate	1 minute
Pro Student	Speaks in favor of the topic	1 minute
Con Student	Speaks against the topic	1 minute
Neutrals	Ask questions, anyone debating can answer	4 minutes
All	Open discussion moderated by chair	6 minutes
Chair	Makes concluding statement identifying major issues	1 minute
Chair	Counts vote by student audience and announces a winner	1 minute

You can adjust this format. For example, you could have just an open discussion or you could encourage neutral students to announce their affiliation with one side or the other.

This format is extremely useful with younger students and is easily accessible to most students (Spencer-Notabartolo).

Positive elements of this format include:

- Informal setting that is not as threatening as giving a speech
- Can involve most of the students in a class in one class period
- Can focus on smaller issues concerned with the material being studied
- Useful activity for introducing future debates

Negative elements of this format include:

- Not all students are involved at all times
- Difficult to use with complex issues
- Not as challenging as a back-and-forth debate

Public Forum

Public forum debates mimic traditional assemblies of people gathered to discuss a controversy. In this debate, no one is required to speak or participate if they choose not to. Instead, a moderator introduces a particular topic and asks for participants. Volunteers choose to speak on the issue and make points to the general body. Often a particular question is presented that is voted on by participants at the end of the session.

Public forum debates represent a great opportunity to encourage discussion and break the ice in a classroom. Because no one is required to speak, participants' anxiety is usually low and allows for a free-flowing discussion that encourages creativity and natural speaking skills. It can also be instructive as a tool for analyzing arguments and fallacies. Public forum debates represent a great way to discuss topics that are close to your students' hearts.

Public forum debates are limited. Because no preparation is required, public forum debates seldom bring new knowledge to the participants. Informing the students about an upcoming debate and assigning them to do research can often resolve this limitation. Occasionally, talkative students monopolize the space for discussion.

Preparation for a public forum debate can be as simple as explaining the activity to the students. But it can become much more involved, with some time needed for research. You may want to type up the format and speaking times for your students. If you are using a group of students that you don't know well, you may want to provide nametags to allow you to keep a list of speaking volunteers. You may also want to prompt a few students to start the conversation.

If you are going to use a public forum debate, you should consider the setup requirement. Public forum debate requires a moderator (often the teacher) who identifies students to speak. Sometimes making a list of students who volunteer and adding their names to the list as the debate progresses is most effective. You will want to carefully explain the goals and format for the event. The important things for you to consider are how long speakers get to speak (one to three minutes is suggested) and if participants get to question the speakers when they are done.

Public Forum

Student	Activity	Time
Chair	Introduces the topic and the rules	1 minute
Citizens	Rise & speak (2 minutes maximum)	30 minutes
Chair	Announces final speeches & vote	1 minute
Citizens	Rise & speak (1 minute maximum)	8 minutes
Chair	Counts vote and announces	1 minute
Radio	Reporter gives story of meeting	1 minute
Television	Reporter gives story of meeting	1 minute
All	Shake hands and congratulate one another	2 minutes

You can adjust this format in various ways to meet specific classroom needs. You might give students assigned roles linked to the issue (characters in literature, figures in history, groups in history, workers, taxpayers, corporate lobbyists, environmental group, law enforcement, local government official, etc.). You can have students sit on the right (agree), in the middle (undecided), or on the left (disagree) of the room. They can move if their minds change during speeches. A vote is not always necessary. For a friendly and positive group you can encourage applause and polite heckling ("Shame") by the audience.

Positive elements of this format include:
- Useful for introducing debate activities
- Easy to organize
- Involves many students at once
- Useful for smaller issues concerning the material under study
- Good format for role playing

Negative elements of this format include:
- Easy for some students not to be involved
- Short speeches make consideration of complex ideas difficult
- Little clear flow of issues as different speakers are focusing on different issues

Spontaneous Argumentation (SPAR)

SPAR debating has been popularized by John Meany of the Claremont Colleges, but has also found its way into a number of college classrooms at top American universities. SPAR debating consists of two debaters drawing a topic for debate out of a hat and then, with a few minutes of preparation, engaging in a quick debate on the subject.

SPAR debating is an enjoyable, exciting, and confidence-building activity. It is an excellent way to reduce speaker anxiety and ensure that students feel at home in your classroom. Because the debate is quick and the audience gets to participate, it is usually a big hit with students. SPAR debates are also excellent tools to get students to practice speaking skills (organization, word choice, metaphors, and logic).

The creativity and excitement of your students limit SPAR debates, so they do sometimes fall flat. The debates do not include any research and can occasionally become more humorous than educational. If you expose students to your expectations and help to guide them, these drawbacks can be minimized.

To use the SPAR debate format, you will need to make a list of topics that you are sure anyone could debate about without any preparation. Seemingly simple topics like crushed ice is better than ice cubes have been very successful. The topics can vary dramatically and fit well with any classroom subject. You need to brainstorm a number of topics that seem appropriate for your students and the subject that you are teaching.

SPAR

Student	Activity	Time
Affirmative speaker	Speaks for one side of the topic	1 minute
Negative speaker	Asks questions of the first affirmative speaker	1 minute
Negative speaker	Speaks for the other side of the topic	1 minute
Affirmative speaker	Asks questions of the first negative speaker	1 minute
Audience	Asks questions and makes comments	5 minutes

Adapt this format to fit your needs. If you would like to eliminate the audience questions or the questions that the debaters ask of each other, feel free. You should be able to time the debates so that your whole class will fit into the time available. You may wish to frame the SPAR debates with a discussion of what you expect in terms of your students' speaking style. Remind them that they are not evaluated on the contents of their argument, but they should be organized, give previews of their major arguments, and have solid arguments.

Setting up a SPAR debate is easy. Either write the format for the debate on the board or, once you are in the classroom, ask for a pair of volunteers to debate. Have the volunteers come up and draw a topic out of the hat. We sometimes allow them each to draw a topic and then pick the topic that they want to debate. If you do this, be sure to account for the adjusted number of topics when you are preparing. Send the students out of the class for a few minutes to prepare. Immediately repeat the process with another two students, so that two sets of students are preparing at the same time. When you call in the first set of debaters, send out another pair so that the students are staggered and there is never a need to wait for debaters to get ready. After each student you should provide a little bit of commentary about their performance and connect the debate to the larger classroom issues.

Positive elements of this format include:
- Very quick
- Dynamic nature may help hold interest of other students
- Short speeches easy for students

Negative elements of this format include:
- Cannot deal with complex topics
- Need to generate large number of topics for short debates

Public Debate
This format allows as many as 29 students to be directly involved in an event that can take place in less than one hour. Individuals have roles so that students are always engaged. Some of these roles reflect those found in a wider social setting, such as the media. Some students will

submit their work (judges' decisions, newspaper reports) in writing the day after the debate if possible.

Public Debate

Student	Activity	Time
Chair	Introduction of motion and debaters	2 minutes
Pro #1	State case for the motion	3 minutes
Con #1	State case against the motion	3 minutes
Pro #2	Expand case for the motion	3 minutes
Con #2	Expand case against the motion	3 minutes
Floor #1	Speak about issues, arguments, new ideas	1–2 minutes
Floor #2	Speak about issues, arguments, new ideas	1–2 minutes
Floor #3	Speak about issues, arguments, new ideas	1–2 minutes
Floor #4	Speak about issues, arguments, new ideas	1–2 minutes
Floor #5	Speak about issues, arguments, new ideas	1–2 minutes
Floor #6	Speak about issues, arguments, new ideas	1–2 minutes
Con #3	Summarize case against the motion	3 minutes
Pro #3	Summarize case for the motion	3 minutes
Floor #7	Speak about issues, arguments, new ideas	1–2 minutes
Floor #8	Speak about issues, arguments, new ideas	1–2 minutes
Judges	Mark their ballots	1–2 minutes
Chair	Counts the ballots and gives decision	1–2 minutes
Debaters	Shake hands, congratulate, & sit down	2 minutes
Radio	Reporter presents radio report	90 seconds

You can easily change the format by limiting the number or length of floor speeches, or by assigning roles linked to the issue. You can make the debate more exciting by encouraging applause and polite heckling ("Shame") by the audience.

Positive elements of this format include:
- Involves many students
- Entire event in one class period
- Allows consideration of moderately complex issues

- Dynamic changes increase attention of audience
- Mixture of assignments, both oral and written
- Floor speeches add focus on issues debaters may have missed
- Excellent format for role playing

Negative elements of this format include:

- Can become a circus-like event
- Important to stay on schedule
- Floor speeches may fragment the attention given to some important issues

Team Debating

Students can be formed into teams of two or more. The formats for team debating differ based on the role of preparation and research in the debate. Debate modeled after American and Japanese policy-making debate requires research and significant preparation. Debates modeled after British, Irish, Australian, and other parliamentary debating are more extemporaneous. This section will discuss some of these formats.

Keep in mind that not all of these formats require any specific team size—teams of a single person or of a number of people are always possible. Debate is a flexible educational method.

Prepared Debate

For the purposes of this work we will refer to all team debate featuring substantial preparation as prepared debate. American and Japanese prepared debate has a formal structure of speeches, periods of questioning (called "cross-examination"), and a particular type of resolution that encourages a focus on significant policy changes.

This is a popular format for both high school and college competitive debating in the United States. In 1964 Russel Windes and Robert O'Neil published their book, *A Guide to Debate*, wherein they define tournament policy debating—"A tournament debate consists of an affirmative team and a negative team meeting under established rules to argue a given proposition. The debate will ordinarily be judged by one or more people . . ."(26). Although this format is most often associated with competition, it can be a valuable format for you to use and adapt for your subject.

The policy debate topic used in these kinds of debates is framed to encourage affirmative advocacy of a significant change in a government policy. Here are two examples of policy-making debate topics:

> The federal government should guarantee an opportunity for higher education to all qualified high school graduates.

> The United States should withdraw all its ground combat forces from bases located outside the Western Hemisphere.

Prepared debate is intended to teach students skills of advocacy, research, evidence analysis, and quick thinking. The purpose is for students to spend some time in building a case or an example of the topic and then encourage clash over the major issues. This can provide the culmination of classroom work or it can supplement a topic that is already being discussed. An added benefit is the group work associated with policy debate. Because debaters will usually work in teams of two, a working relationship is built between partners that can be extremely valuable in a classroom setting. Prepared debate can be difficult for students to master because of the extensive research needed to discuss complex issues with confidence.

Because this form of debate encourages research, you would do well to introduce the debate project and the topic early. Provide a thorough explanation of how the debate will work and the duties of each student. Although larger teams are possible, this kind of debate is traditionally a contest between two pairs of students, with two students supporting an affirmative case and two students presenting negative arguments against that case. First, you will establish teams and topics for the debates. You might want to use the same topic area for all of the debates in a class and suggest different approaches for each affirmative team or you could have different topics for each team. This will increase the enjoyment of the audience as they get to learn about different topics, but will also up the amount of research for your students. Traditional policy-making debate is switch-side, where debaters are responsible for both being affirmative and negative. You may want to draft a schedule for your class that provides for each team debating on both the affirmative and the negative if time allows.

Using the example of the topic provided above: "The federal government should guarantee an opportunity for higher education to all qualified high school graduates," we can look at what a hypothetical affirmative and negative team might argue. The affirmative team might advocate that the federal government provide scholarships to pay for a college education for any student who finishes in the top 40 percent of his or her class. The negative team might argue that this policy change would have disadvantages; for example, the cost to the government would be prohibitive and such use of funds might necessitate a trade-off with social services for the elderly. They can also argue that the affirmative case might dilute the quality of colleges and universities, effectively "dumbing down" the education for all students who attend.

Much of the preparation required for the debate will include guiding students through the research phase. Students will need time and occasionally help both in finding and evaluating information for the debate. It will help all involved if both sides disclose their arguments to each other to aid in research preparation. If you are pressed for time, you might want to gather a selection of relevant articles and provide them to your students to use as either the totality or the foundation for their research.

One of the major goals of this debate format is to encourage clash of ideas. The debate is set up to foster a vigorous back and forth of arguments in an attempt to resolve specific controversies. Therefore, it provides for a constructive speech (where debaters construct their major arguments) and a rebuttal speech (where debaters refute their opponent's arguments) for each student. Consequently, the format winds up looking like a complex back and forth between sides. Below is the traditional policy debate format, which usually takes about two hours per debate. (You may want to change the speech times to fit a single debate into a class period.)

Prepared Debate

Student	Activity	Time
First Affirmative constructive	Builds a case for the topic	8 minutes
Second Negative speaker	Cross-examines the First Affirmative speaker	3 minutes
First Negative constructive	Attacks affirmative case; introduces other issues for the negative case	8 minutes
First Affirmative speaker	Cross-examines the First Negative speaker	3 minutes
Second Affirmative constructive	Defends affirmative case; analyzes new negative issues	8 minutes
First Negative speaker	Cross-examines the Second Affirmative speaker	3 minutes
Second Negative constructive	Continues attack on case and promotes other negative issues	8 minutes
Second Affirmative speaker	Cross-examines the Second Negative speaker	3 minutes
First Negative rebuttal	Same as Second Negative constructive, but handles different issues	5 minutes
First Affirmative rebuttal	Defends affirmative case; replies to major negative issues	5 minutes
Second Negative rebuttal	Summarizes debate, weighs, and compares important issues	5 minutes
Second Affirmative rebuttal	Summarizes debate, weighs, and compares important issues	5 minutes

Once you have given out topics and created teams, your students will create speeches to fill in their time. The first constructive speeches should be 99 percent prepared, while the rest of the speeches will flow off the arguments presented by opponents and partners. When the time comes for the debate, you will want to prepare the rest of the class to be active listeners. If you have assigned them to write a ballot explaining who they believe won the debate, then you can explain the parameters of the assignment. If they are just listening to the debates, you should remind them that they have an ethical duty to be an active, engaged audience and that they would want that kind of audience when they are debating. You should establish some way to watch the time of the debaters. You might want to have a student volunteer to be the timekeeper and use some index cards labeled with the time remaining. Or you can call out the time orally. You may require your students to keep track of their own time during the debate. Finally, you need to explain how the students will be graded/evaluated for their efforts.

Positive elements of this format include:
- Good vehicle for research and directed learning by students
- Complex issues can be addressed
- Teach students about teamwork
- Students challenged to gain deeper understanding of the material

Negative elements of this format include:
- Takes a lot of class time
- Students may not research sufficiently
- Must allocate research and preparation time

Extemporaneous Debate

Extemporaneous debate is modeled after the traditions of competitive parliamentary debating common in many countries around the world. Parliamentary debate emphasizes quick logic, wits, and a persuasive speaking style. Its format is similar to that of prepared debate with several vital exceptions. Extemporaneous debate does not allow the use of evidence to be quoted in a debate and participants are allowed to stand up and pose points of order including questions and brief statements while their opponents are speaking. In addition, topics are traditionally released several minutes before the debate, thus participants must use their mental agility and reasoning powers to interpret the resolutions rather than do research. Competitive parliamentary debaters do engage in research to prepare themselves, but it is of a very general nature.

The chief value of extemporaneous debate is the emphasis on quick thinking and persuasive skills. Students are rewarded for a quick wit and an ability to be inventive while making arguments. Because research is de-emphasized, the format is easy for new debaters. In addition, the audience is traditionally quite involved during these debates, usually letting their opinions on the qualities of arguments to be known by slapping hands on desks (approval) or by mildly mocking bad arguments or saying "shame."

The chief negative to extemporaneous debate is that it does not emphasize research. This format is probably not a good candidate as a final project in a class where research and knowledge of a subject are required. Because the debaters are usually encouraged to be liberal in their interpretation of topics, the direction of the debate is often hard to predict. For example the resolution "A penny saved is a penny earned," could be debated in several different ways. One interpretation might call for consumers to stop using so many credit cards because of high interest rates. Another interpretation could define the resolution to argue that the government should save money by ceasing to pay welfare benefits. The topic could also be interpreted to mean that the International Monetary Fund should cancel Third World debt so the citizens of less-developed countries would not starve because of heavy debt repayment schedules. Topic interpretation almost assures a high degree of randomness in the actual arguments that emerge. Of course, you could certainly provide topics that were more precise to counter this possibility or instruct students to stay with a strict interpretation of the topic.

Points of information are a vital part of the extemporaneous parliamentary debate tradition. They are short offerings of data that clarify the debate. Traditionally, points of information are intended only to convey facts, but in your class you can be as flexible as necessary. The first and last minute of speeches (excluding the rebuttals) are "protected" time where no point of information can be made. During "unprotected" time a member of the opposing team may stand and say, "Point of information" or "On that point" and the speaker may decide to take their point ("yes") or decline to take the point ("no thank you"). If the point is taken, the opposing speaker has less than 15 seconds to ask a question or make a point to which the speaker responds quickly and then moves on with her speech. Good debaters are expected to take points and handle them well. Opposing debaters are expected to remain active throughout the debate by rising for points. Points of information provide an exciting and dynamic component in these debates.

If choosing the extemporaneous format for your classroom, you *must* explain to your students how the debates will occur and have them practice the points of order. You will need to make a list of topics for the debate. You may want to release the topic area to your students to allow them to do background research before the debate.

The precise format for an extemporaneous debate can be any of those indicated in this work. We will review the major competitive formats used as a reference and a guide only. You may pick the precise speech order and lengths that fit your classroom situation.

American Parliamentary Debate

Student	Activity	Time
First Affirmative constructive speech	Presents affirmative case	7 minutes
First Negative constructive speech	Attacks affirmative case; introduces other issues for the negative case	8 minutes
Second Affirmative constructive speech	Defends the case; responds to new negative issues	8 minutes
Second Negative constructive speech	Continues to attack the case; continues with negative issues introduced in first negative opposition speech	8 minutes
Negative rebuttal	Summarizes debate; weighs and compares important issues	4 minutes
Affirmative rebuttal	Summarizes debate; weighs and compares important issues	5 minutes

The format for competitive parliamentary debate varies from country to country. In Canada, the leader of the opposition gives the second opposition constructive speech and the rebuttal. British tournaments have four different two-person teams in each debate—two defending the proposition and two opposing it. Each speaker speaks once, with times of five, six, or seven minutes. In Australian and some Asian tournaments, each team has three members.

Extemporaneous debates require little debate-related preparation on your part, but do require you to make topics and time cards to inform the students of how much time they have left for their speeches. You will also have to prime the audience to be active participants in the drama unfolding in front of them. It is common for parliamentary audiences to become quite audible when they encounter arguments that they like or dislike. The traditional format for positive responses comes when the audience thumps the table repeatedly at the sign of good arguments. Negative feedback is often more outspoken with light jeers from the crowd. Of course, you must decide how much (if any at all) you want of this kind of behavior from your classroom audience.

Positive elements of this format include:
- Emphasizes quick thinking and public speaking
- Requires students to be generally well informed about the topic at hand
- Is easy to organize and stage
- Points of information provide a dynamic and interesting component to the debate

Negative elements of this format include:
- Takes a considerable amount of class time, including preparation for an extemporaneous topic
- Students may not know very much about the topic you have selected, creating a less than optimal debate
- Students may experience communication anxiety because of the extemporaneous nature of the debate
- Points of information, while an excellent feature, require skill of the debaters; in early debates using this format, your students may not have the confidence or skills to use points of information effectively

For more information about parliamentary debating, we suggest you consult two excellent books: *Art, Argument and Advocacy* (2002) and *On That Point* (2003), both by John Meany and Kate Shuster.

Role-Playing Debates

Role-playing debates are persuasive speaking events where a historical or fictitious event is used to establish the framework of the debate. Students may be asked to play the roles of particular characters or interests, or they might be allowed to simply be participants in a particular scene. Blending theater and debate, these events are both fun and rewarding.

Role-playing debates are valuable partly because they allow students to step away from themselves in a debate and give them a role to play. This can reduce anxiety about debating and can clear up what a person's arguments should be. Role-playing debates are also great to encourage imagination and work extremely well with younger students. These debates are extremely easy to integrate into any classroom because all you need is a controversy and a willingness to try a debate.

Role-playing debates require a significant amount of preparation by the instructor. Because the scene needs to be understood by the participants, it helps if everyone has researched the subject beforehand and the stakes of the debate are understood. The instructor must not only provide the scene, but also establish the opinions of many of the participants. Fortunately, this is usually the subject of a lesson the instructor was already planning to prepare.

Role-playing can be a powerful technique when combined with debating. The justifications for role-playing in education mirror, in many ways, the justifications we have been giving throughout this book for debating. Adam Blatner echoes our arguments when he writes:

> Role-playing is a methodology derived from sociodrama that may be used to help students understand the more subtle aspects of literature, social studies, and even some aspects of science or mathematics. Further, it can help them become more interested and involved, not only learning about the material, but learning also to integrate the knowledge in action, by addressing problems, exploring alternatives, and seeking novel and creative solutions. Role-playing is the best way to develop the skills of initiative, communication, problem-solving, self-awareness, and working cooperatively in teams, and these are above all—certainly above the learning of mere facts, many if not most of which will be obsolete or irrelevant in a few years—[what] will help these young people

be prepared for dealing with the challenges of the Twenty-First Century. (http://www.blatner.com)

Role-playing debates require an instructor to find a controversy that has good arguments on both sides. Questions of history are particularly fruitful. One good example includes recreating great trials (or imagining new trials—like putting President Harry Truman up on war crimes charges for dropping atomic bombs on Japan). Another example would be a contemporary debate about the preservation of old growth forests, with the debaters playing the roles of lumber company executive, conservationist, government official, citizen, local business person, etc. Contentious issues in virtually any classroom subject can point us to exciting role-playing opportunities. The format for the role-play will vary with the exercise. If there is a trial, then perhaps the teacher could be the judge, providing each side with opportunity to speak. If the role-play is a meeting, then the teacher could be a person with a proposal that sparks dialogue and discussion.

Role-playing requires that students be given their roles and the situation of the debate and that the parameters of what they are supposed to do be clearly defined. The day of the role-play the students should be able to adopt their characters and not have to worry about what they are doing, only about persuading their fellow students.

Positive elements of this format include:
- Students genuinely seem to enjoy playing the roles given them
- Role-playing debates are fairly easy to integrate into the material being taught
- Any speech order and length can be used

Negative elements of this format include:
- Students may go "over the top" in playing their roles, creating a distraction
- Students may have insufficient information to properly play their roles
- Students may have difficulty "thinking like" someone other than themselves
- Substantial teacher and student preparation required

Mock Trial Debate

The mock trial debate replicates the format of a court trial, with several debaters playing the roles of counselors for particular legal motions. This kind of debating lends itself to a rewarding understanding of how legal norms and ideas come to exist and for students to research legal controversies. This format is obviously the preferred debate format for those who might pursue a legal career.

Mock trial debates encourage students to explore ideas in a rigorously formatted debate process. Because an instructor can use as many courtroom traditions as she would like, these debates can follow closely in the footsteps of the legal system. This allows instructors to teach not only the ideas of the law, but also the formats. Perhaps more important, the mock trial format enables students to see how law evolves and works within a society. The very practice of jurisprudence can help to create a strong understanding of how law permeates a social fabric.

M. Donna Ross has written a variety of short essays on the mock trial technique that teachers might find very useful. They can all be obtained at her section of Debate Central (http://debate.uvm.edu/NFL/rostrumlibmocktrial.html).

The mock trial format has at least two limitations: creativity may be discouraged and occasionally the complex format of the debates can overwhelm debaters. Both problems can be solved if enough attention is paid to the preparation of the debate. If the topic of debate is carefully selected and the preparatory research is guided with faculty input, then students can discover new ideas about the law and feel confident enough to let their own creative ideas flow in the forum. In addition, if an instructor is willing to either carefully explain the utility of the courtroom format or be flexible in the use of jargon, then the second limitation can certainly be overcome.

The formats of a mock trial will model itself on the nature of a country's judiciary system. In the United States, this creates a debate with counsel on two sides arguing about a particular legal case or motion. Often a controversial court case that is being considered is used as the grounds for these topics. By having debaters defend the sides of a legal case, students can research the legal precedents to such a case and then present their own arguments about the law. The teacher or a panel of students might be used as the presiding judge or panel of judges. Sometimes an actual judge can be persuaded to preside over student finals.

Trials can be held about legal issues from the past or present, can concern the guilt or innocence of an accused, or can apply a legal model to a nonlegal issue, for example, "Hamlet is not a hero in Shakespeare's play."

Because a full trial may be quite involved, a mock trial may take more than one class day but can involve many students. All of the roles in a court situation can be filled by students, including media covering the trial.

Mock Trial Debate
Day One: 50 minutes

Student	Activity	Time
Judge #1	Reads charges against the accused	3 minutes
Accused	Makes statement in own defense	3 minutes
Prosecutor #1	States case for the prosecution	6 minutes
Pros. Witness #1	Cross-examined by Prosecutor #2	2 minutes
Defense Lawyer #2	States case for the accused	6 minutes
Pros. Witness #1	Cross-examined by Defense Lawyer #1	2 minutes
Pros. Witness #2	Cross-examined by Prosecutor #1	2 minutes
Pros. Witness #2	Cross-examined by Defense Lawyer #2	2 minutes
Pros. Witness #3	Cross-examined by Prosecutor #2	2 minutes
Pros. Witness #3	Cross-examined by Defense Lawyer #1	2 minutes
Def. Witness #1	Cross-examined by Defense Lawyer #2	2 minutes
Def. Witness #1	Cross-examined by Prosecutor #1	2 minutes
Def. Witness #2	Cross-examined by Defense Lawyer #1	2 minutes
Def. Witness #2	Cross-examined by Prosecutor #2	2 minutes
Def. Witness #3	Cross-examined by Defense Lawyer #2	2 minutes
Def. Witness #3	Cross-examined by Prosecutor #1	2 minutes
Radio #1	Reporter gives story of trial	90 seconds

Day Two: 45 minutes

Student	Activity	Time
Prosecutor #2	Closing arguments for the prosecution	6 minutes
Defense Lawyer #1	Closing arguments for the defense	6 minutes
Judge #2	Instructions for the jury	2 minutes
	[Jury stays in room, but they act as if in isolated deliberation]	
Jurors' statements	Each juror makes a statement of 1 minute	9 minutes
Jury deliberates	Open discussion among jurors	10 minutes
Jury votes	Each juror in turn indicates guilty or not guilty	1 minute
Judge #3	Announces verdict and sentence if guilty	2 minutes
	Congratulations and condolences	
Newspaper	Reporters interview losing side	3 minutes
Television	Reporters interview winning side	3 minutes
Radio #2	Reporter gives story of trial	90 seconds

You can adjust mock trial formats to suit your needs. You can use fewer witnesses, make the accuser and the accused witnesses, create a new lawyer on each side to do all cross-examinations, appoint one student the jury foreperson and have that person announce the decision, have fewer lawyers, and adjust media roles.

In many ways the law represents a model for many debate formats. Mock trial debates can present a challenge and a powerful opportunity for many students to debate about legal issues. In these situations the value of debate emerges for both students and society.

Positive elements of this format include:

- Exciting and dynamic event that is enjoyable to observe and be part of
- Challenges students to become deeply involved in the material
- Keeps the entire class occupied with roles to play

Negative elements of this format include:

- Requires substantial student orientation and instruction about roles
- Requires considerable class time

- Students may not fully understand the nature of legal argument
- Topic choice can be essential to event success
- Cross-examination periods may not be long enough

Model Congress Debate

In the model congress format, students engage in imaginary debates that a body of government might face. This format is a wonderful way to incorporate a large audience in a debate format. We have seen this format used with as many as 300 students and it can be used to create debating opportunities between classes and even between schools.

The model congress format follows the template of the congressional debates in the United States, allowing for a large crowd of legislators to debate about public policy proposals. Traditionally students research and write a piece of legislation that they think should be passed. The teacher may provide suggestions drawn from subject matter being studied. All of the bills are gathered together and copied, with a packet of bills distributed to each student participant. The bills should be distributed early enough to provide time for students to consider and even research the issues raised by their fellow students. Then the students gather in a room and, observing the rules of parliamentary procedure, debate the bills. After each debate, the students vote on the bills to determine if the chamber supports them.

This format is exciting and challenging, providing fast action and an informed discussion about current topics of interest in politics. Students generally enjoy this process because they are able to speak extemporaneously in front of large crowds.

One of the weaknesses of the model congress format is the difficulty in establishing the debates. Because students need to be guided during the research and while writing bills, not to mention in the debate format itself, this format often proves daunting for teachers and students alike. Fortunately, these problems are easily resolved with some preparation. Researching topics is often a simple matter of having students read a newspaper for a week to pick out problems they would like to address and then using a generic template to write bills. One other risk is that mob opinion or the popular wisdom when debating a particular topic may sway students. This risk can be challenged through student discussion about the importance of making difficult decisions and the occasional need to go beyond personal politics when considering arguments.

The setup and format for model congress debates are straightforward. We suggest that students be given a week to research and write their bills, and then turn them in for review by an instructor. After possible revision, students' bills will be copied for all and then distributed or read aloud to the assembled students. At the debating session, we suggest that a teacher serve as the chair to identify students who want to speak about each bill. Whenever possible, let the students drive the debate agenda. Let them suggest which bills they want to debate and then have the author of the bill give a short speech urging support for his or her legislation.

Afterward, allow students brief periods (two minutes or so) to ask questions of the speaker and then open the floor up for participants to volunteer to debate. You must decide if you would like every speaker to have a distinct question-and-answer period or if you would like students to choose whether to accept questions from the crowd. The debate should continue until specified time runs out or until the energy lapses on the topic. Afterward, you should allow students to vote for or against or abstain from voting on the legislation. Some model congress debates have volunteers that run messages. Some model congress debates call upon students to play the role of nations or particular states. The flexibility afforded by this format provides exciting debate opportunities.

A complete handbook on how to hold a student congress session according to the procedures of the National Forensic League in the United States can be found at http://www.nflonline.org/AboutNFL/LeagueManuals.

The model congress format of debate allows large numbers of students to engage in self-driven debates about subjects that interest them. The capacity and speed of the event make it quite popular among students. It is extremely exciting and stimulating, and can fit a wide variety of debate needs.

Model Congress Debate

Student	Activity	Time
Chair (teacher)	Welcome to forum	1–5 minutes
Sponsor of bill	Advocacy speech	2–4 minutes
All students	Ask questions of the sponsor of the bill	2–3 minutes
Any student	Floor speech given in favor of or against the proposed bill	2 minutes

Positive elements of this format include:

- Open format allows students to guide the proceedings
- Students assume ownership of the bills they are proposing and defending
- Bills or motions can be easily drawn from course material
- Many students can be involved at the same time
- Students can negotiate support of one bill in exchange for support of another

Negative elements of this format include:

- Fairly extensive preparation necessary
- Takes a considerable amount of class time
- Member voting may follow a "popularity of the sponsor" formula instead of a "compelling arguments" formula
- Fairly easy for unmotivated students to hide in the crowd

Variations on Debate Formats

Whatever debate format you select, you will have available exciting variants that can spice up the procedures of your debates. These include changing the number of debaters on a team, including panels of questioners, and using debate as an extensive tool to analyze a subject.

Changing the Number of Debate Participants

Traditionally policy and parliamentary debating is done in teams of two, while traditional SPAR debating is done with just a single debater on each side, although these numbers are certainly not requirements. Almost all debate formats work equally well with a single person on each side. Many lend themselves to increasing the number of debaters. This section discusses the logistics of changing the number of debaters in a debate.

Reducing the Number of People on a Team

You may want to reduce the number of students debating because you are concerned about the time each debate will take or because you want to be able to more successfully track the work of individual students. Reducing the number of debaters to a single person on each side makes preparation and debating much easier. The downside is that many students feel increased anxiety when they are solely responsible for a performance. The benefit may be increased flexibility in the classroom and ease of scheduling.

Increasing the Number of People on a Team

You may wish to increase the number of participants to get more students involved or to ensure that everyone in a class gets to debate. A debate format used in central Pennsylvania in the United States has four debaters on each side, with a single debater responsible for a speech. Other possibilities include different students taking responsibility for the questioning and the speaking. You could also increase the number of debaters on a team and shorten the speaking time. It is reasonable to have a three vs. three debates or a four vs. four debates. For these kinds of debates, you may want to have a single concluding rebuttal given by a participant rather than each student giving both a constructive speech and a rebuttal.

Other Format Variations
Panel of Questioners

One variant that has been used in public debates in the United States but is seldom explored in classrooms is adding panels of questioners to whatever format you choose. This student panel would be responsible for researching and asking high-quality questions of the debaters.

This variant gets more students involved and encourages high-level dialogue on the issues. If you decide to make teams for a series of parliamentary debates in your classroom, you might also assign two different students for each debate to be a panel responsible for drafting high-quality questions to pose to the debaters.

Audience Question Time

A major criticism of classroom debates is that the audience loses interest because only a few students are participating during each classroom section (depending on which kind of debate you are doing). Having a period where nondebating students can pose questions and challenge the debaters can be a valuable way to encourage participation among your students.

Multisided Debate

Most debate issues are not clearly black and white. In fact, Deborah Tannen, author of *Argument Culture*, takes issue with the cultural need to create these dualistic oppositions: "I am questioning the assumption that everything is a matter of polarized opposites, the proverbial 'two sides to every question' that we think embodies open-mindedness and expansive thinking" (8). In fact, most debate questions can be best addressed by multiple approaches and answers.

Consider a debate about what the UN position should be on North Korea. One side of the debate might represent a hard-line stance advocating strict sanctions and a vigorous bombing campaign to get North Koreans to rebel against their government. A second side might advocate humanitarian assistance to help rebuild the shattered infrastructure of North Korea and feed starving children. Another approach might offer economic assistance to North Korea in exchange for a commitment to forgo a nuclear program. Yet a fourth position might represent a decided "hands-off" approach, arguing that the best thing that the UN could do would be to leave North Korea alone.

Debate offers a chance to experiment with imagining different worlds. When debaters conceptualize what the world would look like with some significant change, they develop critical thinking skills. These kinds of multisided debates both initiate this kind of thinking and also help avoid the simplistic black-and-white assumptions that many debates fall into.

Multisided Debate

Participant	Activity	Time
Teacher	Introduction	2 minutes
Assigned student	Background	4 minutes
Team a	Side #1 constructive	6 minutes
Team b	Side #2 constructive	6 minutes
Team c	Side #3 constructive	6 minutes
Class	Questions from audience or other sides	18 minutes
Student 1	Commentary #1	3 minutes
Student 2	Commentary #2	3 minutes
Team a	Side #1 rebuttal	4 minutes
Team b	Side #2 rebuttal	4 minutes
Team c	Side #3 rebuttal	4 minutes
Teacher	Concluding remarks	1 minute

Positive elements:
- More than two sides adds detail and dynamism to the debate
- More than two sides adds an element of interest for the audience
- Question period is lengthy and allows for development of new ideas and issues
- 60-minute format easy to insert into a class period
- Rebuttals allow summary and a sense of closure
- Commentary adds issues debaters might be ignoring or neglecting
- Lengthy background information allows the audience to become oriented to the topic and the positions each side will advocate

Negative elements:
- Topic must be suitable for three separate lines of advocacy

- Questions must be specific and relevant
- If audience permitted to ask questions, they should be reviewed in advance or else they may be of poor quality
- May be confusing to some because of the complexity of three different sides

Extended Debating/Return to Subject

A reasonable concern for the instructor is that the debates suggested in this book might be seen by students as a brief respite from the primary goals of the class. We believe that debates not only provide useful exercises, but also can be deeply integrated into course planning. It is entirely possible that debates could be a method by which a teacher orients an entire class.

Consider a history class that was studying the classical Greek and Roman civilizations. The teacher could use different kinds of debates at various times during the class to illustrate major points. A public forum debate on the value of Athenian democracy vs. Spartan military culture, a role-play on the trial of Socrates, and a parliamentary debate on the dangerous expansion of Roman military culture are all possibilities. Debates can illustrate each step of a class. There is no right or wrong way to design a debate as long as it meets the basic definitions we have offered.

Using the same class as an example, it is also possible to return to a single topic of debate throughout the duration of study. If the topic were "Greece and Rome are the cradles of civilization," then this subject could engender a contentious debate at several points during the term. Returning to the same subject encourages students to use and illustrate their deepening understanding of classroom material. At various points in the term, students could debate the importance of African and Asian contributions to knowledge, explore the learned society of Athens that held slaves, and highlight Roman architecture as evidence in an ongoing debate whose resolution is secondary to the educational goals realized. Extended debating revisits a major topic at various points and builds upon previously acquired knowledge. More important, because debates call upon students to incorporate what they've learned into a new performance, such debates can often result in exciting new outcomes.

Conclusion

Debate is a fundamentally valuable tool for every classroom; what is difficult is finding the right format to mesh your needs as a teacher with those of your students. This chapter provides criteria to help you to select a format for your debates. Many more possible formats are listed in the appendixes. Your first task is to pick a format and then map out how it best fits into your current curriculum. Debates should help you as a teacher to realize your students' learning.

Chapter Five

▾ ▾ ▾ ▾

Topics for Classroom Debating

Because so much of the debate process relies on the creation of debate topics, establishing a topic can be stressful. This chapter is intended to relieve those anxieties. Here you will learn how to create a debate topic and frame a constructive debate exercise that will fit with the goals of your class. We survey the debate literature to provide guidelines for topic construction. Then we discuss the three types of topics available (fact, value, and policy) as well as a nontraditional topic approach—reenactment topics.

Topics Set the Stage for the Debates

Every debate is "about" something. Without a topic, debate becomes little more than a bickering session. Having a topic allows the debaters to prepare sufficiently for their presentations and anticipate the arguments of the opposition. The topic informs the audience about what they should expect from the debate and creates a real focus for the decision that the participants are asked to make at the end of the debate event.

The topic also provides an educational theme for your classroom. A poorly constructed topic can result in a debate that focuses on the peripheral elements of the topic. If your goal is to have students learn about the importance of industrial inventions like the cotton gin, then having students debate "Technology has changed human history" would probably *not* achieve your goal. If, instead, you asked students to debate "What technological innovation has aided industry the most?" then you'll achieve your classroom goal. If you are careful in your choice of topics, you can ensure that your students will debate within the parameters you determine.

While competitive academic debating and the information landscape have changed in the last 100 years, the basic guidelines for topic construction have not. It is useful to draw on a number of well-established guiding principles available in debate literature. This chapter will draw on several classic debate texts to provide guidance for topic construction in the classroom. We thank those who came before us for their knowledge. In this text, we are especially indebted to Robert Branham for his ideas on crafting of debate topics.

Guidelines for Topic Construction
Topics Should Explore Important Parts of the Subject Matter

One of the easiest ways to make sure that a debate topic succeeds is to explore an enduring controversy. Many fields of study have such contested areas where people of honest intent simply disagree. Both sides of an issue are often composed of a set of good arguments and thus are not easily reconciled. For example, in the debate about using animals in scientific research, animal rights activists call for alternatives to animal testing. In this case, a debate based on this controversy is well framed because there are two clear sides. Controversies in a field often create good positions for an affirmative team because the team needs to question the conventional wisdom.

Topics for classroom debates can also examine critical choices made by various actors, individuals, and nations. The study of history offers many difficult choices that can become fruitful topics for debate. Literature is also full of critical choices that characters make that can serve as useful debate topics. In the study of politics and government, you can easily find debatable choices about public policy, elections, and legislation.

Topics for classroom debates can also be gleaned from the major areas studied during a class. Short and less formal debates can be used to illustrate issues that are part of the curriculum. Debates do not always have to focus on large issues; they can be adapted through shorter formats to become a way to pursue fairly specific areas of study. The larger topics, involving enduring points of controversy, often come up again and again and might be saved until the end of the class, but you may find it useful to stage several shorter debates that explore parts of the larger issue at several points in the class so that student perspectives and applications can develop and mature. We have had great success teaching issues in social studies, such as the balance of power between state and federal governments, using these themes for multiple classroom debates.

When crafting a topic, consider its research implications. A topic that is too big will make in-depth research impossible, while a very narrow topic will make research a frustrating endeavor. Will students be able to sustain quality arguments on both sides of the debate? Will both sides have the same research burden? These are the kinds of questions you should consider when planning a debate topic.

Topics Should Be Interesting

Not every topic makes an interesting debate. Some questions can be debated, but are of little usefulness when the time comes to make a decision about the topic. The more personally relevant the topic is to the students and to their course materials, the more interesting they are likely to find it.

Many historic, well-known debate topics have failed this first basic test.

William Trufant Foster pointed out in 1945 that some debate topics simply do not lend themselves to exciting debate. Using the example of a debate about the comparative use of iron and coal, he wrote that it was uninteresting "not only because it is undebatable, but also because [hu]mankind cares little how it is answered." He continued by calling for debates to be vital parts of the classroom experience, saying, "The scholastic disputants of the Middle Ages tried to determine how many angels can stand on the point of a needle, but that is no longer a live issue" (10). Foster argues that students should take on the issues that immediately interest them in their classes. Foster's observations are as true today as they were in 1945. Topics should be engaging and student interest is an important variable to consider when designing them.

The easiest way to make a topic interesting is to include your students in its creation. After assigning an essay, you might ask your students to brainstorm the controversies presented. Students can then suggest which of these they would like to investigate further.

Topics Should Be Debatable

Not all topics are debatable. Some topics are simple truisms that could be debated with a great deal of ingenuity, but probably not with any considerable value to the audience or the participants. A topic that has almost all people in agreement with one side becomes either a pep rally or a session for condemning those who hold the highly unpopular view. Likewise, a topic that all would prefer to oppose rarely elicits a good debate.

As well as avoiding truisms, some topics could never really be proven with any approximation at all. Foster offers some terrible debate topics such as: "Sodium contributes more than chlorine to the value of salt" and "Whether angels speak any language; if so, whether it is Hebrew." He reminds us that "a question should offer more than an ingenious exercise; it should offer the possibility of reaching, through argument, a reasonably sound conclusion" (5).

Nevertheless, there may be value in exploring ideas that seem to be universally unpopular. These arguments and ideas can point to the value that is accessible even in the untenable argumentative strategies. For example, Foster suggests: "Men have done more than women to advance civilization" as a topic that in his eyes is undebatable (5), but we think examining the positive and negative contributions to society that the two genders have offered could be quite exciting. When considering a debate about something extremely unpopular, you must reframe the topic to explore how certain ideas came to be popular—or make clear that the debaters are taking positions that do not reflect actual feelings.

Topics Should Have the Affirmative Support Change

In the vast majority of debating formats, the affirmative team (which supports the topic or resolution) gives the first and last speech of the debate. This format is clearly an advantage for them. Giving the affirmative the obligation of overturning the conventional wisdom or existing policy usually counterbalances that advantage. This role is also well suited to the first presentation of the debate, where the affirmative spells out its case. By opening the debate in an attempt to overturn existing belief or practice (the topic being affirmed should be one calling for change), the affirmative has what is called the "burden of proof," which is the way most dispositional communication situations are organized.

Assigning the affirmative the first and last speech clearly gives that side the advantage because they get to introduce the concepts of the debate. On the other hand, they are also responsible to the parameters they have set up. In competitive debate, students will present cases that favor their side, advocating for feeding refugees, aware that they will be able to castigate their opponents as callous for challenging their case. This kind of competitive under-learning can be challenged in the classroom setting by encouraging students to face difficult advocacies and pushing them to use debate to explore the world, not affirm what they already know.

Topics Should Have One Central Idea

Debates are time bound, and the length of a single debate is seldom sufficient to discuss any complex subject in depth. Yet, debate does attempt to embrace issues on a complex level as opponents look for weaknesses in the other side's ideas through the brainstorming stage and research stages. To focus the debate, you should try to constrain the topic to one major idea. This will allow the affirmative to develop a case for which the negative team might be able to imagine arguments in advance, prepare responses, and thus increase the depth of the debate. A topic with several ideas makes preparation more difficult, and the examination becomes obscured. Even if the ideas are related, a bifurcated topic makes the debate a bit shallower by virtue of having half as much time to discuss the ideas. An exception to this rule would be a topic in which two concepts are being compared, such as, "The right to privacy is more important than the public's right to know." Foster provides good examples of topics that have two parts, but still work. Most of them tend to center both questions along the same axis, for example: "Military drill should be taught in the common schools of America, and all able-bodied citizens should be required to serve a term in the army" (11). Both questions of the topic are answerable with the same proposal, so the question encourages a focus on a central idea.

Topics Should Be Elegant

Elegance refers to a stylish crafting that makes a debate appealing and easy to understand. We often admire elegant prose, such as that of Ivan Illich, Leslie Feinberg, or Abraham Lincoln, where much is communicated through relatively straightforward prose. Debate topics should likewise be crafted in a straightforward manner.

Many style guidelines have no better advice than to "use fewer words whenever possible." The topic becomes more confusing when more terms are introduced. Almost any word can be defined in several different ways, so multiple terms make a topic much more difficult to understand, define, and debate. The meanings of the words used in the topic should also be fairly clear. Extremely abstract terms should be avoided whenever possible. All terms contain much ambiguity, of course, but some terms are far more ambiguous than others.

Helping to craft clear, elegant topics is one of your central roles when using debate in the classroom. Often students will toss out ideas that are awkwardly phrased. (One of our students once suggested "Rhenquist rocks" when planning a debate about the politics of former Chief Justice William Rhenquist.)

One of the best ways to promote elegance is to encourage students to think about the goals of the debate as well as the subject. Ask your students what issues they hope will come up in the debate and encourage them to phrase topics that focus on those issues. For example, if students want to debate the harms of pornography, they might suggest the topic "Pornography is the worst evil in the world." This debate is likely to find debaters comparing the ills of pornography to the evils of events like war and child slavery. A class that wants to debate about how pornography objectifies women might be better served by the topic "Pornography does more harm to women than good."

Topics Should Use Neutral Language

Frame a topic so that it is neutral to both sides in the arranged controversy. Loaded language inserted into debate topics will influence the way the debate takes place and is perceived by the audience. If a loaded term is used, the debate may be slanted toward one side or another. Another risk is that the negative side may try to hold the affirmative to the standard of that term, thus confusing the debate. For example, a debate during World War II with the topic, "All nations should join together to fight the Axis barbarians," might be approached by the negative team arguing that the Axis nations of Japan, Italy, and Germany are, in fact, civilized, with health care and public transportation and thus are not included in the topic. *Barbarians* is such a loaded, non-neutral word that an audience attracted to this topic might be biased toward one side or the other before hearing one word of the debate.

Another risk is that people might view seemingly zesty topic choices as offensive. Writing a topic that describes environmentalists as "wackos" or feminists as "man-hating" taints the discussion and skews the outcome of the debate. When a debate topic offends people, some may challenge the language of the resolution, but many more will not participate. Students might refuse to take part or audience members might not show up. This use of negative language is especially risky with a public audience, where a poorly worded topic may make many feel as though they are purposely excluded. With a homogenous audience, debates can quickly become cheering rallies for arguments that everyone agrees with.

Topics Should Not Be too Broad

Because a debate is of limited duration, its topic must focus on a limited set of issues. However, this focus is required only if the debates are isolated and individual instead of part of a series. Often the national policy debate topic in the United States will be fairly broad, but there will be thousands and thousands of debates on this topic, allowing through repetition for coverage of a broad spectrum of concerns. The situation is somewhat different for classroom debating, where a given topic will be debated usually only once or only a very few times.

In competitive policy debate, a single topic operates for an entire year or a semester. In this situation, a broader topic becomes necessary. Robert Branham contrasts the topics of a year-long competition to the needs of a single classroom debate. He writes: "The proposition must be sufficiently limited to permit satisfactory treatment of it in the time allotted." Branham provides the example of "Resolved: that the United States should expand its exploration of outer space" as a topic that cannot be sufficiently explored in a short classroom debate because there are so many different options to explore outer space. He suggests that the topic "The United States should send astronauts to Mars by the year 2000" as a much more fruitful classroom debate (34).

Types of Debate Topics

Debate topics are broken into three different types: fact, policy, and value. This approach allows us to better craft topics to achieve our goals. In debates about fact, students are asked to prove propositions like "John F. Kennedy was killed by Lee Harvey Oswald acting alone." In debates about policy, debaters are asked to propose plans of action to solve problems. For example: "New Paltz is better served by the Green Party" is a policy topic. Topics about value call for debates on value judgments and opinions. "Fast food tastes worse than home-cooked meals" is a debate about values of taste.

Fact Topics

Topics of fact invite the debaters to argue about what "is," "was," or "will be." Debates about fact include some of the most exciting controversies of our time and often appeal to students because they feel they can prove them decisively.

Propositions of fact include "causality, definition, conditions of the past, and predictions" (Branham 34). Debates about causality, for example, "Nuclear energy is harmful to humans," argue that something results in a problem or solution. Debates about definition, such as "Protest is treason," discuss whether something belongs to a particular category. These debates might also cover conditions of the past, historical debates such as "The United States won the war in Vietnam." In a definition debate such as "The killings in Sudan are genocide," the political context can help students explain what is happening in Sudan. An understanding of the various definitions of the term *genocide* and previous genocides become important parts of preparing for these debates. Topics of fact are useful debates to teach the skills of prediction. Students are asked to imagine what might happen in the future based on current knowledge. In prediction debate, students would argue topics such as "Global warming will threaten food security by the middle of the 21st century."

In framing these topics, make sure to include the proper determination of the time period and context being debated. A debate about whether population is rising in a nation must be sure to focus on a particular time period so students will debate about the same things. It is also important to determine which of the above types of fact topics you are dealing with and then insert the proper terminology into the topic.

A topic concerned with causality should include the proper causal terms, such as *causes*, *leads to*, or *significantly contributes to*.

A topic concerned with definition should include the proper classification terms, such as *belongs to*, *is one of*, or *should be defined as*.

A topic concerning conditions of the past should include the proper historical terms, such as the use of the past tense *was* or *did*, or the statement of a period of time that the topic concerns.

A topic concerning predictions should include the use of the future tense, the specification of a particular condition or event to be predicted, and perhaps a statement of time frame so that the debate is not about the unlimited future.

These topics are highly debatable. Our interpretation of facts changes through time and often changes through the process of debate and discussion. Students can come to better understand what they accept as facts and how they come to accept them. Along the way, debates about fact will encourage students to explore how they came to know ideas as facts, understand the categories of knowledge, and better understand causality.

Value Topics

A value topic deals with the evaluations of persons, places, things, or events. The expression of a value topic is the offering of an evaluative term and then the object to which that evaluative term is applied. Often the value term being applied is fairly abstract, dealing with concepts such as beauty, importance, equity, morality, and ethics, all of which are open to wide variations in interpretation.

Creating a value topic can be as simple as finding a topic in the curriculum and asking students to evaluate it. In a history class, trying to grapple with the evil of the Nazi regime, students might debate: "Hitler was the worst leader the world has ever known."

Our experience with arguing value topics pervades our lives when we discuss what we like better and what is right or wrong. Robert Branham points out that we are familiar with value debates because we have often participated in them when we argue about a movie or a meal we might have shared (35). For students, value debates are often comfortable, but in many cases difficult events to evaluate.

We often assume that questions of value need to be resolved in an absolute way, such as that something is good or bad, ugly or beautiful. While this may be the case in some topics, such as "Murder is always immoral," it is also true that values can be debated in comparison to each other, such as "The pursuit of economic prosperity is less important than the preservation of environmental quality." Value debates provide a wonderful chance to engage students and, with some planning on your part, can provide focus and educational rigor.

Policy Topics

Topics of policy concern social or individual action. These topics ask the question, "What should be done?" Examples of policy topics would include debates between candidates to gain the ballots of the voters, debates in legislative bodies about what laws to adopt, and debates about which product or professional service to utilize. Other topics include (Branham 36):

> "The United States should permit the use of human fetal tissue for scientific research."
>
> "All nations should cease the killing of whales."
>
> "Quebec should secede."
>
> "Maine should establish a state-run lottery."
>
> "The city of Lewiston should adopt mandatory recycling procedures."
>
> "This house supports X for president of the United States."
>
> "This university should establish a system of pass/fail grading."
>
> "This house believes that knowledge of at least one foreign language should be required for graduation from this university."
>
> "The university should prohibit racist speech on campus."

In crafting policy topics, keep the following guidelines in mind:

- An action or policy should be specified.
- The agent of that action should be specified.
- The word *should* (meaning ought to but not necessarily will) is useful for indicating the difference between a policy and fact topic.

Because policy debates tend to focus on specific proposals, when writing policy topics, teachers should focus the requirements of the topic on what is necessary for the learning goals.

The three types of topics (fact, value, and policy) are not completely separate; they overlap in important ways. For example, a topic of value will utilize questions of fact (the way things are or were) as well as questions of value (the way things should be). Topics of policy involve knowledge of facts and the application of values in order to determine what should be done (the policy being debated).

Time Period and Reenactment Topics

Topics can be written so that they take place in a specific time period or with the debaters in specific roles. These settings could feature topics of fact, value, or policy. A time period topic would, for example, situate the debaters in a specific period of time (the UN debate over the creation of the state of Israel) and ask the debaters to engage in the debate as if they were living in that time. A reenactment topic, for example, would situate the debaters in a specific situation (a debate about whether an old-growth forest should be harvested for lumber) and ask the debaters to play various roles that would exist in a real debate about such an issue (lumber company representative, local government official, local businessperson, environmental protection activist, etc.).

Time period topics can be extremely useful for studying either actual or fictional history as portrayed in a historical novel. Reenactment topics can be very useful for studying complex social phenomenon where competing interests are represented. These reenactment debates can help students understand the various perspectives of important actors in the situation being portrayed.

In one of our classrooms, we've used a role-playing debate where students are asked to be activists from the late 1960s involved with Students for a Democratic Society (SDS), which was instrumental in stopping the Vietnam War and agitating for black civil rights. In this role-play, the debate focused on women who want to leave the group in order to focus exclusively on women's issues. The debate requires a certain amount of imaginative reconstruction about the life in these times.

When using these topic variations, you must provide additional information to assist students in making the debate a productive event. Keep two things in mind. First, students should be provided with the background for the debate. Be sure to communicate to the students involved that the debate is located in a specific historical and social context as, without some detailed background information, the practice loses much of its value. This preparation might have already taken place through a study of a specific time period in class. Second, if students are to represent specific individuals, provide substantial biographical material about these individuals.

Conclusion

Topic choices frame the focus of the debates and direct the research and preparation of your students. You should devote considerable time to drafting topics, using knowledge of the subject matter as well as the guidelines presented in this chapter. Different kinds of topics produce different kinds of debates, and you can use the flexibility of diverse topics to better engage your students.

Chapter Six

~ ~ ~ ~

Preparing Students for Classroom Debating

This chapter assists teachers in preparing students to engage in classroom debates. Although your students will not need extensive training, they will need to learn some basic procedures and skills. This chapter covers the information students might need for preparing for and executing classroom debates. The chapter is only an introduction, for more information on specific issues, see the appendixes or refer to the bibliography.

Brief Introduction to Debate Skills and Practices Is Sufficient

You may wish to share the information in this chapter with your students, utilizing it during class time or as a resource students can use when preparing for debate. This book is not only aimed at teachers of debate classes, but at any educator interested in using debate as a teaching method.

We realize that you do not have a large amount of time to spend on teaching complicated debate skills. Fortunately, the debate process is easy to grasp, and many of the skills are natural communication practices that humans use daily. Students do not need long periods of instruction on "how to debate" for most of these exercises to be useful. Regardless of their educational experience, everyone can and should debate.

We urge you to de-emphasize the skills of debating and focus rather on the ideas being debated. Our educational model envisions debate as a method of inquiry, one that works in every situation where dialogue can contribute to the understanding of phenomena.

Students often want more concrete parameters for classroom behavior—clear expectations of what they are to do. You can help to reassure students by providing a clear framework of how the debate is to run and what each student will be expected to do in the debate. While the spontaneous energy of debate is often obvious, many participants also learn vital decision-making skills. Because debate is an activity where students define not only the subject but also the process, they have an enormous impact on how the debates operate.

We begin our discussion of preparation with a checklist of behaviors that debaters can use to ensure success and to inspire their performance. Several New York Urban Debate League coaches asked one of the authors to compile a list of characteristics that describe a good debater as well as those that describe a poor debater. Because the debate is supposed to be won by the team who did the "better job of debating," these rather abstract and symbolic characteristics very often translate directly into competitive success. We also think they translate into success later in life. We provide them here for your use.

The "Better" Debater

- Is a gracious winner and a respectful loser.
- Gives strong rhetorical reasons for the probative force of his or her arguments.
- Makes needs of and benefits to others the focus of the debate through her or his arguments instead of focusing on his or her competitive triumph.
- Argues through excellent evidence, but always makes argument the focus, not evidence. Good debaters use evidence to support their arguments and do not assume the audience recognizes the importance of their arguments.
- Debates dynamically, with enthusiasm and commitment.

- Sees the big picture, is aware of how ideas influence one another, and uses those relationships to enhance analysis in the debate.
- Knows the value of having a working command of the debate topic. There is no substitute for knowing what it is you are debating about.
- Understands the need for organization in order to identify the critical tipping points in the debate.
- Projects an image of an intelligent person who is seeking to understand and discover the truth.

The "Less Skilled" Debater

- Becomes frustrated when debate success isn't easy or automatic and loses the benefits of debating through lack of determination.
- Whines that everything is against her or him: judges, situations, other teams, and fate.
- Fails to show respect to all participants—opponents, judges, audience, and hosts.
- Speaks from a position of privilege—demanding that you trust and accept his or her ideas over those of others without demonstrating why.
- Fails to make connections between various issues and arguments in the debate.
- Speaks only in generalities or only in specifics, not understanding that both the big picture and the minutiae are important at all times.
- Fails to have fun in the debate because of an overly competitive nature or lack of interest.
- Fails to pay rigorous attention to the judge's critique, learning neither from failure nor success.
- Fails to focus during the debate, allowing his or her mind to wander and be distracted by outside events.

Discerning who is the better debater can be difficult, requiring you to be carefully involved in the debate's progress and observing each debater's behavior. This list is based on our years of experience as teachers and coaches and is a guide for you to use in your classroom. It is not a list of goals or even a guide to evaluate students, but rather a list of suggestions for attitude.

People develop debate skills through participating in debate; thus, no matter how thoroughly you've instructed them, you shouldn't expect your students to display a high degree of proficiency in their first tries at debating. Rather than focusing on teaching these skills, provide the guidelines and let the students go. These lists of good and bad debating styles can point you in the right direction, but they are not teachable in the traditional sense. Instead, we encourage you to spark the desire in students to follow their own path and discover the natural value of being a positive debater. A brief introduction to debating should be sufficient to allow classroom debating activities to begin. After they begin, everyone learns by doing and performances improve as collective learning accumulates.

Teaching Issue Discovery

Teaching students how to approach the topic of debate is the skill of issue discovery. People usually are aware of their own opinions about various controversies and the reasons they hold them, but they are usually not familiar with the arguments and reasons in support of positions they do not agree with. When students become debaters, they need to take this extra step to determine what the various issues are within the controversy.

Malcolm X describes this process during his time debating in prison. He writes: "whichever side of the selected subject was assigned to me, I'd track down and study everything I could find on it. I'd put myself in my opponent's place and decide how I'd try to win if I had the other side; and then I'd figure a way to knock down those points" (184).

Some students have difficulty discerning which issues are vital to a controversy. An issue can be thought of as an idea or concept that is both essential and unavoidable in a meaningful discussion of a topic.

For example, whether an unborn fetus is a human being is such an issue in the debate about abortion rights. It is essential because quite often the resolution of that issue directs the position an individual has on this question. It is unavoidable because no debater can engage in a debate about abortion rights without discussing this issue. This is not to say that an idea must be absolutely essential and absolutely unavoidable for it to be thought of as an issue, but if it loosely meets either of these standards, it must be considered and prepared for.

Students can uncover the issues in different sorts of resolutions by looking at the basic "stock issues" (primary themes) or "points of stasis" (major arguments) in that type of resolution. Students discover issues through basic methods they can then use throughout their lives. Some of the methods: interpreting formal course material, examining controversies in the field, using brainstorming techniques, and engaging in thought experiments.

Formal course material may provide students with insight into issue discovery, especially if the instructor features differences of opinions and various perspectives when covering the subject matter. Students can react to ideas presented in readings, lectures, and discussions that they find relevant to the topic they will be debating.

Every living and growing field of knowledge has controversies. An examination of these controversies not only leads to the creation of good topics for classroom debates, but also reveals different approaches to the subject that the student may not be aware of and can apply to the debate topic. Instructors should be ready to inform students about such topics and the individual scholars associated with them.

Brainstorming is an excellent tool for issue discovery. This practice involves a small group of people deciding to have a discussion to determine what the important ideas are within a given topic. A public list is created of all ideas presented, and criticism of any ideas is delayed until a later time. The creation of such a list should continue even when the flow of ideas begins to slow because that is the point at which the group's real creativity begins to operate, simply because the obvious ideas have already been brought up—where students are digging and stretching for ideas. After such a list has been constructed, criticism and analysis can begin. Duplicative ideas can be grouped together, related ideas can be put into larger categories, and irrelevant or unacceptable ideas can be excluded. The list that remains is often an excellent survey of the issues.

Thought experiments—where students are encouraged to fantasize in order to better imagine a solution—are another useful technique for discovering issues. While none of us may be as insightful as Albert Einstein thinking about travel at the speed of light while in an Austrian streetcar, this kind of critical and creative imagining can be quite revealing. In a thought experiment you imagine that something has taken place or is true and then you project this idea to other ideas that seem relevant. What if animals could communicate with humans? Would this kind of world necessitate a new relationship between the species?

Much of policy debate involves thought experiments. In a thought experiment about significantly raising income taxes on wealthy citizens, one would imagine that such a program was in existence and then imagine the consequences. The resulting thinking might suggest that the wealthy might move their income out of the country to avoid paying higher taxes, that the use of charitable donations as a tax benefit might increase, that more people might cheat on their taxes, that the additional funds might be poorly spent, and on and on. Most people have very powerful and creative imaginations, and those forces can be harnessed in the process of issue discovery.

Ultimately a good exercise in issue discovery will require additional research by the student debaters. They will need to seek, locate, and prepare to use information that supports their point of view or challenges the point of view of their opponents. In this process, issue discovery is a natural result.

Teaching Speech Organization

Excellent ideas can be sabotaged by poor organization. Similarly, average ideas can be improved and made successful if properly organized. One of a debater's most important goals is to present material in a way that makes logical sense, relates ideas to one another in meaningful ways, and allows the audience to connect responses to the arguments the speaker is answering. Unless ideas work together well and unless the audience understands the answers to the arguments, comprehension is unlikely.

When building arguments and advocacy positions in a debate, basic outlining techniques are important. We suggest breaking up the ideas into the following parts.

Major Points

Divide ideas up under major headings. These major headings might represent major argumentative burdens. Make sure that the major points are distinct from one another. If an idea is unavoidable and vital in coming to the conclusion, it should be included as a major point. Put major points in the proper chronological order: causes before effects, background before conclusions, etc. The statement of the major point should be relevant to all of the points arrayed under it. It is also important to organize speeches into major points in order to help students conceptualize their ideas. You should encourage your students to give previews of their major arguments and to keep all of their important points in their head throughout the debate. The organization of a speech into major points is vital in this process.

Subordinate Points

Include within each major point all the specific points that support it. Some of these subordinate points will naturally group together into further subgroups. This sorting of ideas is crucial to debate success and to becoming a critical thinker. Ideas can be sorted by distinct idea or concept, general or specific nature, different steps in a logical process, or some other coherent way.

Notation

Outlines (and debate arguments) have letter and number iterations so that one level of substructure can be differentiated from another. Major points are often expressed with Roman numerals (I, II, III,

IV, etc.), subtopics of major points are letters (A, B, C, D, etc.), and particulars about subtopics are numbers (1, 2, 3, 4, etc.). At least two particular ideas are necessary to begin a subdivision of any point; otherwise the single subdivision would be the more general point. You need a B to justify an A, and a 2 to justify a 1.

Other organizational guidelines include critiquing arguments by authors and applying certain issues to unique positions taken by the other team. In these instances, organizing smaller groups of arguments is essential. For example, if the affirmative case has stated that corporate agriculture is harmful, the negative will need to organize responses to this assertion. Here are two distinct ways to organize responses.

List of Reasons—Use Numbers. Often debaters will provide a list of independent reasons why something is or is not true. If the affirmative side claims that gay marriage would ruin the family structure, the negative side could come up with three independent arguments why this is not true: gay parents love their children as much as straight parents, studies show that gays can be excellent role models for children, and gay parents often have higher incomes, which provide opportunities for children. Each of these would be a separate idea, not a repeat of a previous idea. Thus, opponents would have to answer each of these separately.

Chain of Reasoning—Use Letters. Often arguments are more complex than one idea and involve several steps. These steps can be thought of as chains of reasoning. Thus, a debater would say that: A. gay marriage destroys the family structure, B. this undercuts our nation's international prestige and leads to conclusion, C. therefore, our enemies are more likely to attack us. Like any chain, it is only as strong as its weakest link. Accordingly, opponents would only have to break the chain at one point, for example, disproving that gay families destroy the family structure. In lengthy chains of reason, the further you get from the original premise, the weaker the argument becomes, as in this case.

Why Do This

It is very important to be able to discern if arguments in a list are independent or if a chain of reasoning exists. Organizing arguments in the ways given above allows you to always be able to tell the difference easily and increase the quality of debates.

As we noted in Chapter 2, the ARE structure of argument is a useful way to conceptualize arguments. In the ARE model, each argument has three components: the **Assertion**, the **Reasoning**, and the **Evidence**. We encourage our students to conceptualize arguments into ARE format while constructing their speeches.

Assertion. This is what the debater wants the audience to write down and remember. It should be relatively short and snappy, and express an argumentative relationship. Assertions should be positively worded and provide some preview of the reasoning. Arguments that explain that something is "good for your health" or "studies show no harmful effects" help audiences to better understand the reason behind an argument. The more expressive label does more than just say, "we win"; it gives a reason why, and giving reasons why statements are true is the basis of argumentation. The assertion gives a statement that expresses a relationship between two ideas and that should communicate those ideas well.

Reasoning. Here is where a debater explains the logical basis of her or his argument. There is a difference between a "claim" and an "argument." A claim states that something is so but does not explain why. Thus, a team could just keep making claims ("we win," "our arguments are better," "our case is true") without making progress in the debate. An argument expresses a *reason* why something is true. It uses some logical principle to compel belief on the part of the listeners. Quite often debaters leave this step out as they write their speeches in an assertion-evidence pattern. They do so at their peril, as their ideas get lost in a haze of quotations, references, and assertions while the audience is left wondering "why?"

Evidence. Here is where the debater uses some fact, testimony, example, or expert opinion to bolster the point being made. Evidence often comes in the form of a quotation or a statistic that has been researched prior to the debate. Such evidence should be relevant and in direct support of the assertion. Formal evidence is not necessary to make an argument, especially if the debater uses some sound logical principle that can be demonstrated rhetorically. A logical demonstration of the argument can also serve as evidence.

An important organizational tool for use during debate speeches is called "signposting." Once a debater has created a series of strong arguments and put them in order, he or she will want to preview those ideas for the audience. Signposting becomes increasingly important as the ideas presented grow more complex.

Transitions between arguments also help the audience follow the order in which the debaters move from argument to argument. Having a coherent discussion of the issues helps the whole debate to move much more smoothly and allows more clashes with the other team. Keep in mind that the language of transitions should mirror the preview presented during the signposting of the introduction.

Signposting and clear transitions allow the audience and other teams to identify the specific argument being addressed within each major argument. Signposting should be done throughout each speech by distinguishing between and labeling each argument. Transitions provide information about which issues will be dealt with next, while also providing the audience time to organize their notes and "shift gears" mentally. One of the most important functions of signposting is to assist everyone in effective note taking.

Teaching Basic Oral Communication Skills

Obviously students will communicate orally during the debate, which will both demonstrate and test their basic public speaking capacity. You need not spend a considerable time teaching students how to speak—they already speak in the classroom and probably use oral communication skills many times each day. Nevertheless, you should share with your students some basic ideas about public speaking that can help to orient their communications.

The primary goal of any speech is clarity and comprehension. Unless the audience clearly understands the ideas, the persuasive potential of those ideas cannot be realized. Good speaking technique also increases the speaker's credibility, because good delivery makes the audience want to understand and believe the speaker. Students should strive to make their ideas clear and straightforward.

Audiences tend to prefer dynamic speakers. Students can increase their persuasive abilities by working on verbal emphasis and ability to engage an audience. Dynamic speakers use energy, enthusiasm, commitment, and variety to move an audience. Debaters who act like they care about the arguments give credibility to their debate performances.

Dynamism can be achieved in public speaking through the application of three delivery principles:

Variation: Be careful not to overuse particular rhetorical techniques.

Emphasis: Use delivery (voice, gestures, etc.) to emphasize and highlight the important arguments and the important words in evidence; speakers should remain within their natural range.

Naturalness: Be genuine. If the audience believes the speaker is faking, they will not want to believe her or him.

These three principles can be applied to the various physical dimensions of oral communication delivery:

Volume: Change it for emphasis but do not talk too loudly or too softly.

Tone: Change it for emphasis but do not speak in an unusual or out-of-character tone.

Speed: Slow down for the important ideas and communicate quickly when attempting to move an audience.

Hand gestures: Used to emphasize important points, gestures make the speaker look more energetic and increase his or her dynamism. The focus of the speech, however, should be the ideas, not the student's performance and significant hand movement can distract from the message.

Face: The face is the most expressive part of the body, and people pay close attention to the facial expressions of speakers. Use facial expressions that match the points being made to avoid sending mixed signals.

Movement: Don't be afraid to move around a bit, but don't stray too far from notes and the podium.

A debate can be thought of as a sort of drama in the classroom; every student debater needs to assume the proper role. First impressions are important. In interview situations, most people are "hired" in the minds of the interviewer within the first three minutes based on their appearance alone. Good debaters who want to assume the proper role should be:

- Competitive (serious demeanor, ready to debate on time)
- Confident (well prepared, up on time, feel good about what they are saying)
- Courteous (friendly, mature)
- Credible (informed, dynamic, of good character)
- Commanding (appropriately dressed, using no street language, unafraid, courteous)

Many of these guidelines are common sense, but they are ideas that we have found useful in helping students quickly become much better public speakers.

Teaching Basic Note-Taking Skills

Taking notes properly (*flow sheeting* or *flowing* is a common debate term) is an essential skill for debaters. To answer arguments by opponents, debaters must be able to write them down so that they can remember them and respond to them in order. Likewise, the flow sheet becomes a set of notes and the text debaters use when they speak. After speaking itself, note taking is one of the most important parts of the debate experience, a skill that many students use throughout life.

Students should prepare their flow sheet by dividing their papers into separate sections for keeping track of the different ideas. This might be different sections of a sheet of paper (marking the page off in quadrants). Many competitive debaters make columns that represent each of the major speeches and take notes for each speech, keeping track of almost every idea presented. Students who keep strong notes can organize their response speeches to directly clash with their opponent's major ideas. If a debater simply writes ideas down as her opponent presents them and then jots down what she wants to say, the arguments will seem disjointed and chaotic. Worse, she might miss a vital argument. Practicing note taking specifically for debates is important.

Here is some specific technical advice to debaters about note taking:

- What should a debater write with? Write in black, because it is easier to read. Use a writing instrument that moves smoothly over the paper, allows you to write quickly, does not smear, and is comfortable in your hand. Try a medium-point pen, though if you write small use a fine-point pen, and if you write large you can get away with a broad-point pen. Always have lots of the right kinds of pens.

- What should a debater write on? Most debaters flow on yellow legal pads. Yellow because it is easy to read (especially with black ink!), and a legal size (8.5" x 14") because it allows for more room to write. Legal paper in pads allows you to have several pages attached together at the top.

- How many columns should the flow sheet have? Note taking in a debate usually involves creating a column on the page for each speech. This format allows arguments to be traced from one side of the paper across the page and throughout the debate. Draw these columns on pages well before the debate starts.

- Having several different note pads is often useful as you can put different kinds of arguments on each one. For example, in a debate about the impact of Japanese nuclear rearmament, students might use a pad to keep notes about military implications, foreign relations, and the cultural debate of a nation that has experienced the nuclear bomb. This use of separate pads allows students to keep notes organized around major types of issues in the debate. Bunches of loose sheets of paper flying all over are undesirable.

- Leave room on your flow. As a speech is given, write down what is being said in that section of your notes and leave space for the argument to develop through the debate. Do not crowd things together. If notes are all packed together on a notepad, you will have difficulty referring to and reading from them as you speak. Don't be afraid to use many pages, with a different major point on each page.

- Use a symbolic vocabulary. People speak more quickly than you can write; therefore, flow will not be a word-for-word version of what debaters say; instead, it will be a shortened and significant version of the ideas being expressed. One useful way to take notes is to use symbols that stand for concepts we commonly encounter in an argumentative situation. By turning opponents' statements into a new symbolic and abbreviated form, you can boil down what they are saying into a form that you can easily write down and keep track of.

Logic symbols include:

↑ increasing or increases,

↓ decreasing or decreases,

= is, or the same as,

→ causes or leads to,

> greater than,

< less than.

Also, all of these can be negated (turned into not) by putting a line through them, so you get not increasing, not decreasing, not equal to or not same as, not leads to or not causes to, etc.

Other debate symbols include:

X for piece of evidence used by speaker,

? no answer to this,

▲ change,

⊖ assertion which should have been proven,

⊗ evidence does not prove argument claimed.

Develop your own abbreviations for common debate terms as well as common terms in the topic students might be debating. If you are making an abbreviation for the first time, try just leaving the vowels out, thus "hospital" becomes "hsptl." As you become more familiar with an abbreviation, you can drop out more and more characters; eventually a single letter might come to stand for a whole complex argument.

Combine logic and debate symbols with debate and topic abbreviations to be able to quickly write down what the arguments of your opponent mean in a way that makes sense to you and that you can interpret to the audience.

If students are having a difficult time taking notes, don't worry about it. Encourage them to enjoy the debate process even as they learn to take notes. Many great debaters have developed their own, occasionally quirky, style of note taking.

Offer this advice for students trying to take notes for a debate:

- Never give up. If you miss something, get the next argument. Once you stop flowing in a debate, you are opting out of meaningful participation in it.

- Try to write down everything you can. Pour your entire attention and energy into this task.

- Ask to see the notes of your teachers and fellow debaters. Learn from them.

- Practice and when you watch a debate try to take the best flow you can.

- Look at your flows and see how many of these techniques you have used. Try to incorporate new techniques to increase your note-taking skills.

- Use structure. Structure and label all the arguments on your flow the same way that the speaker you are flowing is structuring and labeling his or her arguments. Be sure to write down all the numbers and letters you hear on your flow so that you can refer to your partner's or opponent's specific arguments later in the debate.

- Use your partner. Use the other team's preparation time to talk to your partner about arguments you might have missed.

These guidelines should help students take better notes and perform better in their debates.

Teaching Students How to Ask and Answer Questions

For many, the question periods are the most exciting parts of a debate because they highlight the greatest moments of clash. Below we discuss audience members asking questions of debaters, debaters asking questions of each other, and debaters answering questions. In this section we help to craft strong questions that will result in the answers debaters need.

Questions may serve the following objectives:

- To clarify points
- To expose errors
- To obtain admissions
- To set up arguments
- To show the audience the debater's skills and entice that audience into *wanting* to support that debater

Too many debaters tend to ignore the value of good questioning technique, focusing instead on their arguments. Remember, in many formats a substantial portion of the entire debate is spent in question-and-answer periods—it should be a meaningful and essential part of the debate. If nothing else, debaters tend to underestimate the influence question periods may have on the audience. Audiences love the question-and-answer period because it is a chance to clarify arguments and assertions and draw distinctions. Questioning periods are some of the most valuable ways to draw contrasts between sides. Behavior during the question period will indicate to the audience just how sharp and spontaneous the debaters are. Invisible bias always occurs in a debate and audiences like the sharpest team to win. Good, effective question periods can play an important psychological role in winning the audience's support.

As in all oral presentations, speakers should be dynamic. The debaters should have questions ready; they should answer questions actively and with confidence whenever possible. The image they project will be very important to the audience. This question period is the one opportunity the audience has to compare opponents side by side.

Guidelines for asking questions include the following:

- Ask a short, focused question designed to get a short answer.
- Indicate the object of the question, what it refers to.
- Don't advertise the intent of your argument or make it too obvious—the answerer might preempt the argument you are trying to build.
- Don't ask questions that you know the other side will answer in a snide manner. For example, you should never ask if your opponents think they are winning an argument, they will inevitably answer in the affirmative.
- Make questions seem important, even if they are just an attempt to clarify.
- Be polite. If the respondent is rude, audiences will notice.
- Approach some points from an innovative direction to trap the respondent.
- Avoid open-ended questions; they allow a respondent to make a short speech.
- Face the audience, not the opponent.
- Integrate answers into arguments made during a speech whenever possible.
- Try to build up a chain of questions that can get you some advantage.

Guidelines for answering questions include the following:

- Give a concise answer whenever possible.
- Refer to something already said whenever possible.
- Answer based on the position of your side in the debate so far, because that will keep options open.
- Qualify answers with words like *often*, *sometimes*, and other limiters.
- Be willing to exchange quotations read into the debate.
- Answer only relevant questions.
- Address the audience.

The question-and-answer portions of a debate can be exciting and dynamic, and can reveal the abilities of the various participants.

Debaters should use these periods actively and strategically to forward their own side of the debate and to better understand the ideas presented.

Teaching Students How to Judge a Debate

Students can better understand the debate process when they also see it from the judge's perspective. While an audience member can observe and learn from the performance of others, putting students in a position to evaluate others assists them in understanding what they must do to gain a positive evaluation when they debate. Knowing that a ballot is due as homework can also encourage audiences to pay close attention to the debates.

Judges can assume several different roles, which are explained in Chapter 8. The judge can take on the role of determining whether the debate influences her opinion (and at the end judges vote for the side they most believe in), he can evaluate the presentation skills of the two sides, or she can judge the debate based on who did the better job of debating.

In the "better job of debating" role, the judge tries to determine not which side is "right," but which side did the better job in the debate. The judge strives to be as objective as possible, realizing that no debate decision can be totally objective. Thus, the judge should try not to allow his opinions to influence the decision, rather he should attempt to suspend judgment and listen to the ideas presented. The judge should try to avoid argumentative intervention in the debate and base the decision purely on what the debaters argued and articulated. Just as the student debaters would not want the instructor's evaluation to reflect a specific ideological bias but rather the skills shown by the students, student judges should attempt to do the same.

This "better job of debating" model requires three major qualities of a judge: diligence, fairness, and knowledge about the debate topic. Judges have a responsibility to listen to the arguments shared in the debate and to evaluate them through contrast and analysis.

Student judges should also be diligent and attentive. Judges should attempt to be active listeners, trying their best to understand the debaters' arguments. This active listening involves taking copious notes during the debate, attending to the speaker, and trying to avoid distractions. Judges should also give nonverbal signals that indicate attention and put the debaters more at ease.

Student judges should be as fair as possible. Absolute objectivity is not possible, since background, education, parents, knowledge of the subject matter, and language skills influence every person. Individuals should be aware of their own strongly held opinions, as well as their political and moral beliefs. Just being aware of bias can help individual judges to keep their biases in check. The judges' goal should be to evaluate the debate going on in front of them. The process of judging the debate is not one of comparing the performances to a set standard but one that compares the performances of all the sides presented.

Student judges should have some knowledge of the topic being debated. Students make good judges in this regard because they tend to know many of the same things as other students. Students have been in the class studying the subject along with the other students, and thus judges and debaters have some common ground of understanding the issues. Each student will, of course, know different things about the subject at different levels of detail.

Student judging is a valuable way to increase student empowerment and audience involvement in the debate. Student judges can provide vital feedback for fellow students and can help to increase the skill level of the debates in the classroom.

Helping the Affirmative Prepare a Case

Students generally enjoy building their own case to support the debate topic. They get to decide what they want to talk about and what they want to do. The ideas are in their control. They get to think in strategic terms about how they wish to organize the debate. They can set traps for negative teams, hide answers to their arguments, and lure opponents into supporting weak arguments. Affirmative debating is a great place to learn and develop communication strategies. Debaters can exercise their advocacy in preparing their case for the topic. They can decide what they want to stand for, what they want to advocate, and how they want to present their ideas. In some contexts, students might have a chance to propose changes in a public forum where other people can consider, oppose, support, and test their ideas. The skill of learning to build a strong affirmative case to support a side of a debate is one of the best outcomes of debate. Students will need to stand up and be advocates in their adult lives, and now is the time to get the training they need.

Students selecting and preparing a case should use research and care in organizing their ideas. Students may wish to select approaches for their case based on the strength of the literature associated with the question. They will need good evidence to support their case. Does the case idea have articles and books written about it? If so, they can learn to marshal the data and facts to fulfill their purpose. They should not be concerned if there is a lot of evidence about their idea. Because they initiate discussion, they can almost always stay ahead of the opposition if they know the literature. Students need to read broadly and holistically to understand the controversies in the field. Familiarizing themselves with a body of knowledge in preparation for the debate enriches the students' encounter with the subject.

Students should not be discouraged if evidence goes against their case—there probably are no truly perfect ideas. They can learn to anticipate the negative arguments, but they also want the preponderance of evidence to be on their side of the issue.

Although not essential, encourage your students to choose a case approach that they believe in. Certainly advocacy of attitudes not held by the debater can be intellectually valuable, because students will have to challenge their own beliefs. But when time comes to advocate, finding a position that students can really get behind can be useful in translating their ideas into strong debate arguments. This approach can also maximize the student utilization of the debate work, because it is something they are likely to discuss in other forums.

Research may be one of the most important skills students will learn in debate; when building an affirmative case, students must focus their research to find the best evidence. Students should go to the library and start by doing a search for the central ideas of the debate. They should scan the articles and book chapters they find looking for good arguments and support. They must not start reading whatever they find or they will never get anywhere. They need to scan what a library has, see what the best materials are, and read them first. They should make sure to look for all kinds of literature on their subject, including books, professional journals in the area of research, government documents, Internet sites, general periodicals and newspapers, and specific prints put out by specialty groups in the field.

Once they have found a variety of materials, they should sort them and start scanning the best items first by looking at the chapter headings and finding the ones likely to have what they want. When they scan a chapter, they should read the first few paragraphs and the last few paragraphs. If that information looks good, then they should scan the chapter one paragraph at a time. They should scan a paragraph by reading the first and last sentences. If those sentences look good for their research area, then they should read the entire paragraph. This way they find the paragraphs that are really needed, not hundreds of pages of irrelevant material. Of course, students should still approach the subject holistically, attempting to understand the ideas presented in their background materials.

Students should not forget to look up the keywords about their case in the index of the book. They should also scan articles and other publications for keywords. Using keywords, they can scan the vast bodies of literature available to find exactly what they need to win their debate.

Using holistic reading, students should make sure to find and note the negative evidence and arguments as well. They will not understand their own case fully until they understand the arguments against it. Students should pay attention to the evidence and arguments that they need but are not finding. They will have to do a special search for such information or else figure out a way to argue the affirmative case effectively without it.

The student debaters are now prepared to write their first speech to introduce their advocacy of the debate topic. The affirmative case is the audience's first impression of the side, and thus must be particularly strong. The presentation must give a good impression of the debaters and their ideas.

Debaters should choose language carefully to explain their case to the audience, using colorful but sophisticated language. They should also put in strong statements explaining what their arguments prove and why their arguments are important.

In the beginning of the affirmative case, a team member should read the resolution and then give two or three sentences that explain the underlying thesis. It is always a good idea to have the judge on board with the general ideas before presenting evidence and minor arguments.

Students will want to present their major arguments in a clear and organized way through the identification of several "contentions" or major issues. They should keep their contentions few, clear, and match them with the topic's stock issues. Word the contentions clearly and simply so that judges and the audience can write them down easily. Avoid having too many subpoints; make the ideas sound big, not fragmented and trivial. Students should gather their arguments in meaningful groups, thus all the arguments about why the proposal solves the problem should be presented in one section of the speech.

Depending on the type of debate in the class, students should format their speech. For example, in a debate about adopting a specific policy, students should try this pattern: problem, cause, solution, and feasibility. This structure will make sense to a judge and to most people.

In Chapter 5, four types of topics are mentioned: topics of fact, topics of value, topics of policy, and those of historical reenactment. Each of these approaches might utilize a different format in the presentation of the affirmative case.

In a topic of fact, the debate is about whether something is or is not true. These topics generally fall into one of four different categories: claims of causality (smoking causes lung cancer), definition (birds are descended from dinosaurs), conditions in the past (better to be an Athenian than a Spartan), or predictions (missile defense systems increase nuclear proliferation). While no debate can determine the absolute truth of a fact, a debate can help to establish the social relevance of a fact as a working idea (Branham 35).

An affirmative case on a topic of fact might have the following major contentions:

- Explanation of which type of fact resolution it is (causality, definition, past events, or prediction) and establishment of a procedure for how to prove that sort of claim
- Establishment of the fact through the use of various forms of proof
- Anticipation and refutation of potential opposition arguments

In a topic of value, the debate is about the evaluation of something. Topics may describe something as good, bad, ugly, beautiful, great, mediocre, etc. These kinds of topics are most often found in the areas of religion, philosophy, ethics, and art. An example of a value topic would be, "The death penalty is immoral." Generally a value topic contains an evaluative term (*immoral*) and an object of evaluation (*death penalty*).

An affirmative case on a topic of value might have the following major contentions:

- Explanation of the evaluative term and how to prove whether that term is applicable
- A criterion for the analysis of that value. If the debate was about quality of life, one team might define quality of life as safety and security
- Anticipation and refutation of potential opposition arguments

In a topic of policy, the debate is about whether the specific proposal of the affirmative team should be adopted. These kinds of topics are most often found in the areas of politics, international relations, government, institutional reform, and personal planning for the future.

An example of such a topic would be, "The national government should adopt a guaranteed annual income." Generally a policy topic argues that, on balance, it would be better to adopt a policy suggested by the affirmative.

An affirmative case on a topic of policy might have the following major contentions:

- A problem exists.
- The present system is not able to solve this problem.
- The affirmative will outline and explain a specific plan.
- The specific plan will reduce the problem identified.

An affirmative case on a historical reenactment topic will vary dramatically based on the parameters of the assignment given. Students may be called upon to use the formats of fact, value, or policy topics, or perhaps intermingle the three. Such vital interchange makes this debate format all the more exciting and educationally rewarding. These are the general guidelines that a teacher can provide to students who are developing their affirmative case for almost any debate.

Helping the Negative to Refute a Case

One of the defining characteristics of debate is the clash of ideas; it can also be one of the most difficult parts of debate for students. Specific disagreement on central issues is what judges and audiences look for in deciding who did the better job of debating. The center of that clash experience is the negative team's analysis and refutation of the affirmative case. Here are some basic guidelines to help the negative team in attacking the affirmative case.

Utilize Challenges

Debaters should utilize challenges to disassemble their opponent's arguments. A challenge is an argument that indicates inadequacies in the opponent's arguments and urges the rejection of the argument. A challenge specifically identifies logical and developmental inadequacies in argumentation and then reevaluates the argument based on these inadequacies. Failures by the affirmative to deal with challenges and fill in inadequacies means that the negative reevaluation of the argument stands.

The format for an effective challenge is simple and direct:

- *Specify the lacking element.* Something is missing or imperfect about an argument. Perhaps an argument lacks a logical step, involves an argumentative fallacy, or confuses the specific with the general. These elements can be highlighted in attacking the affirmative case.

- *Demonstrate the objection's importance.* Now that a problem has been found in a particular argument, the argument must be reevaluated based on this new finding. The error that many debaters make is in assuming that because an affirmative argument is not perfect it should be rejected. Rather, it is far more credible to say that the argument is not as strong or lacks relevance to the point it is trying to prove. This approach is much harder to answer than mere pleas for perfection. If such challenges are not answered by the affirmative, then the negative can begin discussing why this inadequacy indicates that the entire argument is logically inadequate. The important points to remember are how to reevaluate an argument based on the challenge and the extent to which the challenge is not responded to by the affirmative.

Indict Affirmative Evidence

Negative debaters should indict affirmative evidence as inadequate. Evidence is the support upon which many arguments rest. The negative team *must* undermine this evidentiary support by addressing major inadequacies in affirmative evidence. Here are some simple techniques for indicting evidence:

- *Match the evidence with the claim.* Often the claim that the affirmative speakers use to support argument is much broader and stronger than the actual wording of the evidence. Negative speakers should monitor the actual content of affirmative evidence as closely as possible and then launch challenges against important pieces of the offered evidence that seem particularly vulnerable or important.

- *Attack the strength of evidence.* Probability is a continuum that begins at "absolutely will not happen" and runs to "absolutely will happen." Few ideas exist at either end of the spectrum and most fall somewhere in the middle range. It is essential to analyze and identify the qualifiers contained within the evidence. Once again, the challenge serves as the appropriate mechanism for dealing with this situation.

- *Question timeliness and relevance.* In general, recent evidence is better than less recent evidence because it takes into account later events. However, depending on the context of the debate, timeliness is very important for some evidence and not so for other evidence. Competing evidence about the yearning humans have to be loved and respected would not be decided based on one piece being six months more recent. In contrast, competing evidence about Algeria's intention to acquire nuclear weapons must be very timely, especially if the situation has recently changed. Lack of recent evidence on the part of affirmative debaters should be pointed out and criticized only if events are likely to have changed since the evidence first appeared.

- *Qualify sources.* The reason we use evidence in a debate is to back up our arguments with expert fact and opinion. High school and college students usually are not subject experts on the topics that they debate, thus they often attempt to quote subject experts to bolster their claims. Negative teams should demand source qualifications while at the same time reading qualifications for their own sources. A quick and easy standard to be established is that without qualification, evidence fails in comparison to any other contrary argument. In debates where credibility of sources is in contention, the negative side should ask the audience to opt for qualified negative evidence over unqualified affirmative evidence in any instance where sources conflict.

- *Point out source bias.* Often those who write about important topics are fervent believers in a specific approach to the controversy. Some sources have direct vested interests in making certain statements ("US foreign policy is promoting peace," says the US secretary of state; or, "My new invention will replace the current gasoline engine," says Wallace Minto, inventor). Everyone who has an opinion is not a biased source, and some source bias is rarely grounds for rejecting the evidence entirely, but serious source bias should be pointed out and the strength of that evidence should be reduced.

- *Check source conclusions.* Many scholarly sources tend to evaluate controversies thoroughly, dealing with all of the relevant issues on both sides and presenting their unique take on the issue in their conclusion. Students should examine the conclusions of several authors on a controversy so that they can understand the direction of scholarly research on a subject and not misrepresent the work of an academic field.

Negative teams must be prepared to disagree with conditions of harm or damage that affirmative teams may claim. The negative team *must* reduce the impact of the affirmative claims or the persuasive weight of the affirmative case will simply overwhelm any other discussion. These claims of harm or damage usually are phrased as qualitative claims (the type of harm) or quantitative claims (the extent of harm). At times debaters might claim both. Strong negative debaters are prepared to challenge either type of claim.

Qualitative claims are usually thought of as those not readily confirmable by numerical evaluation. Freedom, equality, justice, are all important concepts, but they can rarely be evaluated in numerical terms (such as 11 percent more justice or 25 percent more equality). Debates of qualitative claims usually require only a single instance of violation; for example, one instance of suppression of freedom of speech offers enough material for a debate. Negative debaters must be prepared to challenge qualitative claims.

Techniques for attacking qualitative claims include indicating the following:

- *The number of people affected.* Indicate that this qualitative impact occurs in a small number of cases. When freedom is compromised in an individual case, it is unfortunate. However, this qualitative concept has a numerical dimension as it would be far worse if millions of people had their freedom compromised. In many debates about cultural values, the number of people whose liberties would be infringed is relatively few, but the claim is that the infringement would be a slippery slope. Negative debaters need to consider how many people would be or have been affected.
- *The amount the value is infringed.* Negative teams must indicate that qualitative infringement of the value is small. There is a

difference between the violation of privacy that comes from a neighborhood watch and a wiretap placed in citizens' homes. Negative debaters have to articulate the degree to which a value is violated. For example, the affirmative may claim that high school students are not allowed to write what they want in their school newspapers and that this is a violation of the First Amendment. But there is a difference between a high school newspaper being asked not to publish a sexist article and a teacher's censoring articles because they were unfriendly to the school. Because the degree of violation has yet to be determined, the negative team must make sure that the discussion of this incident does not elevate itself to an affirmative claim that the entire weight of the First Amendment should be given to this argument.

- *A loss is not a preferred value.* The negative team may stress that those experiencing qualitative losses do not mind. Freedom, justice, privacy, and other rights are only as valuable as individuals make them. If people value privacy, then its loss might be serious. However, if they do not value privacy, its loss would hardly be noticed. If individuals did not seem to mind experiencing the affirmative qualitative impact or did not protest against it, then they can hardly be said to have been victimized. Negative speakers should attempt to force affirmative teams into proving a claimed preferred value or the negative should demonstrate that these qualitative elements are not important to those experiencing the deprivation.

- *The affirmative is trading off other values.* The negative may also try to indicate that by affirming one value another is compromised. Many values that we hold dear trade off with other values that we also hold dear. Some values can be said to be "mutually eroding," in that achievement of or movement toward one may reduce achievement of or movement toward another. Liberty and security, privacy and community, equality and justice, these are just a few of the values that can be seen as mutually eroding in some situations. Negative debaters can contrast the value gained by the violation of another value and thus de-emphasize the violation.

- *Cultural bias.* The negative may assert that affirmative values are not very important because they are too culturally embedded. The controversy over whether values are universal or relative need not be fully explored to realize that some value claims are very much based in a specific cultural context. For example, claims of national superiority or cultural dominance are arguments that are very difficult to disprove or engage because of the potential for offense. These values, of course, would be less important than more broadly recognized and globally accepted ones. Denial by the affirmative that this was so might lead the negative to make a charge of ethnocentricity against the affirmative.

Quantitative claims (those easily evaluated numerically, such as dollars, tons of gold, numbers of human lives, etc.) have distinctly numerical dimensions and are often best analyzed in terms of their numeric dimensions:

- *The number of times an event happens.* Obviously, an event that costs 10,000 lives is more significant than an event that costs 1,000 lives, or even 9,999 lives; three accidents at nuclear power plants are worse than one. Negative debaters must make the affirmative prove a number with evidence and then try to reduce that number or reduce the significance of those events. However, in no case should that number be inflated, and negative speakers should be consistent in repeating the agreed-upon number.

- *The significance of each instance.* Evaluate each instance of impact the affirmative describes for its seriousness. Many impact claims may be of wildly differing severity. Cancer and the common cold are both illnesses, but they are hardly comparable. Something may happen to one million people, but if what happens is not very serious, it can hardly be seen as tremendously important. This tactic makes it easier for other negative arguments to outweigh affirmative claims.

- *Probability.* To the extent that the affirmative is claiming some impact in the future, they must indicate the probability of that event. Impacts should be evaluated by the risk that they might occur. Debating about the horrible consequences of an asteroid slamming into the Earth is largely irrelevant if all parties agree that the risk of such an event is nil. Too often future scenarios are evaluated as being 100 percent or 0 percent, when the reality should be somewhere in between, especially if the negative is clashing substantively with affirmative claims. For example, the affirmative team may have slightly better evidence that nation X will attack nation Y than does the negative team, but that does not mean that X will attack Y, only that the probability that X will attack is somewhat greater than that it won't. The harms of that scenario can be reduced accordingly. Negative teams must take into account the probability of affirmative arguments and attempt to reduce the perception of the risks.

- *Time frame.* Events that are coming up sooner tend to claim more of our attention because our understanding of them is much firmer than events that are more distant in time. We can imagine what might happen in a few weeks, but so much might happen within a few years that it is hard to imagine those events. We know less about the distant future than we do of the immediate future, thus we are better able to act in relation to it. This is traditionally called "future discounting." Thus, negative debaters should challenge affirmative scenarios for their time frame, "When will this happen and how long will it take?" Smart negative debaters will suggest intervening events that would change the arguments of the affirmative case.

- *Reversibility.* Losing your wallet and losing your innocence are two different types of events. One can be reversed (you can get a new wallet, identification, money, etc.) but your innocence, once lost, cannot be regained. We usually think of events that can be reversed as less important than events that cannot. This is a logical distinction, because mistakes made in terms of reversible events can be repaired while mistakes made in terms of irreversible events cannot. For example, some evidence indicates that once the Amazonian rain forest is chopped down, it will not be able to grow back and repair itself, thus making such destruction more important than some other ecological disaster that can be repaired. The negative should point out if affirmative scenarios are reversible while negative scenarios are not to better refute the supposed consequences of the affirmative case.

- *Moral imperative.* Some quantitative benefits or harms may be explained away by contrasting them with the concept of moral necessity. For example, a high paying job might be forgone because it involved producing a toxic chemical that would harm people where it was stored. There may be no doubt that money is good, but we may be morally required to forgo it in some situations. Negative teams need to challenge which moral imperatives are truly necessary. Perhaps the toxic chemical being produced might significantly benefit humankind. In many cases, the application of moral imperative involves a variety of other moral claims, many of which are debatable.

- *Voluntary risk.* Some situations involve risk, such as cigarette smoking and car travel, both of which are voluntary. Both, however, have different degrees of necessity—a person might need to travel by car in order to work, but few people's employments require smoking. When debating the risk, negative debaters should label the risks that are voluntary. Some situations involve involuntary risk, for example, being killed by an intruder in your home or having your water poisoned by a polluting factory. Traditionally, this concept of risk has been contrasted to the value of personal freedom. Philosopher John Stuart Mill, for example, thought that as long as you damaged no one else, you should be free to damage yourself. More current thinkers have maintained that although voluntary risk is different from involuntary risk, the former, while not a social good, was not nearly as serious as the latter. The negative should feel free to argue that affirmative impact scenarios involve voluntary risk. Although such argument would not eliminate the affirmative scenario, it might make it easy to outweigh the affirmative with negative scenarios that involved involuntary risks.

- *Percentage of the total.* One way to make something seem small is to compare it to something big. While 3 percent of the population affected by some malady is still an impact scenario, it does not seem nearly as important given that 97 percent of the population was untouched. This tactic, however, is only marginally effective and needs to be used in combination with others in this section.

- *Comparisons through time and space.* Descriptions of impact scenarios are always statements based on expectations and are trapped in time and space. We do not expect a level of sanitation today, for example, that we might have expected during the Middle Ages, thus what seemed like a clean city to individuals of the 14th century might seem quite dirty to us.

    Comparisons can be useful in reducing the apparent magnitude of affirmative impact scenarios. For example, while things are not perfect, they may be: a. better than at any time in history; or, b. better than in any other country in the world. In both cases, negative arguments based on this concept might be characterized more as pleas for perfection than as legitimate impact scenarios.

Affirmative policy proposals are only as valuable as the problems they can solve. One of the most fruitful attacks a negative team can undertake is to challenge the ability of an affirmative case to solve the problem outlined. If a policy is not workable and will not yield positive results, there is little reason to adopt it. If the problem isn't solved, the affirmative gets no credit for simply identifying the problem. Negative teams probably won't prove that the plan will be completely useless in solving the problem, but they ought to make the results of the plan as small as possible.

Here are some basic techniques for attacking affirmative solvency. Let's use the example of a plan that requires school uniforms because they will reduce school violence and improve academic achievement.

- *Force the affirmative team to quantify.* Even the best affirmative solvency evidence will not claim to solve 100 percent of the problem. In fact, most affirmative teams can only find evidence that indicates that "some" or "much" of the problem will be solved by the plan. Point this out and start specifying amounts—the plan will only solve 30 percent of the problem, less than half of the problem, etc. Make them *quantify* their solvency; if they can't suggest a high number with evidence, the negative should suggest a low number.

- *Attack specific approaches.* The affirmative will use a specific technique to solve a problem. Acquire and use arguments that indicate that this approach is not effective. Knowing in advance what another team is specifically going to propose can enable students to directly research specific proposals.

- *Attack their solvency evidence.* Often the affirmative will find an example of something that has been done before and then say it should be done on a national level. Just because school uniforms helped academic achievement in an upper-class neighborhood in Chicago doesn't mean it will work in Harlem, South Central Los Angeles, or Las Vegas, Nevada. The place where it was tried might have been atypical, the study size may have been too small, the thing being measured may have been very unspecific ("better learning environment," what does that mean?), and the study was probably carried out by researchers who picked only the best schools and the best teachers to be involved. If students volunteered to be in the program, it has more chance to succeed than if students are forced into it. Any time the affirmative tries to generalize their solvency from a small example you can make these kinds of arguments.

- *Find alternative causes.* Most things have no one single cause, like school violence. Uniforms only deal with one small cause of school violence (gang-related clothing, supposedly), while the other causes of school violence (poverty, media, poor conflict resolution skills, violence at home, etc.) remain unchanged. Find those alternative causes and show how the plan does nothing about them.

- *Argue that people won't comply with the plan.* If the affirmative policy has not been adopted because people don't like the plan or don't want the plan, then those same people will want to sabotage the plan. To create this argument, first find a reason why people will want to sabotage the plan (gang members will hate the uniforms) and then find a way for them to sabotage the uniform requirement (they will adopt new and different gang markers, such as hairstyle, gestures, etc.). The result is that uniforms fail to solve gang violence.

Many other techniques of refutation exist, and negative teams should use a variety of approaches. In policy debates specifically, negative teams have other strategic options, such as counterplans, disadvantages, and critiques. In value debates, negative teams are given value objections. These are discussed in more depth in Chapter 5.

Helping Students Disclose Arguments Before the Debate

You can improve the quality of classroom debates by encouraging student debaters to engage in pre-debate disclosure. Pre-debate disclosure is a process whereby each side makes their major arguments known to the other. Each side would then have time to prepare their response to the other's arguments.

Disclosure is a very valuable process, especially for relatively new debaters, because it enables students to prepare and research the specific issues to be raised in the debate. It will improve the discussion of the major issues and will also ensure that debaters are more relaxed going into the debate because they are not as concerned about being surprised and unprepared. While disclosure may or may not be fruitful in a competitive situation, it is extremely valuable in an educational context.

Disclosure is useful only when it is properly implemented. Some debaters will want to avoid full disclosure, believing that refusal will improve their performance. You can avoid this problem and use disclosure successfully by following some simple guidelines:

- Require disclosure to the other team
- Require a date by which disclosure must be accomplished
- Specify the level of detail required in the disclosure
- Warn debaters not to add major new elements after disclosure

Online Assistance for Student Debaters

A number of Internet resources are available to assist debaters. The resources mentioned here have been developed by one or both of the authors and are available on the Web.

For general materials to assist debaters in preparing we recommend: Debate Central, housed at the University of Vermont and facilitated by Dr. Alfred Snider. The site can be found at http://debate. uvm.edu. The site offers sample debates streamed on video, teaching texts, topics, and research help.

Conclusion

In this chapter we have attempted to guide you through the process of creating a classroom debate. We have helped to establish your expectations of what a good and bad debater are, and how to navigate some of the problems you might face when creating debates in your classroom. By giving you an outline for working through the basic skills needed to debate and helping affirmative and negative teams create their arguments and speeches, we hope this chapter can be a vital resource for your debates.

Chapter Seven

Staging Classroom Debates

In this chapter we attempt to give practical advice for staging class-room debates. We discuss logistics—scheduling, staging, and timing classroom debates—and make suggestions for leading discussions after the debate. Debates can also be documented through videotape and then used to train future classes. Finally, we discuss how to use debate events to enrich your school and community through publicity, public staging of events, and outreach activities. These outreach efforts can be extremely useful in gaining the support of the public and your colleagues. If more teachers see how useful debate as a classroom technique is, then the method may spread.

Planning and Scheduling Classroom Debates

Time is the most critical variable in planning and staging classroom debates. If you stage a 45-minute debate involving four students, assuming some start-up and close-down time, and that you need to get all 20 students in your class debating during the term, you will need five hours of class time; for a class of 30 students, you would need more than seven hours. You may need to adjust the format you are planning to use to suit time constraints. In planning and schedul-ing debates, make sure you have allowed enough time.

Planning for the use of debates in a class must begin early, prefer-ably well before the term begins. A simple formula is to take the time of a single event, multiply that by the number of students involved, and then divide by the number of students in each debate.

Thus, a series of 20-minute one-on-one debates with 5 minute total start and stop times to serve 30 students is represented by:

$$\frac{20 \text{ min.} + 5 \text{ min.} \times 30 \text{ students}}{2 \text{ students in each debate}} = 6 \text{ hours } 15 \text{ minutes}$$

The length of your class period is also critical when planning for classroom debates. Whenever possible, a debate event should not take place on two separate days. The attention of the audience and the focus of the student debaters will be dulled by such a break in the action. For example, if you have 50-minute periods, it is unwise to schedule two 20-minute events and half of another 20-minute event. The format you choose for the debates must fit your available time.

You should schedule some time for the transition between events as well as take into consideration the fact that such events rarely start precisely on time. This is called "up and down time," the time students need to sit after speaking, rise to give the next speech, and change the cast of characters from one debate to the other. We recommend that you schedule some time for class discussion of the debates, which is where some of the most potent learning can take place.

Forming teams and topics as early as possible in the term can facilitate scheduling. Once teams and topics are arranged, a schedule should be printed and distributed to all students. You should also post the schedule in your classroom.

Save time at the end of a sequence of debates or the end of the term for make-up debates. Inevitably one of the members of a given debate team will be absent through no fault of his own, and you have to allow for this in the schedule.

If a classroom debate simply takes too much time to fit into your schedule, some alternatives exist. Debates can be held outside of class and videotaped so that you can watch them when time is available. Debates can be scheduled outside of class and nondebating students can be assigned to act as judges and complete ballots about the debate.

Physical Arrangement of the Classroom

The physical space in which the debate takes place is important for creating a proper environment for observation, attention, and presentation. Fortunately, almost any classroom will do. If it is large enough for the number of students in the room, it is appropriate for staging a debate.

Certain factors should be kept in mind when setting up a classroom for a debate. With some formats, such as a trial, these may not be appropriate, but for the vast majority of formats these arrangements should be sufficient. These elements include placement of debaters, location of the speaking area, orientation of the audience, and placement of the timekeeper and others officiating at the debate.

The debaters should be placed at the front of the room facing the class. If there are two teams they can be located at the right and left front of the room. If possible, each team should have a table, with the teams and tables facing the audience. Have the participants write their names and the topic on a blackboard or on sheets of paper that can be taped to their desks.

The speaking location should also be at the front of the room, but is often best placed between the two teams. The speaking place then becomes a sort of "common ground" while each team occupies only their appointed spot when they are not speaking. If at all possible, a speaking surface, such as a podium, lectern, or even a music stand, should be provided. This speaking surface can hold notes and other materials while the speaker addresses the audience. Do not, however, allow the podium to obscure the speaker; it should be adjustable for different heights. If possible, put the school symbol or perhaps a design created by the students on the front of any podium or lectern.

The audience should be comfortably seated during the debate and face the debaters and the speaker at all times. If possible, the audience should have access to desks or tables so that they can take notes and work on ballot comments during and immediately after the debate.

Appoint a designated timekeeper, who should sit near the front of the room and be easily observable by the speakers. A stopwatch can be used, but the preferred timepiece of debaters is the countdown timer found in any cooking supply or electronics store. Such a device indicates how much time is left for the speech and emits a beeping noise when time has expired. The timekeeper should make sure that the debaters are aware of their time remaining through the use of large timecards, holding up an appropriate number of fingers, or just calling out the number of remaining minutes. Make sure the time-keeper is attentive and precise. When the time is elapsed, the speaker should finish that sentence and sit down.

Announcement of and Warning About Debates

The beginning of each debate session should involve the announcement of the topic to be debated and the participants so no misunderstandings can arise later. If more than one debate event is scheduled during that class period, whichever debate has all participants present should begin. Don't use a "first debate" and "second debate" distinction unless all are present.

Have one debate's cast of debaters available on "stand by" in case someone from one of the debates is not present. A "stand by" team is ready to debate if needed. With such a team, you will rarely have a situation where valuable class time set aside for debates is not used. If you need to use the "stand by" team, schedule the incomplete team for the next class period.

The end of each debate session should feature an announcement about which students will be participating in debates during the next class period. This practice gives ample warning to the less-than-diligent students and clarifies any misunderstandings about the schedule.

Preparation Time

Preparation time is those periods in the debate between the end of one speech and the beginning of another. Instead of allowing students to decide when and if to take a moment to prepare the next speech, in debates about complex subjects make sure to allow each side a set number of minutes to use during the event as they wish. During a debate of four or fewer speeches, preparation time will be primarily used before the second speeches. Alternatively, you may want to eliminate preparation time and encourage students to speak extemporaneously.

We find that preparation time is valuable for students to help them gather their thoughts and consult with their teammates. We have also found that preparation time provides the teacher with an opportunity to talk to the class about the debate. You can provide comments (usually positive) about tactics and arguments used that you want the class to note.

During preparation time, students think about how to answer specific points made by the opposition and often write out in shorthand some of the arguments they hope to make. During preparation time, members of the same team may confer about ideas and strategies for the next speech.

The amount of preparation time given to each team is determined by several factors. If the teams do not disclose their arguments to one another before the debate, additional preparation time will improve the quality of the debate. If the subject matter is complex, additional preparation time might be useful. In general, the longer the speech, the more preparation time necessary. Very little preparation time is needed for a short three-minute speech, while a speech of eight or ten minutes requires far more preparation.

Students should be advised to save their preparation time until later in the event, but to always use all available preparation time in an effort to improve the quality of the last speech.

The timekeeper should call out the minutes of preparation time for each team as they expire. The timekeeper may also hold up cards showing the debaters the number of minutes remaining. Once a team's preparation time has expired, their speech time should begin whether they are speaking or not.

Timing and Continuity

Each debate is a fairly intense exchange of ideas and information. Critical advocacy of this sort is stimulating but can be taxing to individuals unfamiliar with it. Therefore you should schedule a short break between debates. Breaks may allow students to finish ballots and notes, prepare for the next debate, and perhaps even use the facilities. Breaks will also keep audiences more attentive. Make sure students know how long the break is and rigorously enforce that time.

Discussion After Debates

Often a classroom debate will generate ideas and questions students will wish to pursue. This can be done by scheduling time after each debate for students to ask questions, express their own opinions, and introduce new ideas related to the theme of the debate. This can be a very important learning opportunity for students as they become personally involved in the issues under debate.

Discussion periods should begin with a request for questions and comments from the audience. If no one speaks up, the instructor should have a series of questions ready to ask the class and the debaters. Such questions might include:

- Who made a better presentation and why?
- Who had stronger arguments and why?
- Who had stronger evidence?
- Did you learn anything new in this debate?
- How has this debate made you reconsider your previous stand on this issue?
- Was there an important argument missing from this debate?

Be sure to guide your class to positive commentary on the debates. Because students will have just performed, they will be anxious about the judgments of their peers. Their classmates' responses can cause a lot of stress for participants. Recognize this and help provide positive comments to balance out criticisms.

Another form of class participation is to invite members of the audience to give brief one-minute speechs in support of one of the sides. These can be given during the debate, just before the closing speech of each side. These are known as "floor speeches" and are described in Chapter 4.

Videotaping Debates

Videotapes can be a highly useful tool that you can use in general debate and argumentation training and to address specific issues students may have (Barker 1). If you have captured a good example of a classroom debate on tape, it can be used later to show to other students as a model of the process. There is no perfect debate, so choosing one that has some errors can be useful. Students need to see that mistakes are made and that the process is never perfect. Often they find such mistakes comforting. When showing such a debate to your class to demonstrate the process, it can be useful to have students react as if the debate had actually taken place in front of them.

Encourage students to take notes on the debate they observe on tape. After the debate, invite a discussion and perhaps even some floor speeches for students to express their own points of view. Students can then cast ballots on the debate. It might also be useful for them to write out ballots to accompany their voting. These ballots can then be collected, examined for the purpose of giving brief comments on the way in which they are written, and then returned ungraded to students.

Videotapes of debates are also highly useful for participants to observe themselves. If you can arrange to have a simple VHS or DV camera in the classroom during debates, simply start taping as the debate begins. You can require each debate participant to provide a blank VHS or DV tape to use for that particular debate. Students can then take the tape and share it among themselves to watch their own performance.

Most of us are not totally familiar with how we appear while making presentations and speeches. Viewing themselves on tape can be very useful in revealing to students how they present themselves and how they sound and can have far more impact than any list of critical comments and suggestions you might provide.

Some of the features students commonly identify include:

- Verbal pauses ("um," "ah," etc.) that they normally do not hear
- Distracting gestures and physical behaviors
- A lack of gestures and physical movement
- Monotone voice quality (our voices always sound a bit better from within the resonating chamber of our skulls)
- Lack of clear organization in dealing with major points
- Clumsy phrasing of arguments and points
- Insufficient explanation of arguments and ideas
- Failure to address major points made by the other side
- Failure to summarize the arguments in the debate to aid in decision making by the audience

Videotapes of debates can also have other important uses. You can use them to document what you are doing in your classroom. Administrators and superiors who are promoting innovation and pedagogical developments will find such tapes an impressive demonstration of your efforts.

You can also use videotapes to encourage your colleagues to experiment with debates in their classrooms. When they see a short debate, they better understand debate's potential value.

You might also be able to broadcast the results of your classroom debates. Many communities have public access cable television stations that broadcast videotapes produced by the public. Usually state law in the United States requires cable companies to provide an outlet for "public" use of the airwaves, so this service is required rather than an act of generosity. These stations are often eager to receive "serious" content, and this is exactly how your videotape debates will be perceived. Beginning and ending credits can be attached to your tape and it can be aired easily. Such exposure will provide considerable publicity to your efforts and you will reach a potentially large audience.

Students also love appearing on television, and they often find that people in the community recognize them on the street and mention that they "saw them on television." We have engaged in many hundreds of such programs, and they have been very potent mechanisms for publicity and promotion as well as education about the topics being debated. Even if members of the community merely flash by your program while they are "channel surfing," they are prone to comment "that teacher who hosts debates is on the air again." This is precisely what has happened to our students in television programs that we both produce at our own schools (see Snider).

A final use of videotapes is as archived material. Years later they provide an interesting (and often entertaining) documentation of student performance. Our experience is that past students often want to see such tapes of their youthful activities. Videotapes of past students are also of interest when they gain some notoriety or run for public office, but we would advise against sharing them with the media or political opponents.

Inviting Outside Observers

Classroom debates can be educational for the participants, but they can also be very informative for observers. Students say that they learn almost as much by watching debates as being in them. Thus, you should occasionally invite others to observe your debates.

Invite several categories of observers to your debates: administrators and supervisors, other teachers, students who are interested in what you are doing, parents, potential supporters and contributors, and perhaps those outside of the school who are interested in the debate topic. You can provide invitations with a schedule of debates so that members of the school community can drop in unannounced and see what the debates are like.

We recommend gaining the assent of the students before inviting outside observers into the classroom. Your students will then feel that they have a degree of control of "their space," and you can be sure that students are prepared.

Do not invite outside observers until the students are comfortable with the debate process. While students are rarely at ease during their first debate, they become more relaxed as they gain experience, and, after several debates, outside observers should not be too distracting.

Outside observers should remain onlookers. They have not been a consistent part of the discursive community you are creating and as such have not "earned" their right to be full participants. Therefore, we suggest that they not be allowed to engage in discussions, ask questions, or give floor speeches. We often find that students resent being questioned by an "outsider" who has not been through the same experience. This is especially true of observers who are likely to be highly opinionated, such as parents of participants and those vitally interested in the topic being debated.

After outside observers have seen your classroom debates in action, make sure to have a brief meeting with them to get their reactions and feedback. This exchange is an ideal opportunity for you to spot previously unnoticed problems, to receive positive feedback for your classroom activities, and to invite them to support or become involved with your work.

Publicizing Debates

If you want people to see your debates, you will need to engage in some simple publicity. Publicize debates only after you are sure that your students are ready to be observed. Make sure to get the permission of all participants before extending your classroom debates into the public sphere. You may reap substantial rewards from your efforts to publicize debates. There is obvious value in connecting the goals of your classroom with larger community issues.

Basic publicity should provide simple information for interested parties, such as time, place, and topic area. It may not be advisable to provide the names of the students participating to avoid people attending because they want to see "Jill debate Bob," which is not the proper motivation for such observation and can put specific and unwanted pressures on those individuals. Always provide a contact telephone number or e-mail address so that interested observers can contact you.

Debate events designed primarily as a showcase for outside observers would, of course, be more widely publicized than your classroom activities.

Here are several easy ways to publicize these classroom events:

- Simple posters produced from any word processing program can be hung in your classroom, outside the classroom, in areas where students and teachers gather, or other high-traffic areas
- E-mail messages to those who might be interested, including any listserv that exists to provide information to those in your school
- Inclusion of the information in the daily morning announcements made in many schools
- Inclusion of the information in any schedule of events for your school

Think about creating a template for such announcements that can be used over and over again. You would then merely have to insert the time and topic.

Staging a Showcase Debate of the Best Students

If your students have staged a particularly good debate in the classroom, it might be worthwhile to consider restaging this debate in a more public way. As we have indicated, debates can be useful and educational for observers as well as for participants—a real justification for staging one of your stronger debates in a more public way.

Just as art students have exhibitions, students who engage in debating deserve their own exhibition. We have found strong support within schools and colleges for showcasing student efforts in a positive way. The format need not be changed for a showcase debate; however, the staging should be considerate of a larger audience, perhaps with a public address system and a more formal introduction of the topic and the participants.

There are a number of examples of venues for such an event. They include:

- A secondary school assembly. Often schools are looking for good assembly programs and have scheduled times for such events. You may well find that a showcase debate will be very welcome.
- An event coordinated with parent and teacher organizations. They are often in search of ways to showcase the work of the students and the school.
- An after-school event targeted at students.
- A demonstration of debating given to a group of administrators, a school board, a university board of trustees, or even another school.
- An event organized for a community group that is interested in the topic being debated.

Publicity for such an event should be increased as necessary and designed to promote that specific event to potential audiences. Listing the event in local newspapers, newsletters, and community calendars is extremely useful. Publicity for such events is most effective if it takes place three to four weeks before the event itself and is continuous up until the time of the event.

Taking Student Debaters Out of the Classroom

Considerable potential exists for taking your debate activities beyond the classroom and beyond the school. Here are two potential venues for debate outside of your institution.

Most communities have service groups or social clubs composed of citizens who gather to network, socialize, and work on charitable projects. In the United States many of these groups have luncheon meetings once a week or once a month. Members of these groups are almost always in search of a program to fill that meeting. Your students could provide a very short debate on a topic of interest (one they are already using in the class), followed by a discussion with the audience. These groups can be contacted easily with a one-page letter offering your services. You will be surprised at how welcome such an offer will be.

These groups can often provide an excited audience, an established venue, and perhaps a free meal. The benefits of this sort of activity are plentiful, including public education, excellent training for your students, outreach from your school into the community, networking with community leaders and businesspersons to enhance future job prospects for students, cultivating supporters for your programs and efforts, as well as excellent publicity.

Most communities also have radio programs that can be characterized as "talk radio." These stations feature both syndicated and local programs that discuss important issues and invite members of the listening audience to call in. These stations are usually looking for topics and programming, especially for local originating programs. A small group of students could go to the radio station, engage in a short debate on a topic they have previously debated, and then answer questions telephoned in by the listening audience. Radio stations can be contacted easily using a one-page form letter offering to stage such an event. Such an event provides a great experience for your students, enriches community discourse about important subjects, provides publicity for you and your school, and helps educate citizens about the values of public debate.

You can host a public debate that you invite the community at large to attend. This involves selecting a germane public controversy, publicizing it through the media and word of mouth, and then presenting a debate in a community venue—community centers, churches, or schools. The benefits of these kinds of debates include sparking discussion about issues, encouraging participation of audiences, and publicity for the educational value of debates.

More information about public debates can be found in Chapter 10.

Conclusion

In this chapter we have attempted to provide a comprehensive, although somewhat clinical, examination of how to stage educational debates. Although we have given many suggestions, we encourage each teacher and organizer to use his or her own best judgment in turning a potential debate into a real debate. Through your exploration and your students' growth new ideas and practices will emerge.

Chapter Eight

~ ~ ~ ~

Audience Involvement
in Debate

One of the most critical objections to classroom debates is that they focus classroom energy on a few students and leave the rest of the class to listen to the debate. Recognizing this challenge, we dedicate this chapter to techniques you can use to involve all of your students in classroom debates.

In this chapter we explore ways by which the audience can be used to improve the debate process and how the debate process can benefit the audience. We discuss the needs, obligations, and potentials of the student audience for classroom debates. Students can also serve as participants, judges, and critics as well as mere observers. The audience actively listens, contributes, and engages in the decision process at the end of the debate.

Students as Audience

Students watching a classroom debate face different pressures. The entire debate situation calls on them to be critical of the arguments they hear and the performances they see. The role as critic is new and different for many of them, and they engage in it tentatively at times or too enthusiastically at others. Students often feel a sort of unity with each other, as they all have to engage in debates and perform in front of the class. These pressures may seem contradictory but can be used in a mutually reinforcing fashion. The discomfort students feel at engaging in something different and risky, like debate, can be dealt with by heightening the sense of mutuality they feel as they learn how to be supportive of each other.

What the teacher wants to create in the audience is a communicative environment that is comfortable and safe. Students standing up and answering arguments made against them need to look out on an audience of friendly and supportive faces. We advise all teachers who plan to use debates in the classroom to remember to make this point to students, and our experience shows they take the advice to heart. The teacher should try to model the proper behaviors to create such an environment, which should be, at the same time, active and questioning.

If serious critical comments need to be given to the students who are debating, we advise that they be given in private and kept confidential. The challenges of being a debater are substantial, producing significant feelings of vulnerability in students. Limiting overt public criticism early in the term is proper. Students seem able to handle criticism, but it is better understood and absorbed when given in private and never in front of other students immediately after a debate. A better way to make public oral suggestions is for the teacher to summarize several debates with a list of areas that need improvement. You can also focus on the positive elements of what students have done. By highlighting successful tactics, students receive positive reinforcement that creates a friendly learning environment. Criticism does not frighten students; it is public, individual criticism about their personal performance that intimidates them. You should reassure students that they will not be criticized in public.

At the conclusion of each debate the class applauds the debaters for their efforts. Although this may happen spontaneously at the end of the first debate, we advise that you begin to applaud and without fail your students will follow along. This gesture establishes the procedure and helps create a positive, supportive atmosphere.

Not all students know exactly how to behave in a debate. The situation may be new to some of them, and they may respond in unusual and thoughtless ways. The teacher must maintain control of the situation and the audience. Strict discipline is not essential, but we believe the instructor should intervene (either during class or privately after class) when certain basic standards of behavior are breached.

Basic standards of behavior in a classroom debate are:

- Respecting the individual
- Respecting difference of opinion
- Retaining the freedom to communicate ideas

Student Audience and Note Taking

A useful way to engage the classroom audience is to invite them to take notes during the debate. Taking notes intensifies listener's focus, helps students retain ideas, and dramatically improves their comments and ballots after the debate. We have outlined note-taking methods in Chapter 6.

In our experience, note taking allows students to understand and interpret the complexities that emerge in any debate. Notes are a graphic representation that allows the audience to understand arguments and issues that have been clashed with and or ignored by one side or the other. Unlike some debates we see in everyday life (political debates come to mind), refusal to answer arguments made by opponents is a serious error in formal debate. Notes make such occurrences obvious.

Notes also allow discovery of relationships between ideas. Notes make it easier to discover when an advocate or a team is in contradiction, another serious error for any debater. Audience members can point to two different places in their notes when an advocate or team has made contradictory remarks.

In an effort to monitor student notes, give suggestions on improving notes, and make sure students are trying to take good notes; instructors can ask students to turn in their notes with their ballots after a debate. These notes can be reviewed, graded, and returned at the instructor's discretion. This process can also provide a number of teaching opportunities that explore the vital parts of a debate.

If you wish to grade notes taken during debates watched, do so quickly by scanning the notes. We suggest evaluating student notes based on the following criteria:

- Detail in transcribing the arguments
- Complete notes on all speeches
- Proper format and organization (as indicated in Chapter 6)
- Recognition of vital or weak arguments

Students as Judges and Critics

Student judging can present a wonderful opportunity not only to involve students more fully in the debate process, but also to learn about the intricacies of scholarly topics.

Our classes are filled with young people, and peer pressure has a powerful effect on them. We often focus on the negative aspects of peer pressure, but in classroom debate it can be used in a positive way. In our experience students can teach each other many valuable lessons, with comments from students often producing action and learning.

Peer pressure sets the stage for students as judges and critics of classroom debates. Students become responsible for learning in the classroom, which fundamentally transforms the learning process of your class. Instead of a situation where instructors stand in judgment of student efforts and performances, in classroom debate everyone present, students and instructor, becomes the audience, the evaluators, the critics, and the judges. In our experience, students work harder when they do not want to disappoint their fellow students. Students will not only be more diligent but will also be better behaved in general. This process goes a long way toward creating the safe intellectual environment we mentioned earlier.

Students often ask for criteria to use in judging the debate. There is, of course, no correct answer, so you might want to give different answers based on educational goals and the nature of the subject matter. You could use one or more of several models, and you should suggest those you deem most appropriate. One possible option might be to point your student toward the "better debater" lists in the Appendixes or to material in Chapter 6.

In the "your opinion" model, students would vote for the side that presents the arguments they most believe in. This is not a vote about their fellow students' performance. This kind of evaluation can be useful in debates about issues of fact and on controversies for which students do not have a firm set of opinions.

In the "better job of debating" model, students would vote for the side that does the best job of arguing their case, not on which side they personally believe to be correct. Students are asked to judge the performance that has taken place, not to use the debate as a measure for truth. This criterion is useful in communication strategy classes, which study such topics as argument or persuasion.

In the "better presentation" model, students would vote for the side that did the better job of presenting their ideas in terms of delivery, organization, and composition. The evaluation is of the debaters' performance more than the debate's content and is useful in a public speaking class.

These various models can be merged in interesting ways. We often urge our students to vote based on a balance of argument and presentation, recognizing that a good presentation assists the argument and that a good argument is far easier to present effectively.

Instruction to audience judges is very important to the success of the classroom debate experience. Instructors should decide which model or models make the most sense to them and are most appropriate for the debate's subject matter. The suggested judging model should be communicated to the audience before the debate.

Audience Ballots

Although having the student audience write out ballots on the classroom debates is not essential, we suggest it as a valuable practice that increases audience attentiveness and prepares each student for her or his turn as a debater in front of the class.

Some guidance is appropriate for students who write ballots. These guidelines make this practice more productive for both the writers and the debaters.

Ballots should always be civil. Criticisms should not become personal insults. Students should feel free to criticize ideas, but must not criticize individuals. Students should be encouraged to conduct themselves on the ballots as they believe their instructors would conduct themselves.

Students should be encouraged to evaluate reasons given and arguments made, rather than rely on simple "impressions" to make their decisions. It is not very revealing to write comments like "seemed to make more sense" and "seemed to know what she was talking about"; instead students should focus on specific ideas, facts, and arguments. This engages students in a deeper form of analysis and critique than most citizens use when considering persuasive messages they receive. The ballot-writing process can serve as a method of training students in critical thinking.

Students should be encouraged to include considerable detail in their ballots. Some may want to include a small number of ideas and considerations on a ballot in an attempt to make the task easier. However, debates are complex communication events that are rarely determined by only one or two ideas. The more detail students use in explaining their decision, the deeper their analysis of the debate will be.

Students should be encouraged to weigh the various issues offered in a debate. Very few debates have one side getting their way in all of the arguments. Usually each side has done a better job on some of the arguments, and a student must weigh the various arguments. For example, in a debate about reforming medical care, a team may win that a problem exists in the current health-care system that needs to be addressed but may not win that their solution will be very useful in addressing it. In this case, even though they have "won" the argument about a need to act, the action they support does not effectively address the problem. So they would not "win" that debate. Students need to be encouraged to discover which issues have been "won" by which side, and then see those issues in relation to one another to decide whether to vote for or against the topic being debated or the teams making the arguments.

Student ballots can be given to the debaters after the debate for inspection, a very important part of the learning process. Debaters can compare the different reactions of the student judges and will be especially impressed by the comments found on a number of ballots. In our experience, students read ballots from their peers much more intensely than they do those from an instructor because of the novelty and multiple perspectives.

We believe that student ballots should have the name of the student judge on them, because students need to be responsible for their comments. Names will temper their remarks and allow student interaction, as one student might ask another to explain a point she or he made. However, if you believe that comments will be more pointed and more useful if they are anonymous, offer anonymity as an option.

Audience Questions

In some formats, and at the discretion of the instructor, students can be encouraged to ask the debaters questions at the end. This process can reveal strengths and weaknesses in the arguments, explore important issues ignored by the debaters, clarify arguments, and provide the audience with personal interaction.

Questions can be taken at various times during the debate. One option is for questions to come before the last (summary) speeches by both sides. This question and answer period raises issues important to the audience so that the debaters can take them into account in their final speeches. This practice does, however, interrupt the flow of the debate.

Questions can also be asked at the end of the debate. This arrangement allows for a longer question-and-answer period, the questions can also cover the full range of the debate without interrupting its flow.

Questions can come from the entire audience or a panel of students selected to ask questions of each side. If anyone can ask a question, less attention and care is given to each question asked. If a panel of students is assigned to the task, the questions will be fewer but they are likely to be more serious and well thought out. Students who perceive asking questions as their "assignment" are likely to take it seriously and put more effort into it.

In any debate, questions can be asked verbally or submitted in writing. In a public debate where the feelings of the audience about the issue are quite intense, you may find that asking for written questions is advisable; this technique permits the screening out of hostile questions and questions can be easily alternated between sides.

In a classroom debate, questions can be either verbal or written. Written questions (submitted during the debate) are easy to ask, tend to be a bit less personal, and can be edited so only the best questions are used. Verbal questions tend to take longer, are personal, and provide a feeling of open discussion. We encourage you to choose the option that best meets your class's needs.

Audience Speeches

Instead of or in addition to questions, audiences can be invited to give short speeches, commonly known as "floor speeches." These speeches give the audience a chance to join in the debate and make their views known.

Floor speeches are generally used instead of question periods and are placed at the same points in the debate. Floor speeches are best inserted either before the last two speeches or after the debaters have finished. Floor speeches are times for audiences to make their decision.

Make sure audiences are aware that they will have the opportunity for floor speeches. An announcement at the beginning of the debate allows the audience to compose their floor speeches before they give them and thus improves the quality of the speeches. When the point in the debate for the floor speeches is reached, the instructor or debate moderator asks for the audience to deliver their remarks.

Floor speeches are generally one minute in length, thus allowing a number of people to give their views. You should also make an attempt to stagger the speeches in terms of which side they are in support of. As one student is delivering a floor speech, those waiting their turn can be asked which side they support so that a balanced presentation of view is achieved. No student should be allowed to speak more than once.

Generally volunteers for floor speeches will be few until one person has actually asked to give one. Once a member of the audience breaks the ice, others often come forward as they observe the procedure going smoothly and they have mentally organized their remarks. If no student comes forward, teachers should be encouraging and patient, trying to get one or two students to agree to speak.

Floor speeches should have a limit based on the time allotted in the schedule. Do not have too many floor speeches because they may dilute the debate itself.

Media Roles for Students

Students can become involved in debates in ways that will seem obvious. With some planning, you can assign students realistic roles that simulate crucial parts of public dialogue.

One role that students will be familiar with is the role of the media. Newspaper, radio, and television journalists often cover events and relay stories about that event through their respective media. You can appoint students to represent the media.

Students who represent the media are assigned to cover the event. During the event they take notes and prepare their story. This can be especially useful during role-playing debates. If a debate about locating a paper mill in a community features representatives of the public, representatives of the corporation, environmental activists, local leaders, economists, and others, the media story can indeed be lively and entertaining.

Radio reporters might be asked to present a short (one-to-two minute) stand-up at the end of the event, while print media reporters might file a story that would be available the next day. If the equipment and the knowledge are available, students might be assigned to be a television news team (reporter, camera operator, sound technician) and then edit together a two-minute television story of the event that students could watch. These media reports are useful as summaries of the event, but they can also educate students about the challenges that journalists face in trying to report a story objectively. You could also raise the issue of objectivity if you assign two reporters with different ideological viewpoints.

Students can also play the roles of concerned citizens who have a stake in the conversation or who would be adversely affected by a change. Teachers should consider the opportunities to include students wherever possible, which will maximize creativity and support.

Announcement of Voting

Students may be asked, based on instructor format design, to vote for one side or the other and to write a ballot explaining their decision. You do not have to call for a vote or ask for ballots, but we recommend this practice. A debate calls for a decision, as our definition indicates, and voting and balloting provide this point of decision.

Voting can take place immediately after the debate. When the speeches are concluded, there can be a brief pause, and then the instructor can ask for a show of hands, count them, and announce the decision. Although immediate and exciting, this process creates some stress and tension.

Alternatively, voting can take place when ballots are turned in. The instructor can receive the ballots at the beginning of the next class, inspect the ballots, and then announce the result in the class after that—giving a two-class delay in announcing the results. While less immediate, this process provides feedback about the decision while avoiding some of the attendant stress.

The announcement of voting can be either general or specific. A general announcement of voting involves the instructor indicating which side received the most votes, but not indicating the victory margin. This method is a bit less precise but does avoid having to announce that the negative won the debate on nuclear disarmament 25 to 1. A specific announcement of voting would indicate who "won" the debate and would also specifically indicate the vote count. This announcement can be a good indicator of whether a "close" debate occurred, as a 14 to 12 decision would indicate, but it can also indicate a debate clearly won by one side, such as a 24 to 2 decision.

Conclusion

Classroom debating is an activity not only for those students actually debating, but also for the entire class, who make a productive and substantive evaluation of the arguments and points raised. Audience involvement, as suggested in this chapter, can contribute to creating learning opportunities for all students every time a debate takes place.

Chapter Nine

Evaluation of Classroom Debates

In this chapter we cover the purposes and methods of evaluating classroom debates. After choosing the type of debate that fits each classroom and setting up the debate, a teacher faces one last hurdle: How to evaluate student performance? You may not use this entire chapter, for instance, if you were not going to evaluate students on their persuasive skills, only on the content of their arguments. We believe that this chapter can both help you set up a framework for grading your students and provide you with some innovative ideas about how to involve the audience in the classroom debates through evaluation and get students more excited about the process.

Because debate is fundamentally a subjective event, judging students' performance is difficult. In addition, many teachers are not familiar with debate. This chapter presents some criteria to help you evaluate your classroom debates. It is divided into two sections: the philosophical basis of evaluating debate performance and some pragmatic teaching methods to help you evaluate your debates. This chapter also offers guidelines for students to evaluate their peers.

Purposes of Evaluation

This section looks at the purposes behind evaluating debates. It explores some ways to determine if your students have become involved in the subject matter as well as how to evaluate debate-related skills, preparation, and arguments.

Evaluation of the Exploration of Subject Matter

For most classroom debates, the value of the event is found in the opportunity it offers to students to use the knowledge presented in the classroom. One of the primary challenges a teacher faces after a classroom debate is determining if the students have engaged the material of the course in a suitable manner. Have the students involved connected with the subject matter of the course? This section helps teachers to answer that question.

Much of this evaluation is common sense. As an instructor in a subject, you will probably be aware if students misunderstand a concept. More difficult is evaluating how much they have absorbed. Because debates are specialized, it is difficult to test whether a student is familiar with a wide spectrum of information.

One possible solution is to vary the scope of the debate topics. Rather than having a specific subject such as "This House believes that the UN should send peacekeeping troops to Macedonia," you might want to pick a more general topic that allows students to draw on the themes that you have worked on in class. You might have a public forum debate on the topic "This House believes that the UN should act." This kind of open-ended topic allows students to develop arguments using material from class discussions. It can be a very rewarding experience to see a debate unfold around classroom subject matter. For more information on constructing debate topics see Chapter 5.

When you are using a debate as a replacement for a test of your students' mastery of a body of knowledge, your concerns are different. In this case, you are probably using the role-playing or policy-making debate formats, because those formats require in-depth preparation, and you are probably looking for a sense of completeness of information, a feeling of comprehension that comes through in the debates.

To prove that they are familiar with the material, students need to understand their responsibilities, which include providing topics ahead of time and having a list of ideas to cover when they debate. If you have a template of the content you would like to see in each debate, then you should include those expectations when introducing and judging the debates.

Students can also show their familiarity with a subject matter through research. When you evaluate students for their research preparation for their debates, you may want to focus on these core questions:

- *Did the student use classroom information and the shared knowledge base of the students?* These debates do not occur in a vacuum. The entire class should be aware of the concepts you have worked on throughout the class. Students' ability to seamlessly integrate this kind of information shows participation throughout the class and also a sense of involvement with the materials.

- *Is the research recent?* Many students will do research, but they will often use old or out-of-date texts to support their arguments. The importance of this qualification varies with the kind of debate topic. If the question is largely historical ("France was complicit with the Nazi"), then current information may be unnecessary. However, if the subject is a hot political topic ("Asian economies are heating up"), then recent and diverse sources are important. Keep in mind that even historical debates changed dramatically with discovery of new information and publication of new arguments. The fields of archaeology and religion are constantly in flux based on new findings that call for dramatic changes in the way experts view their areas of expertise.

- *Is the research complete or are there large gaps of knowledge?* If you are familiar with the topic, then you will see this flaw in research almost immediately. Even if you aren't familiar with the literature on a particular topic, it is likely that a debater's gap in knowledge will be exposed in the course of a debate, often because the other side will bring it up. Remind your students that arguments about recent and relevant sources can be important parts of the debate.

- *Is the evidence presented biased in some way?* While researching their topic, many students will encounter advocates who make strong, even bombastic, arguments. Often the best quotations for debate evidence come from people who have a decided interest in the outcome of the discussions. These people may be fiercely biased and willing to twist ideas and evidence to support their own views. Remind students that this kind of evidence exists and should be supplemented with other kinds of research.

Evaluation of Debate Skills and Preparation

Debate skills are natural abilities that grow as a person becomes more involved with the process. Quick thinking and confidence develop as your students participate in more debates. However, student preparation and practice can augment this process. You may want to evaluate your students on their debate skills; the following questions may help you grade your students' performance. We assume that most of your students don't have much of a background in debate, therefore, the focus of this section is on those skills that they can augment with practice and preparation.

Does the Student Seem Persuasive? Persuasion is a skill that emerges through a combination of confidence and practice. It involves not only the content of arguments, but also presentation and delivery. You might note if your students are watching the audience when they speak, commanding the attention of the audience, or simply reading from notes? Does your student have a powerful delivery? Does she vary her tone and voice to call attention to her arguments? All these skills make up persuasive ability and can be cultivated through practice. You should be able to tell if a student has not practiced her speech, taking into account that the student may suffer from speech anxiety and, even with preparation and practice, still have a difficult time persuading the audience.

One of the best standards for evaluating persuasive speaking is the amount of time students put into their word choices. Visualization, the use of metaphors, analogies, and powerful words are all indicators that a student has taken his debate preparation seriously. If a participant took the time to work out the phrasing of a particular argument and make sure that she was explaining herself fully, then she should receive credit for being persuasive and well prepared.

Is the Student Well Organized? Organization is an important skill in presentation and delivery. Does your student seem prepared to give speeches and does he have notes and ideas prepared to follow the information path no matter where it goes? Depending on debate format, students need to be prepared to move in an unusual direction. In this case, you can evaluate the flexible thinking that emerges in such a situation.

Organization also shows in speeches themselves. Do your students' speeches fit the time parameters given for the assignment? Dramatically short speeches and extremely long speeches are symptoms of a lack of preparation and a poor organization strategy. Your student's speech should begin with a preview informing the audience of what she is going to argue. In addition, the speech should stick with the major points that have been previewed. The speech should flow and each argument should be distinguishable. Clarity of purpose and implementation are all signs of good organization. Even with impromptu debates, like SPAR and parliamentary debate, students should organize their speeches into major arguments and give a preview of them. Regardless of how much time students have to prepare, you can evaluate their preparation based on the organization of their speeches and arguments.

Does Your Student Focus on the Central Ideas of the Debate? One of the most important skills that debate teaches is the ability to discern important from irrelevant arguments. Often students become excited about an idea or distracted about a particular subject and spend a lot of their energy focusing on what they know or what they think is vital, while ignoring core issues.

One of the easiest ways to check this is to think how you expect the debate to occur before you get to the classroom. If you have an idea of what the major arguments are in a debate on "Animals should have rights," then you will be prepared to evaluate what kinds of arguments your students put forward. One essential question is whether students connect their ideas successfully to the resolution.

There are exceptions to this kind of analysis. British parliamentary debate rewards willingness to take on difficult interpretations of the topic. Thus, if you were to interpret a resolution so that you had an easy burden of proof, you would receive fewer points, but if you carved out an extremely difficult series of arguments, you might get significant credit. Even with this standard in mind, you can analyze the connections and justifications that students make to tie arguments together.

Evaluation of Arguments

Entire textbooks are written to explore the quality of argumentation, so we will not pretend to cover all the vital information in this short section. Instead, this section is a primer to help instructors who do not have as much experience in evaluating public arguments.

There is no clear-cut right or wrong way to argue. Often textbooks decry certain kinds of arguments as not logical or sound, when in certain situations those kinds of arguments are extremely successful. Many sources decry arguments based on emotional grounds. Consider this section from Lunsford and Ruszkiewicz's book, *Everything's an Argument*. "Untempered by reason, emotional arguments (and related fallacies such as personal attacks and name-calling) can wreak havoc in democratic societies divided by economic, racial, religious and philosophical differences" (43). Placing the blame for social breakdown at the feet of emotion-centered argumentation is shortsighted. In reality, every kind of argument can be used in a good and bad manner and there is nothing particularly villainous about emotional argumentation. In fact, many circumstances call for emotional reasoning. Inspiring a crowd or speaking at a funeral are clear examples.

When you are evaluating the arguments in a debate, you should feel confident that you already have all the training you will need. Life has prepared you by facing hundreds of arguments and questions every day. You can listen to a debate and make judgments about the arguments with no additional work needed. Because your classroom debates will be on subjects about which you are well informed, you will be able to give a valid critique because you can provide specific suggestions about the content.

What follows are some tips that we use to evaluate arguments in our debates. These tips, thematic templates, may help you in your classroom by allowing you to look at arguments that are quickly presented in a debate. You can use these questions to evaluate any argument. You can also use our debate evaluation sheet in Appendix 1.

Do the Arguments Presented Relate to the Rest of the Arguments in the Debate? Many debaters prepare arguments that they envision as central to the debate, only to have the material move in a direction they had not considered. A good debater will follow the path of argumentation and make relevant arguments. Unfortunately, many students will simply continue to make their prepared arguments, regardless of relevance. You should always check to make sure that the arguments presented in your class relate to the debate, because even seemingly strong arguments can be peripheral to the main points presented.

Consider the example of a debate about affirmative action. An affirmative student might justify race-based preferences for entry into colleges and universities by arguing that multicultural education is valuable for all participants and that white students are at a disadvantage without a multiracial learning environment. A negative debater who responded by arguing that current generations should not be held responsible for previous generations of intolerance might have a strong argument, but it is not relevant to the claims made by the affirmative debater.

Does the Argument Have Assertions, Reasons, and Evidence? In Chapter 2 we talked about using the ARE (Assertion/Reasoning/ Evidence) format. We find that conceptualizing arguments in this manner not only helps students build their arguments, but also can help you evaluate them. Most problems in debate arguments come down to a failure to use the ARE format. At the same time, you should be prepared to reward your students for their innovative use of evidence in this format. Stories, anecdotes, poetry, pieces of art, and references to common knowledge can all be used as high-quality evidence to augment traditional pieces, such as quotations and statistics.

Have the Students Correctly Assessed Causality? The concept of causality is both a valuable and risky element in student debates. Students are quick to recognize that arguments based on causal connections can be powerful. However, be aware of two risks when exploring causal arguments. The first is the impulse to extend lines of causal argument to their extreme in order to make a stronger impact. The second is to simplify causality to a single cause for an event. Both of these notions will be profiled in the following example.

Consider a debate on the topic: "We should go back to nature." A debater who was supporting the affirmative might argue that Western industrial civilization is doing great harm to the Earth by cutting down the rain forests to furnish Western cities with lumber. Her causal chain of reasoning might include the idea that cutting down the trees prevents them from engaging in photosynthesis. The lack of oxygen causes pollution-laden areas to become unbreathable "dead zones" and turns these former rain forests into deserts.

While this is a powerful argument, and she has included elements of truth in each of her steps, several missteps of causal logic emerge. For example, the leap from the loss of photosynthesis to the loss of oxygen in certain areas assumes that oxygen is a regional product rather than an atmospheric element that flows easily from one place to another. And while many climatologists agree that cutting down the rain forests may lead to desertification, the reason is not that there won't be enough oxygen, but that the soil underneath rain forests will become too dry without the complex system of roots and the foliage cover that slows evaporation.

This debater attempted to take the scientists' line of argument too far in order to persuade her audience. Rather than using the causal arguments that were supported by her evidence, she wanted a powerful impact that could be used to win the hearts and minds of her class. The risk of drawing out lines of causal argument to their extreme is that your original claims, which might have had merit, become lost in the hyperbole of your vision.

Similarly, many debaters (including the one in the example above) simplify causality in an attempt to make their claim stronger. What causes clear-cutting of the rain forests? The above debater attempts to claim that there is one single cause to the cutting down of the rain forests—Western industrialized cities and their need for lumber. This attempt is a significant simplification of the causal chain. In fact, we can point to myriad causes when we consider this question. Some believe the need for countries to export lucrative crops has caused them to cut down rain forests in order to get more land to cultivate. As our global populace increases its demands for fresh meat, forests are cut down in order to provide pasture for beef cattle. Many believe that local populations cut down trees in rain forests to find places to live as local population explodes. To cite the Western desire for lumber as the sole cause in the clear-cutting of the rain forests is a simplification.

On the other hand, all claims of causality are subject to these kinds of criticisms—there are usually a variety of causes for any event. The skill of a good debater and a good teacher is to evaluate where the primary responsibility for causal chains lies. In the above example, we can agree that the local people who are carving areas out of the rain forests to live and grow a few crops are substantially less responsible than are multinational corporations that clear-cut thousands of acres to grow coffee for export. Exploring causality requires us to look at the scope of causal responsibility.

What Are the Implications of the Arguments? Ignoring implications is very common. Many debaters are content to make their arguments by explaining their reasons and supporting their assertions with some evidence. They may build an entire case and never talk about the implications of their arguments. The single biggest failure of a debater is the lack of a solid explanation about why his argument is important. Many debaters become so involved in the minutiae of winning that they forget to answer the more fundamental question, "So what?"

Explaining the impact of arguments is vital to understanding why we are debating at all! Consider a debate about Russia–China relations, where one side of the debate argues for increased engagement of Russia and China. Many debaters might argue that the advantages of such a policy would be increased information sharing, reduced military tension, and civilian exchanges to increase social understanding. Yet, the implications of this argument could be much more. The unspoken element is: what happens if these moves fail? A conflict between two of the world's most powerful nations. Even a cold war between these two superpowers might be catastrophic. To engage in this debate without exploring the significant implications of the argument ignores the stakes of this dialogue. It is vital that debaters recognize and be prepared to discuss what the greatest implications are for the debates in which they participate.

Evaluating arguments is simultaneously simple and complicated: simple, because you have all the fundamental tools you need; complicated, because each argument contains nuanced elements that you can draw out using some of the tools that we have explored in this section. By looking at the relationships between arguments, the value of the ARE format, questions of causality, and the implications of the debate, you can add to your own understanding of argumentation and feel more confident in your ability to evaluate debate arguments.

Methods of Evaluation

This section explores some of the various methods of evaluating debates. We will look at five methods that implement the ideas we have discussed in the above section. We encourage you to explore different kinds of evaluation in your classroom debates—use your own experiences to guide you to the kinds of evaluation that work for you.

Student Ballots

Student ballots are a way to evaluate the debaters and get students involved. They consist of assigning a written justification of what debate team each student believes won the debate. If you looked around while students were giving presentations to the class and found students napping or looking out the window, then you may assume that the student audience is intellectually absent. Student ballots provide a way to pull the rest of the class into the debates—especially if the ballots themselves will be graded.

Debates are a good educational experience for the participants and the audience. A student can never receive enough experience in evaluating arguments and judging performances. If students are required to be active listeners and take careful notes during the debate, they will get involved in the debate and experience the arguments and ideas. Even more powerful, they will have to take their time and compare the merits of arguments. As the audience, they will have to contrast the relevance of arguments, the clash between ideas in the debate, and the evidence in order to make a decision.

This process will probably be difficult for your students at first. Because they do not have any experience in this area, they may feel frustrated by the open-ended nature of the ballot. Therefore, we advise that in the beginning you provide a form for them to use. You can write the same categories listed above on the board and explain the goals of the evaluation. After some experience of watching debates, you may want to assign every student a take-home written assignment to explain his or her decision to you.

You must decide if you will consider the ballots when you grade the student participants on the debate. On one hand, the student ballots can show how effective the debaters have been in persuading an audience. On the other hand, if there are personal difficulties between students, the ballots may be marred by illegitimate influences. If you decide to use the student ballots when assigning a grade to the debate, you should get the audience's comments to the debaters, who will find them extremely valuable. If you decide to give copies of the audience ballots to the debaters, you should make sure that the class knows this ahead of time and writes respectful comments. For more on this subject see Chapter 8.

Teammate Evaluations

It can be very difficult for students to participate in group work. Despite the benefits of group work as a pedagogical tool, many students are critical of the process because they view the preparation burdens as uneven. We have had many students who have privately complained about the division of labor while preparing for a debate. One solution is to use debates that do not require teamwork or to focus on spontaneous approaches. In addition, you could use team-mate evaluations to help remedy this perception of imbalance.

Regardless of student perception, we believe that team preparation is extremely valuable. When students work out ideas together and prepare to debate, they can create a kind of synergy that enhances this process. Teamwork is a vital skill used in most debate formats. Working as a team in a debate is critical to individual success.

If you assign students to prepare for debates in a team format, we advise the use of teammate evaluations. They inform you if one student did significantly more work than the others. They also alleviate the stress associated with teamwork, because the students have the opportunity to vent any frustrations. Moreover, they inform you of your students' preparation levels.

Using Your Own Ballot

Your own ballot can be an extremely valuable artifact for learning. As you judge the debate, you should take notes on all of the goals of the debate listed above. Your notes or a more polished version of your perception of the debate can be extremely valuable for your students. If students spent a lot of time preparing, they want to know how they did and where they can improve. The teacher ballot provides the feedback they want.

Checklist for Evaluation

You may feel uncomfortable using a free-form ballot or the typed evaluation sheets like the ones included in Appendixes 1 and 2. The second one is focused not so much on debate performance as on mastery of the subject as demonstrated in the debate. A checklist evaluation form might be the correct evaluation tool for you. The checklist format provides a template for you to use as a standard method of evaluation. You can list all the goals that you have for the debate and then create a scale. It could be as simple as checks, check pluses, or check minuses. It could involve using letter or number grades, or a scale of boxes that you can check off. If you do use a checklist, you might want to include space for a few comments to explain why someone receives a particular evaluation.

Evaluation of Improvement Through Repetition

If you successfully integrate debate into your classroom, you might want to have more than one debate. You can also explore the possibility of using an extended debate format where debaters return to a particular subject throughout the term. (For more on this subject, see Chapter 4.) If you decide to have multiple debates in your class, then you might want to consider grading students through the lens of repetition.

If students debate more than once, their skills will improve. That should be a factor in your evaluation. You may want to use the successes and failures of earlier debates as the foundation for the grade of the next debate. If a student failed to organize major arguments in the debate, that might be a goal for the second debate. If a student was soft on research, then another debate might be a great opportunity to work out those kinks. You might want to have a single grade for all debates, and allow students to work on getting that grade up by reworking the areas that need improvement. If you take this approach, it would be valuable to keep each student's evaluation sheets together to allow you to compare performances in different debates.

Conclusion

Evaluating debates can be extremely difficult because it is hard to quantify a performance and even harder to know exactly how to interpret the diverse goals of a debate project. This chapter helps to organize these goals and skills of debate into a template that teachers can use to evaluate debates. If a teacher goes through section one and selects the core goals to stress in the debate and then selects a method of evaluation, then that teacher will be well suited to judge the debates in his or her classroom.

Chapter Ten

~ ~ ~ ~

Putting On a Public Debate

In this chapter we will discuss how educators can extend debate skills and the learning environment into the community. We focus on the pragmatic needs of teachers who would like to move the debate experience into the public sphere. This chapter is also a useful resource for students who are coordinating and creating public events.

Power of Public Debates

Public debates are powerful because they can simultaneously create a space for people to deliberate and to disseminate ideas. Public debates create a forum for community members to reflect on a subject (even if it comes in the form of a student wondering what could be important enough to count for "extra credit"). They also offer a chance to make those ideas public and spread new concepts and opinions among a larger audience. Ideally, each person attending a public debate will extend the debate to others. In this way a public debate creates a powerful learning environment where ideas are discussed and deliberated, and participants feel empowered through their own involvement.

Public debates are valuable for students. Putting on a public debate requires the application of many skills that are part of classroom learning. The work needed to organize a public debate often makes previously abstract classroom skills concrete. For many students, practicing writing a press release for some event that never happens is difficult, but with a real public debate to promote, they become excited about the exercise.

For audiences, public debates offer media-free space for autonomous public deliberation. Students and citizens alike have little time or opportunity to discuss issues deeply with others. In a world where opinion makers tell their audience that they aren't smart enough to participate in their dialogue, the public debate is a radical departure. Public debating requires audiences to listen and engage with the messages of speakers—the goal isn't simply to inform or to persuade, but to create an earnest dialogue.

Persuading the Class to Participate

Public debates can be most simply thought of as a period of time where some students or community members will have a targeted discussion, usually on a predetermined topic. Public debates use the formats and ideas in the rest of this book but include an invited audience.

Here is an example of a public debate:

> An 11th grade English class might stage a debate on the subject of immigrants' right to a driver's license. They spend a 50-minute class period researching and brainstorming a list of arguments on both sides. The teacher then assigns students several articles on the topic as homework so the entire class understands the issues and the stakes involved.

> The students plan the structure of their debate. They develop a two-on-two debate with four students volunteering to participate at the forum. Other students volunteer to be a panel of questioners. After making a list of what they need to accomplish for the debate, the class breaks into committees to cover all that they need to do (publicity, documentation, facilities, media) and plans a schedule of the debate performance including the time limits.

The students choose to put on a debate at 7:00 on a Tuesday evening, reasoning that this would be a time and day convenient for the target audience, parents, and community members. They then contact the local newspaper and television stations to publicize the event. Students cover the town with flyers, and on the Tuesday evening, more than 100 community members show up for the debate.

The students videotape the event and they transcribe and publish the text of the debate in a local community magazine. For the next two months, the letters-to-the-editor page of the local paper is alive with people talking about the issue.

Public debates provide an incredible opportunity for students to interact with community members. But the public nature of this kind of debating can scare students (and teachers)! When you introduce the idea of the public debate, the class may resist the project. Students may be afraid of speaking in public and fear making a mistake with people watching.

Tell them that they will have much of the creative control of the project and that together they can overcome their fears. With practice and support any student can be a debater. Tell the students that some vital roles don't involve standing up on the auditorium stage: They can serve on a panel of questioners or write an op-ed piece for a newspaper after the event. If the entire class becomes a research think tank working over ideas and controversies, the likelihood of someone making a factual error in a debate is small.

You must listen to students' concerns as they begin to prepare the debate. Some of their issues might be vital to the success of the project. We recommend that students do much of the "heavy lifting." If the students are in charge of the work, then the project will be relevant and applicable to their lives.

Planning Stage

To succeed in the planning stage, you will need to create a list of roles that students can play so that you can include everyone. We encourage you to have the students brainstorm a list of what they think are the important tasks to be done. If you succeed in empowering the students in the planning stage, the entire process of producing a debate will be educational.

At this stage you should envision what the debate might look like so students can get involved. The traditional public debate features two sides clashing before an audience. This model is a bit limiting, so you can spice it up. Perhaps you might want to add an audience question-and-answer period or consider a panel of student questioners who have prepared targeted questions for the debaters.

You can use all of the formats described in this book for public debates. Of particular interest might be multisided debates or public forums that can create significant audience involvement.

Researching

Researching a public debate is a great opportunity to teach research skills to the entire class. At the University of Pittsburgh, the public debate program creates a research dossier of all the articles on the subject of the debate. The dossier is usually bound and shared with all of the participants. During this stage all the students can do research and bring ideas to the table. Because this is a public debate, it is vital that students focus on bringing ideas to the public, not necessarily competing to defeat each other. This research is shared with the entire class, providing a common language for students to discuss the issue.

Part of the research work centers around finalizing the subject of the debate. Students working on a debate about a proposed local jail might not know exactly what the topic wording will be until they research the subject. So students should focus not just on acquiring information, but also on presenting the central arguments found in their research to the rest of the class. As students present these arguments, they should organize them into pro and con on big sheets of paper.

Brainstorming arguments with the entire class is vital for the success of the project. If the nondebating students feel like second-class citizens at this stage, you will create an educational experience that only works for some. The students who promote and coordinate the debate need to be a part of the issue-construction phase. Involving everyone is also useful because all the students should be able to discuss the project with others. Eventually, the students who are debating might need to fine tune their speeches with additional research, but most of their ideas should be presented to the class early on.

Selecting and Supporting Debaters

Some of the students will be on stage debating at this public forum, perhaps teamed up with expert advocates. Selecting these students might be a simple matter of people volunteering. You might also encourage students to wait to select debaters until after the brainstorming. Ask the students to suggest who they think might be capable advocates for either side.

You might need to provide specific support to debaters, whose anxiety is likely to be higher than the rest of the class. Students might need extra practice or a chance to talk about their fears.

The debaters should be responsible for creating a speech and also presenting the ideas to the class. Teachers should encourage students who are debating to be accountable to the rest of the class for their research and ideas.

Organizing the Event

One immediate question is *when* to put on the debate. Ask the class to consider when would be a good time and date to put on the event. Consider your audience when answering this question. Is your debate something that would be of interest to the rest of your school? If so, then you might want to schedule the event at the end of the school day to encourage students to go directly to the debate. Consider if any other events (sporting events, plays) are scheduled for the time you are considering; will those events be attractive to your hoped-for audience? You might best schedule a debate on school uniforms that will feature a school administrator for 3:00 in the afternoon on a school day. But in scheduling a debate about sprawl and development that the class hopes will attract working people, storeowners, and community leaders, you must consider conflicting community meetings and choose a time (usually in the evening) when your target audience can attend.

Your public debate might be just for your school. If you can get several other classes to attend, you can share curriculum planning with the other teachers. For example, history classes could debate the causes of World War I. Perhaps several science classes could coordinate a debate about the nature of chaos theory in the sciences.

If your debaters are particularly polished, you might want to present a debate to the entire school body. Keep in mind that presenting to peers is often the most difficult audience young debaters can imagine. You may want to consider including roles like moderator and questioner that can maximize student participation and minimize speech anxiety.

You must also find a venue and reserve the space. The obvious location is an auditorium or large classroom at the school. You might need to reserve the room far in advance. Also remember that a custodian or security guard may need to be on hand to lock and unlock the room if the debate takes place in the evening.

Promoting the Event

Promoting the event takes planning, again centered on who your target audience is. When we hosted a public debate about animal shelters at the University of Pittsburgh that asked "Can Pittsburgh become a no-kill city?" the target audience was animal shelter staff and volunteers. We made an explicit attempt to invite community members who we thought might be interested. This meant making sure that the date we picked did not conflict with other activities in the shelters.

Advertising a public debate should begin with the students' ideas. Let them develop a list of people who might be interested in the topic and strategies for how to reach them. Students with some computer knowledge or graphic design savvy might be in charge of making a poster (or a series of posters) to promote the debate. They could hang these in the school and around the community. Students could also create flyers (often sheets of regular 8½ x 11" paper), which they could use in face-to-face promotion. Don't forget to promote the debate in shared places where many different people go such as supermarkets.

Flyers may not reach all community members, so you need to consider contacting the media. Is there a community message board or public access television on which you can promote your event? Perhaps local radio stations might be willing to announce the event. When promoting a debate about drug education programs, we had our two debaters stage a five-minute debate on the air. The station received so many calls that the debaters were on the air for almost an hour arguing the issue. The debate was packed.

You should also consider promoting debates on the Internet. If local newspapers or news services have Internet community calendars, you can publicize your event there. But given the large number of "spam" e-mails that people receive, getting people to read your message grows harder and harder. Ask the webmaster of organizations interested in the debate topic to post your event or share e-mail lists. In a debate about the United States lifting sanctions on Cuba, groups concerned about U.S.–Latin American relations would be appropriate, but if people perceive your e-mail approach as heavy-handed or biased, you will have difficulty pulling in an audience. A well placed e-mail and press release can make a big difference.

Creating a press release offers another wonderful teaching moment. If you give your students examples of press releases, describe how to develop them, and help the class craft the message, then the students will develop skills that will make them more media savvy.

Debaters and Experts

Although you might want to have a subject expert play a part in the debate, having the students involved is essential. One of the more fruitful formats is to pair students with experts so that student voices and ideas are given the same weight as those of the experts. It is often extremely profound for students to experience a peer voice expressing strong arguments and have them considered alongside the voices of experts. Consider a debate about Israel and Palestine that included spokespeople from the two groups. Matching up each side with a student (or two) creates a moment of empowerment when students realize their own ideas are on par with those of experts.

A Word of Advice for Teachers: Troubleshooting

Despite your attempts to create self-sufficient learning environments where students take responsibility for the entire event, some part of the debate planning may break down. Consequently the debate facilitators (including students) must check in regularly to make sure that the process is working and, where necessary, you may need to volunteer your help.

We have encountered a few trouble spots in our work. Often students have a tough time finalizing a date and reserving a room. These vital logistics might need a teacher's touch. Some students have trouble getting outside advocates to participate in the debate, and you might need to help support students who are having difficulty getting through to a desired speaker. These problems might be addressed by a coordinator or with the help of more students.

You should help the debaters by walking through the arguments they are developing. Specific feedback on their speeches and arguments will help them become more comfortable talking in front of an audience. They will also need practice responding to questions and to their opponent's arguments. The research phase should help with this process because the entire class will have a good understanding of the arguments that both sides of the debate will present. Consider pairing up debaters with other students who will challenge them or role-play audience members with questions.

Helping student questioners requires you to guide them in developing varied and interesting queries that don't duplicate each other. The debate may contain a particularly contentious aspect, like how much a program will cost, that the students view as central.

Encourage them to parse this and consider how they can ask more than one question about it. Students might also need help balancing questions so that both sides of the debate receive equal attention.

During the preparation periods, encourage student questioners to think about the importance of their role. They bear the responsibility of explaining the significance of a discussion. Because they have researched the issue and are well informed, they have knowledge of aspects of the topic that neither side may want to discuss. It is their duty to bring attention to those complexities and nuances. The goal of questioners is not to "trip-up" the debaters, but rather to push them to view the topic through new lenses.

Mapping out the debate from start to finish is vital to make sure that nothing has been missed. Students will need to make a minute-by-minute agenda of what will go on in the debate. This will help to ensure that every detail is taken care of.

A walk-through with or without arguments/practice speeches is beneficial for all participants. If the event is going to be filmed, looking good might be an extra incentive to encourage students to practice.

Documentation

One of the most empowering parts of a public debate is when students document the event and then spread the ideas and discussion so that what was temporal becomes permanent. The *process* of the debate becomes an intellectual product that can have impact beyond the experience of the debate itself.

The easiest kinds of documentation are videotapes and transcriptions. Encourage your students to record the debate. Videotaping can be as simple as a single student with a camera on the corner of a stage. If people have access to a computer with video-editing capabilities, a few video cameras capturing the event from different angles can be easily edited into a powerful presentation. Audio recording is easy to store and distribute over the Internet. The audio of a debate can be easily recorded and then converted into an electronic music format like Mp3 and made available from a website. Photographs are also useful documentation of the event. The class might consider appointing a few students to be photographers using digital cameras to record the debate.

Transcribing an event makes the debate accessible to newspapers and magazines. Equally powerful are student-written opinion pieces about the debate issue or process. See if the local newspaper would run a section from the debate transcript and a commentary by one of the students.

Sharing the event with the public requires planning. Of course a class could distribute videotapes of the debate but this might not be the most efficient way to disseminate the ideas articulated. In several debates we have organized, local newspapers have been interested in running sections of the transcript in the next day's issue. Some journals and magazines might be interested in running the entire text. Talk to the media to get a better idea of what formats they use to highlight such programs.

Real intellectual value is achieved by teaching students not only ideas, but how ideas become part of the public sphere. Encountering their own words and ideas in a magazine can be an empowering moment for students.

Transcription is difficult, largely because it is tedious and requires that someone closely check the final transcript. The other difficulty is that transcriptions are most appealing to news agencies right after the debate. So the expected turnaround time for transcriptions is extremely quick.

Don't let this deter you, however. We believe that the benefits of transcription outweigh the difficulties and would like to provide you some tips that we have found useful when transcribing debates. If a newspaper would like to run some highlights of the debate text, then consider simply transcribing those sections and leaving the rest for later. Just remember to keep the video/audiotape of the complete debate as backup. Transcribing two 700-word sections of a debate will take two people a few hours. You can make task even easier by assigning each student in your class the responsibility for transcribing a single question or a single speech. If the transcript is going to be published, you or a group of students should take responsibility for checking the text.

When preparing transcriptions for publication, avoid focusing on the experts you brought into the debate. Remember to include student comments in media representations and encourage reporters to focus on the students rather than reinforce the message that experts have all the answers.

If a local television channel or school network wants to run a tape of the debate the next day, preparation is relatively simple. You need only add a title page identifying the debate, the date and time of the original event, and the sponsoring school/class. Do not try to edit the tape. Save your editing for when the tape is going to be shown in a class or when the video is put on the Internet for download.

The 2004 Summer Scholars program at Marist College used public debate as the center of two intense weeks that taught students not only how to create debates but also how to videotape, edit, and publish video to the Web. Knowing that we were only going to use short sections of the videotape made it easier for students who were filming the events.

All of these examples of after-the-debate publication require that someone talk to the editor of the newspaper or the manager of the television station. Include your students in the discussion of what to do with the video/audio and text from their debate. They might know of a local newspaper that would be pleased to publish sections of the debate. Many students are quite savvy about video/audio and the Internet. Consider this part of the debate instruction as an opportunity to reach those students.

Examples of Public Debates

You may wonder how to fit public debate into already full curricula. Here are several models for public debates that require different amounts of time.

Public Debate in a Single Day

A high school history class is having a stimulating conversation about gay marriage. Some students are arguing that gays and lesbians should have the right to marry based on the idea of equal rights. Others are arguing for a norm of social good that positions gays as bad parents and therefore assert that gay marriage would be bad for the future of society. Arguments are flying as the class heads into the last 20 minutes.

Suddenly the teacher interrupts and asks if the students would want to continue this debate after school. When some of the students respond that they would, the teacher quickly proposes a public forum on gay marriage that afternoon. With quick agreement, they get to work.

One of the students makes a quick flyer to publicize the event, and the teacher copies it for distribution. During the lunch period, students make announcements and encourage friends to come to the afternoon debate. The event is added to the announcements at the end of the school day and within hours dozens of curious, argumentative students gather to discuss this issue.

The teacher acts as a moderator and the participants agree on a few ground rules. Students must take turns speaking, personal insults are out, and speech time is limited to two minutes. A list of students eager to speak quickly grows and the debate kicks off.

Public Debate in a Week

A music teacher has been having a running debate with a number of students about copyright and the new ease of downloading music with computers. The teacher, who is also a musician, makes a living by selling CDs of his music. He argues that downloading is theft. When students offer him copies of music that they think he will like, he refuses them, explaining that he thinks it is taking money away from artists whose album he did not buy. The students argue that artists make money from tours and sharing their music will make them new fans who will attend the artists' concerts.

One of his enterprising students finally challenges him to defend his ideas in a public debate, and they agree to debate the issue in a public forum. The teacher and the student decide to debate at a local coffee shop where they often perform during an open microphone. The coffee shop owner is excited to have another event and quickly agrees. They make some flyers to promote the event and call the local radio station to ask if they can announce the debate. A few well-placed e-mails to local musicians and among the network of music students help to ensure that the coffee shop is filled with people ready to argue.

The debaters agree that they don't need a moderator and quickly settle on a format where each will speak for five minutes and then share the microphone with the audience. At the end of the forum the debaters will have five minutes to summarize.

Public Debate in a Month

As part of the syllabus of a college class on freedom of speech, a communications professor has students organize and participate in a public debate on limitations to freedom of the press. The class agrees on the topic: "Limitations on freedom of the press are necessary in times of war."

During the preparation weeks, students reserve the auditorium at a large family center in town. They chose this place to encourage community members, not just students, to attend the debate. A group of students volunteers to promote the event; they create a flyer and record an announcement for the event that they take to different radio stations in the area.

The editor of the local newspaper agrees to join students debating on the negative side of the topic, and a professor from the political science department agrees to join those students advocating for the affirmative. After a long discussion, the class finds that only four students want to debate in the public forum, so they create a debate format that uses three people on each side. Wanting to keep the event to approximately 90 minutes, they decide to keep the speeches relatively short (five minutes each). Their format looks like this:

Introductory comments	Student moderator	5 minutes
First Affirmative speaker	Political science professor	5 minutes
First Negative speaker	Newspaper editor	5 minutes
Second Affirmative speaker	Student advocate	5 minutes
Second Negative speaker	Student advocate	5 minutes
Audience questions		30 minutes
Third Affirmative speaker	Student advocate	5 minutes
Third Negative speaker	Student advocate	5 minutes

The class decides to videotape the debate, and the campus television station agrees to edit the event down to an hour and run it on the campus television network. Students from the class coordinate the filming and reserve equipment from the media center.

Conclusion

Public debates are a wonderful educational opportunity for students. No other educational model can duplicate this active and collective learning atmosphere. More important, the ideas that emerge from this kind of debate are directly connected to some section of the public (e.g., school audience, community members). This dual process of challenging and amplifying ideas makes public debates a vital part of the teaching curriculum, one that should not be overlooked.

Chapter Eleven

Using Debate in
Specific Subject Areas

Art

Humans have been making art for as long as we have been alive. Art is a fundamental impulse of all societies, and every historical epoch and every nation in the world have a vibrant culture of artistic achievement. Great controversies over music, poetry, theater, painting, sculpture, and graphic art have rocked the world. Debates about style, format, and content have long been a part of the art world. These issues make for fruitful subjects for debates.

Murray Edelman, in his book *From Art to Politics*, positions art not only as a creative impulse in our society, but also as a building block of our very consciousness. He writes:

> Art creates realities and worlds. People perceive and conceive in the light of narratives, pictures, and images. That is why art is central to politics, just as it is central to social relationships and to beliefs about nature. . . . Because they create something different from conventional perceptions, works of art are the medium through which new meanings emerge. (7)

According to Edelman, art is a fundamental part of who we are as humans. His argument points to the importance of art not only as an aesthetic concern, but also as a socio-cultural-political topic. Debates can point us to new understandings not only of art, but also of who we are.

Why Debate Is Valuable to Art Classes

Art classes seem to be subject areas where one would learn the skills of artistic production and debate might not fit in. We believe that debate can contribute a valuable sense of history and importance to a subject matter as well as introducing students to artistic movements they might never have encountered otherwise. Debates about art can provide the context of a student's own artistic efforts and explore subject matter that might be controversial or new to the student body. Debates are a great way to get students excited about projects and teach them background information. While some teachers may believe that the purpose of art classes is to provide the skills to create art, we believe that, inevitably, perspectives on art are produced as well. Rather than try to inculcate subtle value judgments about artistic styles or artists themselves, why not have a debate in the class to help illuminate ideas?

Using debate in art classes helps teachers explore the difficult line between theory and practice. Christopher Knight wrote this polemic in the *Los Angeles Times*:

> For art students, practice is more important than theory because being an artist is not a scholarly discipline. To approach making art as a scholarly discipline is to attempt to establish an authoritative society of learned persons—to establish, in other words, an academy. The goal is academic art. Art has always been a difficult fit with school because making new art does not conform to objective criteria that schools can readily test and evaluate. That's one reason most art schools are bad art schools. They emphasize technique because technique fits the demands of pedagogy and testing for the typical academic curriculum. The color wheel doesn't change, and an excellent spot weld can be measured. (C7)

When facing this quandary of how to teach art, debate addresses technical and even practical ideas as well as theoretical innovation. Through debate, this polarization between theory and practice that Knight complains about can be resolved. Instructors can teach the theories of art concerning the practice of art and the outcome can be both scholarly and critical.

Sample Debate Topics for Art Classes

- Art cannot escape politics.
- The artist does not really matter.
- Art cannot be defined.
- Public monies should not finance art.
- Censorship can never be justified.
- The good life is best measured by aesthetics.
- We should dramatically increase public funding for the arts.
- Life imitates art.
- Art imitates life.
- Government censorship of public artistic expression is an undesirable infringement of individual rights.
- Advertising degrades the quality of life.
- Sculpture has a more beneficial effect on the intellect than painting.
- Modern art is less moral than art of the Middle Ages.
- Drama contributes more to mental enjoyment than the study of real life.
- Gunpowder has done more for the benefit of humanity than poetry.
- The critic does more injury than good.
- The composer is greater than the author.
- The recent history of the stage proves that spectacle is of more importance than intellect.
- Fashion is art.
- Tibor Kalman was right.
- Changes in art predict changes in society.
- Art follows the lead of society.
- There is no such thing as obscene art.
- Artists should avoid politics.
- The art market turns great art into just another commodity.
- X was a superior artist to Y.
- X is a superior work of art to Y.

Sample Debate Formats for Art Classes

In this section, we profile three model debates for a variety of art classes. These models are not the most important subjects nor suggestions of where to begin. They are meant to help you understand the role of debate in the classroom.

Teaching an Introduction to Art class is difficult because of the scope of information an instructor needs to provide to students. Add to this the lack of interest that students sometimes show when facing a new trial, and you can have a frustrating first few days. Why not begin the class with a role-playing debate about the innovations and impact of new kinds of art? Divide the class into five groups and assign each group an area of art to think about and defend. Stage a role-playing meeting where students represent different, perhaps controversial, kinds of art in a public forum: rap music, collage, slam poetry, video game animation, and graffiti writing.

You might want to set the scene at a meeting for parents of students enrolled in the school. There might be a movement afoot to revoke funding for art classes (a common occurrence in the United States). You could position the students to defend the value of each area of art or talk about why it is valuable to defend all kinds of art regardless of content. Another approach is to have students decide which category of art is least defensible and which might have to be sacrificed if funding is cut.

Teaching Graphic Design, a class whose purposes seem tied to commercial advertising, provides significant space for debates. Consider a debate on the topic "Resolved: Designers should use their skills to fight against consumerism." This topic would pit student against student to discern the stakes and purpose of what they are studying and can have a lasting effect on a student.

Consider this quote from "Psycho Design" in the magazine *Adbusters:*

> But design-based behavior modification doesn't have to be ultimately banal and destructive. In the right hands, it can be used to do something much more interesting than just speed up consumer purchasing cycle. Take everything you know about design and throw it out. Try to take a completely dif-

ferent tack. Instead of obsessing on the glitz, the salability, the cool of the object you're designing, think about other, perhaps opposite, psychological states your design might induce. Instead of increasing desire, you attempt to reduce it. Instead of saving time, you s-t-r-e-t-c-h it. Maybe you design a car that a whole neighborhood can share, a chair that eventually tells its user to get off his butt, a radio that even a child can repair. Maybe you forget about planned obsolescence and start designing products to last a hundred years. You give your designs a human, not only a commercial significance. Some fun, huh? Once you break out of the consumer design box and start playing with the ecological and psychological dimensions of design, the can of possibilities explodes. (53)

In the same issue, California Institute of the Arts Graphic Design Professor Jeffrey Keedy attacks this vision of activist designers:

In the context of graphic design, anti-consumerism is a radical idea precisely because it doesn't make much sense. The graphic designer as anti-consumerist is a lot like the liquor company promoting responsible drinking, or the tobacco company discouraging underage smoking—maybe they're sincere, but it's hard to believe. Perhaps the bursting of the e-commerce bubble and the sudden interest in anti-consumerist design is more than just a coincidence. Are the designers who lost their jobs designing Websites for the home delivery of butt toners now designing Websites about the butt toner industry's use of sweatshop labor? (46)

In this magazine whose content contributes to this very question, the issue of whether graphic designers should use design to fight against consumerism is an exciting debate. While *Adbusters* paints a picture of activist designers whose lives revolve around creating new and positive meaning through design, Professor Keedy believes that this outpouring of activist sentiment comes because designers have lost their jobs.

The value of this kind of debate is that it highlights the stakes of a class. What is the purpose of a class on graphic design? Why should the students care about what happens after they learn the skills that the class promises to teach? What do you most want to share with your students about why we do these things, not just how? Debates can help teach your students to think about issues that affect what they are learning.

Conclusion

Debates in art classes can be vibrant, exciting, and challenging. Teachers should keep in mind that one of the greatest strengths of debate is that it is extremely flexible. Students should be encouraged to use pieces of art as evidence in their arguments, to explore radical and exciting new ideas, and to push the boundaries not just in their creations, but also in their thoughts. Debate can expose controversies in the artistic community and public policy and illuminate ideas.

Civics, Politics, and Government

Classes that explore these topics are some of the most debate-friendly educational opportunities. In the questions of how we govern and are governed and how our nations are created and sustained are found some of the most exciting debates. Debates take existing controversies and allow students to become knowledgeable about the importance and the difficulties in making decisions. Through debate, participants can work through the very foundations of national identity and discover the meaning and importance of civic life.

Why Debate Is Valuable to Civics, Politics, and Government Classes

Debate allows students to learn about public policy and explore the intricacies and meaning of government decisions. Debate also provides an incentive for students to learn more about their nation's laws. Through debate students become aware of the value of the civil society that may or may not constitute their nation and learn about the process of governing. Public issues come alive through debates. When students find their voices, they discover that the perception that governing is easy falls quickly to the wayside.

Debate teaches students to question and understand government policies and the social norms that guide a nation. Through this interrogation classroom debates inform students of concepts that are often hard to teach. A role-playing debate can get at the historical context that informed the creation of a law; a parliamentary debate can help teach students to rely on their own voices to question state norms. As a teaching tool, debate encourages critical thinking about the value and importance of national norms.

Students who might otherwise be uninterested in a class about government and the workings of society might find debates an exciting way to become engaged in the topic. Because debates are active, they allow students to express their own opinions. This expression can be liberating because students get the opportunity to see how their ideas match up against the very laws that define a nation.

Some may see debate as a dangerous teaching methodology that encourages the questioning of governments. We believe that is a faulty view. Debate certainly teaches students to ask difficult questions and express themselves, but we believe that this form of expression makes those institutions grow stronger. Through debates, students often come up with a perspective that verifies the value of existing government policies and norms. Debate does not necessarily challenge the state; often it conveys the value of government norms and the realities of political decision making.

Sample Debate Topics for Civics, Politics, and Government Classes

- We should tax the monarchy.
- Royalty is irrelevant.
- Nations of the Western Hemisphere should form a permanent union.
- The U.S. Supreme Court, on balance, has granted excessive power to law enforcement agencies.
- The realist worldview does not adequately represent the world.
- We should assist other nations through foreign aid.
- The power to tax is the power to destroy.
- We should support a two-party political system.
- Only the elite can successfully manage national affairs.
- We support the strong state.
- We believe in the separation of church and state.

- We should use force to make peace.
- We should reject big government.
- Strong dictatorship is better than weak democracy.
- We should support sanctions for citizen nonparticipation in the democratic process.
- We should have term limits for national officials.
- One person's terrorist is another person's freedom fighter.
- Negative political advertising is significantly detrimental to the democratic process.
- We should support strong laws to protect the flag from desecration.
- Old enemies can become new friends.
- The public deserves the politicians it elects.
- Collectivism is better than individualism.
- We should support open borders.
- Justice in country X can be bought.
- We should support social unity over cultural diversity.
- Special interests have ruined democracy.
- The right to privacy is more important than the freedom of the press.
- Freedom has been taken too far in the Western world.
- We should dissolve the House of Lords.
- Results are more important than character in national leaders.
- Compulsory national service for all qualified citizens is desirable.
- The judicial system has overemphasized the rights of the accused.
- Country X is justified in providing military support to nondemocratic governments.
- Significant government restrictions on coverage by the media of terrorist activity are justified.
- Membership in the UN is no longer beneficial to country X.
- Significantly stronger third-party participation in the national elections would benefit the political process.

- Violence is a justified response to political oppression.
- UN implementation of its Universal Declaration of Human Rights is more important than preserving state sovereignty.
- The national news media impair public understanding of political issues.
- More severe punishment for individuals convicted of violent crime is desirable.
- Country X should adopt the cabinet-parliamentary form of government.
- The national government should significantly strengthen the regulation of mass media.
- More rigorous academic standards should be established for all public elementary and secondary schools in one or more of the following areas: languages, arts, mathematics, natural sciences.
- One or more of the existing restrictions on the freedom of press and speech should be curtailed or prohibited.
- Initiative and referendum are the best form of legislation.

Sample Debate Formats for Civics, Politics, and Government Classes

A debate on the topic "One person's terrorist is another person's freedom fighter" is virtually guaranteed to be an exciting exercise in the classroom. Because of the long-standing controversy about this topic and the possibility that someone in the class has been personally affected, we advise some preparation.

By guiding research, the topic can be addressed in ways that minimize the real possibility of students becoming angry in the classroom. Teachers can help point students to different examples and ideas that can broaden the focus rather than fixate on a particular political struggle. It is also important to provide a fixed time period in which students can express themselves and their opinions. This topic, like others in these areas, must have a pressure release valve, where students in the audience who are bursting with excitement to make an argument or ask a question are allowed some moderated time. You might suggest that students write reaction papers to the debate to allow some time and the use of the written word to temper heated ideas and allow emotions to cool.

Consider this topic of terrorism as the subject of a researched parliamentary debate. The affirmative team or the government must present a case that someone can legitimately see every terrorist as a freedom fighter. The militant Palestinian group Hamas might be the focus of their arguments. Developing their arguments, they might want to use examples of the Irish Republican Army, the Jewish militants who rose in the Warsaw Ghetto, or the African National Congress of South Africa who fought against apartheid. Each of these groups was labeled terrorists and as having some value by citizens of these nations. Remind students that they are not only fighting against the logic and arguments of the other team, but are also challenging the conceptions of their audience.

Crafty negative teams could identify some tactic (such as killing civilians or using anonymous bombings) that differentiates terrorists from freedom fighters. They might also pick a single group of "terrorists" who they believe are indefensible and try to prove that they are the exception to the perception that what some see as terrorists others see as freedom fighters. However, we believe that this approach will fall victim to the argument by the affirmative that regardless of our negative perception of terrorists, someone out there perceives their actions as justified in the fight for freedom.

Instead of these approaches, a negative team might want to interpret the resolution in a new way. An opposition team could argue that terrorists are defined not by their affiliation, but by their tactics, and that some members of the Irish Republican Army are freedom fighters, but others who engage in assassination, for example, are terrorists. By coupling these arguments with the argument that these kinds of tactics actually discredit an organization, an opposition team could define the debate to give themselves some debating room. Another approach might be to claim that the ownership and use of nuclear weapons define terrorism because these powerful weapons hold the entire world hostage. In this case, the debate could be about the ownership and use of nuclear weapons by the United States, because that country is the only nation to have ever used nuclear weapons in wartime. By creatively interpreting the debate, students can find new arguments for and catch their opponents off guard.

Conclusion

Through debates on these kinds of topics the very nature of who we are as citizens emerges. By exploring how governments create and change laws, the value and virtue of those laws, political possibilities and realities, as well as civil norms and dialogue, students can become involved and excited about these topics. As an educational tool, debate illuminates these complex issues and fits well within the classroom curriculum.

Criminal Justice

The study of criminal justice is full of opportunities to debate. In every nation's complex law enforcement system is the potential for important and powerful debates on legal, tactical, and ethical issues. In this section, we explore the value of debate to the study of criminal justice as well as some of the possible debate topics and formats that can be used in the classroom.

Why Debate Is Valuable to Criminal Justice Classes

The study of criminal justice is a fundamental pillar of any society. As law enforcement officials are being trained, the complexity of their relationship to the law, the citizenry, and the government are constant points of dialogue. Debates contribute to these studies by helping students relate the topics they are studying to their own lives, thus encouraging them to appreciate their roles in the community and to become aware of their own power.

The criminal justice classroom is filled with nuanced, subtle concepts. Many of these ideas seem so minor that they may slip by your students. Because the details of law are so important, future law enforcement officers must be made aware of the complicated concepts, history, and justification for laws, rules, and regulations. These ideas can be brought into clear view by judicious use of role-playing debates and by debating the complexities of these themes.

As future law enforcement officers, your students must be made aware of their role in the communities in which they work. Using debate, students can take turns making arguments from the citizens' perspectives of problems with various law enforcement tactics. Consider a public forum debate about a civilian review board for police officers in a community of color. Your students can work out some of the ideas that might arise and then be more sensitive to these ideas when they are on the streets.

Awareness of their own role in law enforcement and society is often difficult for students. Uncertainty about what kinds of jobs they will be expected to perform can contribute to a sense of frustration. Classroom debates can help to work out these anxieties by exploring the goals and philosophies of law enforcement. One exercise we suggest is to bring up common concepts such as justice and peace and have your students explore what they think these ideas are. By providing students with the opportunity to express themselves about these issues, you can help position them in the community and prevent future difficulties. By using debate to help future law enforcement officers be sensitive to many perspectives, they are better prepared to handle a variety of ideas, opinions, and situations that will arise in the course of their careers.

Sample Debate Topics for Criminal Justice Classes

- We should always protect personal rights.
- We should have some limit on freedom of speech.
- We should curtail police powers.
- The police should have additional powers.
- We should allow for vigilante justice.
- Victim-offender reconciliation should be explored.
- Justice is more important than peace.
- Nonviolent drug offenders should not be jailed.

- Corporal punishment is essential for juvenile delinquents.
- We should liberate the jails.
- Power is fluid.
- The rights of the accused have been increased too much.
- The exclusionary role for evidence should be eliminated.
- In criminal justice, human intelligence is more important than machine intelligence.
- Police should only be armed with nonlethal weapons.
- Guns should be outlawed.
- Punishment is as important as rehabilitation.

Sample Debate Formats for Criminal Justice Classes

A model congress debate format works well for criminal justice students. Guiding the students to represent themselves in a parliamentary or congressional format and using *Robert Rules of Order*, you can involve many students and have a free exchange of ideas.

Select a topic like "Resolved: Nonviolent drug offenders should not be jailed" and assign two students to be primary advocates in favor of the topic and two students to be primary advocates against the topic. These students are expected to present a variety of arguments and data that will provide the foundation of the debate. You might assign a pair of information-laden articles for the rest of the class to read in preparation.

As moderator, you direct each of the primary advocates to speak for a few minutes and then take questions from the audience. Afterward you can build a list of students who want to speak on the topic. Remind students that they can accept questions after they finish speaking. Encourage students to speak multiple times and keep their speeches short, perhaps a minute or so.

You can set up several debate topics in a single class, assigning different students to become primary advocates. If you want to invest more time in the project, have the students research their topics for a couple of weeks and then encourage each student to present a change in criminal justice policy that he or she thinks is important. Have the same format of questions and speakers. After each debate, ask the students to vote in favor or against the change.

Do not worry too much about the format or the rules. Students speaking out of order or a lull in the debate is part of the natural process. Instead, focus on keeping the ideas flowing in the classroom.

Conclusion

Teaching criminal justice is more than simply conveying information to students. Teachers of criminal justice need to impress on students the ideas and themes that will save their lives and the lives of the citizenry. Along the way, students need to learn about ethics and to reflect on their own positions and privilege. Debates help us to become aware of the meaning behind rules and laws and to teach students to explore their own role in society.

Current Events

Current events is an exciting area for teachers and students to explore emerging controversies. The potential for heated discussion points to debate as an excellent pedagogical tool for teachers. This section discusses the valuable intersection between debate and the current events classroom.

Why Debate Is Valuable to Current Events Classes

Debate is valuable for current events classes because it provides new perspectives on subject matter. Debates allow students to examine and challenge topics that might receive scant attention from the various media. The very nature of debate forces students to clash with news stories that are emerging; spontaneous criticism comes when a person is forced to defend a seemingly indefensible argument. Minds are often lazy, finding easy paths. Debate pulls students into positions where their minds are challenged, intrigued, and forced to look critically at ideas.

Imagine a debate that occurs on the day after a political protest turns into a major riot in your nation's capital city. Your students are assigned to debate this riot, with some of the students responsible for defending the rioters. The students are aghast. The entire nation, the newspapers, their parents, and peers all appear to be criticizing these rioters. How are they supposed to defend this position? After a period of frustration (and perhaps guided by a strong teacher), they discover some of the protest's root causes. Perhaps they find some reference to police violence during the rally. Slowly they begin to understand that the rioters who seem crazy have firm political beliefs and might have been pushed into a rioting situation. The students then find that they are looking forward to the debate. Because successful debates hinge on the recognition of multiple sides, each with its own value and support, debates call upon students to explore new terrain within topics.

The flexible formats of debate allow students to explore controversial topics in depth. As new and exciting world events emerge, there is a tendency to sketch them in the broadest strokes. Because media sources and experts often give short shrift to the complex background that inspires these events, students expect a simple background template. Debate can challenge this kind of understanding. Because debate is a teaching method that can be used in almost any situation, it can encourage the need to get beyond simplistic understanding of issues and reach real explanations. Perhaps as a lead-in to a classroom unit on anti-immigrant racism, debate can expose prejudicial norms. A role-playing debate where students represent the opinions of different parties on an emerging political scandal can put students in the hot seat and bypass sensationalistic journalism. A model parliament or congress might require students to exhaustively research an upcoming piece of legislation.

Because students are responsible for the content of the debate, they strive to discover ideas on their own, rather than being led to these ideas. Students who participate in debate often realize that they are supposed to support a side that they have little or no knowledge of and jump into a process of self-exploration. A teacher can accelerate this process by inculcating research skills, thereby providing students with the tools they need to explore most topics.

Debate allows teachers to fit complex ideas into structural contexts. It might be very difficult to teach students why good ideas so often fail in our public arenas. With debates and role-playing debate exercises, students can discover the difficulties in making changes within a constrained system. Students can also integrate historical precedent and ideas into the debates, providing a long view of how and why political problems exist and continue to plague politicians.

Sample Debate Topics for Current Events Classes

- Country X should unilaterally disarm its nuclear weapons.
- The European Union should coordinate European immigration policies.
- Immigration is a plague.
- We should free the people.
- The future is now.
- The Balkans should fix their own problems.
- The international community should prosecute war criminals.
- All nations should act to forestall global warming.
- Russia/China should withdraw from Chechnya/Tibet.
- It is better to combat terrorism by reducing its causes than by fighting its symptoms.

Sample Debate Formats for Current Events Classes

A possible debate in a current events class might be about the Middle East peace process. This kind of complex topic is difficult to broach in traditional classroom situations. Simply conveying information about the political makeup of the Middle East is extremely difficult given the number of players and the intricacies of their political justifications. While many education professionals layer knowledge of geopolitics, international affairs, culture, and religion to try to give an overview of the Middle East, debates can help students to become engaged in this topic.

If a current events class were to use debates as a recurring event and the Middle East peace process were a central topic, students could seamlessly connect their debate skills with the real knowledge about the subject. The class might start with a public forum debate where students could voice their opinions and expose their level of knowledge about the subject. Using these ideas as foundations for a debate, the teacher might assign readings that explore the issues of the peace negotiations, the justifications for Israeli control, and the Palestinian arguments for statehood. After some research and discussion, a multisided debate on the same issue where students represented various factions of Israeli doves and hawks, Palestinian militants and moderates, the United States, and Syria might help them envision the complex issues in this drama. Later in the class, the teacher might assign a parliamentary debate about the role of Israeli settlements in the peace process. The class might also pursue the foundations of the controversy by debating historical land disputes from both the Jewish and Arab perspectives.

By using debates as a tool to learn about the issues and returning to the subjects, students will build upon their own knowledge. Their understanding of issues and ideas will culminate in knowledge that they have not simply memorized but have a deep commitment to. This process surpasses traditional teaching methods in creating understanding.

Conclusion

Debates about current events mesh with teaching goals: to encourage students to become interested and involved in issues. Through debating, students become aware of issues and can also conceptualize them in a complex manner. Debate helps students understand the contexts, difficulties, and constraints that result in modern policymaking decisions.

Economics

Economics is central to the lives of students, but many fail to understand how important. Debating economic issues may help them realize the relevance of the subject.

Why Debate Is Valuable to Economics Classes

Economic issues are well suited to debate for several reasons. First, debate can help students examine and understand economic theories. Second, economic decisions are interlaced with all major political decisions. As debate teachers and trainers for many years, we understand that every government policy has a cost, or savings, or an effect on human economic behavior, or some of all three. Teaching students to integrate economic decision making into their political decisions through debate can be highly useful. Third, a large portion of the public misunderstands economics. Some consider it a highly technical science, which is what some in the financial world believe it is. Others believe that it is an arcane art, which some in financial circles also believe. Other citizens merely consider economics impossible to understand, predict, and control. Debate destroys some of these presuppositions and allows you to introduce and analyze economic concepts as an area of intellectual inquiry.

Finally, we also believe that understanding how markets and economies work is vital for leading a full life. A critical understanding of economics might save someone from a stock swindle or teach a student to consider the ethical dimensions of the impact of free trade around the globe.

Sample Debate Topics for Economics Classes

- Income from investments should not be taxed.
- The value added tax is an essential fiscal tool for any national government.
- Agricultural subsidies by the European Union and the United States victimize poor farmers in developing nations.
- John Maynard Keynes was right.
- Karl Marx was right.
- Monetary policy alone is insufficient to manage a national economy.
- We will come to regret the creation of a global free market.
- Indigenous peoples cannot long survive integration into capitalism.

- Computer-based trading has increased the volatility of markets.
- The U.S. Social Security system can be saved through X.
- Company X is a better investment than Company Y.
- The high level of fossil fuel used in Nation X should be significantly reduced.
- Tradable carbon permits should be used to reduce carbon dioxide emissions.
- Development is suicide.
- Economic growth can be sustained forever.
- Businesses should uphold ethical standards.
- We should implement the Tobin Tax.

Sample Debate Formats for Economics Classes

Use topics, formats, and settings creatively to examine the material you wish to discuss in your classroom. Here are a few suggestions.

First, you could use the mock trial format. The class can put a major economist, such as Karl Marx or Milton Friedman, on trial, claiming that the widespread application of his theories was destructive of people, resources, and ecosystems. You could also set the debate in a specific historical period. This is a good way to engage students in the challenge of examining earlier economists. You can stage trials in a variety of ways and easily involve a large number of students. For example, you could stage an elaborate two-day trial involving the entire class or a 30-minute trial with two competing student advocates. Alternately, you could stage a trial over a series of days, with a part of it presented each day.

Second, you can stage a debate about various business models. The debate can compare two firms in the same business, using any format that fits your needs. You can assign students to research these firms and then argue that one of them follows a superior business model. This type of debate helps students understand how major firms are organized and operate, and how businesses are integrated into the broader economy.

Third, you can stage a public forum debate or a public debate on whether economics is a science. Ask half the class to research the pro and the other half of the class the con of the statement. Both debate formats will allow many students to participate and encourage stimulating exchange.

Fourth, stage a public debate on a topic relevant to the students. Ask the students to debate an economic policy of your choice. For example, students from nations that have just entered the European Union could debate, "Entering the European Union is economically disadvantageous to country X." This type of debate can be very involving for students and demonstrate the relevance of economics to their lives.

Fifth, students can use a short two-on-two format to debate specific policies: economic policies, tax policies, minimum wage laws, youth employment regulations, etc. Assigning each debate a different topic is both instructive and entertaining. You can assign topics at the beginning of the term and schedule one short debate at the beginning of each class *or* you can stage them consecutively over several class periods.

Sixth, stage a role-playing debate about the trade-offs often identified between the benefits of high economic growth and the health of the ecosystem. You can develop a specific scenario for economic development that has both profound economic and ecological consequences. You can then assign students the roles of community members, corporate developers, government regulators, environmental activists, investors, workers, etc.

Conclusion

Debate can be very helpful in studying economics. Beginning students can access basic economic principles by debating them. Advanced students can demonstrate their specific knowledge and expertise during debates. Debate will also give them better communication and reasoning skills to "sell themselves" as economic practitioners.

Education
Why Debate Is Valuable to Education Classes

Debating has a special relevance to the field of education as a classroom method and as a way to provide training in specially related subjects of study. As a method of teaching content and a process for learning skills, debating can help teachers to become more aware of important issues and ideas. This section is a guide to debating in an education class.

The learning model debate is useful to all education students and professionals. The relationship of gaining information, trying to use it, receiving feedback, and beginning the cycle again is one that expresses the ongoing process of learning. Using debates, students take class information, use it in their performances, receive critical response to their work, and then use that new knowledge. This process is very similar to the process of becoming a teacher, where an educator learns a subject, uses it in his or her own teaching, and then evaluates the success of the teaching process. The debater knows that no issue can be fully explored, no discussion is ever complete, and the debate never ends. In the same way, education is a lifelong process.

Debates create a good atmosphere for disagreement in the classroom. Intelligent people of good will can disagree about a wide variety of issues, and students as well as professional educators are advised to incorporate that fact into the classroom. Too many classrooms contain only one voice—that of the authority figure hired to supervise it. Educational debating can create what Robert Branham has said about debate in general, that the process demonstrates the "harmony of conflict." When extra voices are added to the classroom, the solo becomes a chorus and a bright opportunity for learning through involvement.

Debating in the education training classroom can show future educators how to use the process effectively in their own classrooms. The debate format is widely applicable to many educational subjects and opportunities. Some of our best mentors are those who taught us processes that we could use over and over again. We hope that integrating debate into the education classroom begins a lifelong appreciation of this form of learning.

Marshall Gregory, a professor of English at Butler University, suggests that when teaching, practice plays a fundamental role. Professor Gregory argues that too often education students become too attached to a particular method of teaching and fail to recognize the student-oriented nature of education. He explains that although practice is vital, it needs to be aided "first by criticism, the ability to see the imperfections in the performance so far, and second by imagination, the ability to visualize the performance or the skill not as it is actually being done now but as it might be done in the future, differently and better, after more practice" (74–75). Teaching future educators how to orchestrate debates and think critically suggests that debate might be invaluable for the education classroom.

Educators need to watch continually for opportunities to train students at all levels in critical-thinking skills. As explained in Chapter 1, the future will call for critical-thinking skills that go far beyond memory and data retention, and debating is a way to train teachers to do what they will be trying to teach students: how to solve problems and analyze complex situations. We have found that teachers who are concerned about critical-thinking skills and learn about debate as a method to teach them become ardent supporters of the process. We urge education-training professionals to consider debate as an important teaching tool.

Sample Debate Topics for Education Classes
- The grading and evaluation system should be radically changed.
- The educational system should not be divided into age groups.
- Students should advance at their own pace.
- Increased reliance on distance learning should be avoided.
- School should be voluntary.
- Teacher certification should be strengthened.
- Colleges and universities have inappropriately altered education practices to address issues of race or gender.

- Higher education has sacrificed quality for institutional survival.
- The government should guarantee an opportunity for higher education to all qualified high school graduates.
- Lesson plan X needs to be revised in a major way.
- Single-sex schools offer a superior secondary education.
- The government should support religious schools.
- Parents should be able to choose the schools their children attend.
- Standardized testing is unfair and discriminatory.
- Being a teacher is an unwise career choice.
- Students should be required to pass a competency test before graduating from secondary school.
- Schools place too much emphasis on sports.
- Ability grouping should be used in schools.
- Many students should not go to college.
- Teachers have a higher responsibility to their students than to their government.
- Teachers should refuse to teach material they strongly disagree with.
- Academic freedom is more important than teacher accountability.
- Every secondary school should have a debate team.
- Vocational education is a thing of the past.
- Students should not prepare for only one career.
- The college experience is better after being in the military.
- Offensive speech must be controlled in the classroom.
- It is vital that teachers use the Internet to create educational opportunities for their students.
- Use of the Internet has led to a deterioration of student research skills.
- Elementary and secondary schools should require school uniforms.
- In higher education, the tenure system has outlived its usefulness.

Sample Debate Formats for Education Classes

A variety of formats and methods are suggested for the education classroom. We urge that you draft or have your students draft specific topics and also that you allow your students to debate more than once in a term so that they have more chances to polish their skills.

Education students can debate about competing lesson plans and education methods. A proposal can be made, disclosed to the other team, and circulated to the class, so that students in the audience can criticize as well as give suggestions for improvement. The teams should switch roles during the term, which allows students to learn the curriculum from two vantage points and provides very real and tangible suggestions from those debating them. Alternating roles is a good way for students to share curriculum projects during the term.

Debates about the big issues in the field of education are valuable and can be framed around such topics as education design, implementation of education ideals, or the definition of an educated person. Students can research some of the critics of modern education practice and then stage a debate in which they represent the views of one critic on the affirmative, with the negative team defending current education practice. These kinds of exercises can reveal very important philosophical, pedagogical, and epistemological concepts.

Debates can be staged about education reform. Education is at the top of many political agendas, and many specific reforms have been adopted. A heated debate about an issue like charter schools and school vouchers can bring out new and exciting ideas in a class. Debates about these reform issues can relate to the content of the course or to important current events. How education can be designed, delivered, implemented, evaluated, and reformed are all useful areas for debate.

Conclusion

Almost every part of this book attempts to prove the point of this small section: debating is an exceptional educational technique. We trust that, among educators, debate will find a receptive audience.

Environmental Studies and Earth Sciences

The study of environmental science offers many opportunities to debate. Controversies over environmental policy, the toxicity of pollutants, and scientific proof of events like global warming all present exciting platforms for your students. In addition, very little tradition of public debate exists in these subject areas. Science is a fundamental part of our public discussions about issues as diverse as food safety and the protection of endangered species. Study of these issues can excite and stimulate students by integrating debates into the classroom.

Why Debate Is Valuable to Environmental Studies and Earth Sciences Classes

Debates can contribute to the educational climate of your earth science classroom by stimulating students to learn more about topics and driving them to see the importance and meaning of what they are studying. Debates in the environmental studies classroom convey to students the complexity of scientific issues and the public policy implications of scientific discourse. Debates in science classes play a very important reflexive role where students explore the sometimes dangerous implications and ethical responsibilities of scientific research.

Debates are exciting. When students have a framework for their debates and some sense of their topic, they begin to enjoy the process. Debates allow students to use the knowledge they have spent so much time and energy acquiring. Debates encourage students to look at issues from different angles, discover ideas they might have previously discarded, and see common knowledge as possibly flawed. Because debates are active, participatory, meaningful events, they encourage students to see your classroom as a thriving place where learning is exciting.

The scope of scientific knowledge and the potential impact of scientific debates can sometimes elude students. Understanding the relationship between the moon and the tides is valuable, but many students will not grasp the powerful implications of this knowledge. Through debates, students can realize and articulate the essence of this phenomenon. For example, students debating the use of tidal forces to generate energy can draw a picture of the intense power associated with planetary pull, explaining (as much to themselves as to others) the significance of that relationship.

Debate can foster a complex view of environmental issues. Much of our knowledge about scientific issues is simplified for easy public consumption. The intricacies associated with causal chains of scientific meaning are flattened so they can be explained in a chart or a quick paragraph. Global warming is a good example. Global warming is usually portrayed as a simple cause-and-effect event where the Earth's temperature increases because the build-up of carbon dioxide traps the sun's rays in the Earth's atmosphere. There are actually dozens of other feedback loops that affect the global warming process, including the role of trees and plants—which exchange carbon dioxide for oxygen—the importance of sea water temperature as a heat trap, and the role of nitrogen dioxide, another pollutant that emerges with carbon dioxide that actually seems to cool the Earth during the night. All of these relationships increase and decrease the processes called global warming. Yet, they are usually not mentioned in the popular science literature. The debate process allows students to resolve such complicated relationships. In researching their topic, they need to understand the complexity of any scientific issue and be able to explain it to an audience, a vital training process for future scientists and a valuable part of a scientific education.

Debates encourage reflection about complicated issues. Despite the perception that science is neutral, it is actually often used for political or social gain. Ethical reflection about the role of science in our society is important. Consider an intense study of the migration, eating habits, mating, and status of an endangered species of caribou that have been hunted to near extinction. The study is well funded and is intended to help scientists understand how they might help this species of caribou. After the study is done, poachers use the published data to position themselves along traditional migration routes and gain an advantage to hunt and kill the caribou. We believe that science has a responsibility to connect to the workings of the rest of the world. This connection means engaging in debates that many would urge science to avoid, such as the ethical debates about animal experimentation and the questions of epidemiology relating to AIDS and HIV. Scientists must recognize that because they are respected, they have power to influence the use of their findings. Debate is one of the few avenues that we have to discuss newly created knowledge. Debate is relentless and critical—as a process, it pushes us to examine possible disadvantages that can emerge and recognize the costs and benefits associated with research results.

Sample Debate Topics for Environmental Studies and Earth Sciences Classes

- We should sacrifice economic growth for the good of the environment.
- The value of natural resources is found in their exploitation.
- Spaceship Earth is crashing.
- Protection of the environment is a more important goal than the satisfaction of energy demands.
- The world should significantly increase the development of the Earth's ocean resources.
- The power of science is dangerous.
- The government should regulate genetically modified crops.
- Planting a tree saves a life.
- We should place culture above science.
- Person X is the most important scientist of her or his time.
- Creationism should be taught in schools.
- The nation should protect its estuaries from pollution.
- We should accept the Kyoto Accord to combat global warming.
- Immanuel Velikovsky's theory of catastrophism should be accepted.
- An asteroid strike destroyed the dinosaurs.
- Earthquake prevention is a waste of time and money.
- Earthquakes can be predicted.

- Toxic waste flows to the poor.
- A shift in the Earth's poles did take place and can happen again.

Sample Debate Formats for Environmental Studies and Earth Sciences Classes

Here are two examples of debates that might be successful in your earth science classroom. The first is a three-sided debate about genetically engineered crops. Using this format, students can see the myriad perspectives on public policy for science. The second debate is about the nature of environmental racism, the unequal distribution of toxic waste. This debate highlights the ethical ramifications of scientific inquiry and the complexity of making environmental policy.

Debate Number One: Three Sides of Genetically Engineered Crops. The issue of genetically engineered crops is one that evokes a lot of scientific bluster and not a lot of analysis of public policy. The science of genetic engineering is thousands of years old. For centuries farmers have bred various strains of grain to gain hardier, more successful, or higher-yielding crops. This natural science has evolved into a high-tech science of gene-splicing, where scientists connect the genes of seemingly disparate entities (like fish and tomatoes). Genetically engineered crops have elicited a massive response from activists, consumers, multinational corporations, and national leaders. One of the exciting aspects of this debate is that it has many sides. Therefore, we have created a debate that explores this situation.

By setting up a three-sided debate, your students benefit from a greater interplay of and a more complex exchange of ideas. Side one argues that genetically engineered food is wonderful and should be completely unregulated. Side two argues that genetically engineered food should be carefully regulated to minimize any danger. Side three argues that genetically engineered food should be completely banned because of the danger it already presents. Through the interplay of these three perspectives, the debaters and the rest of your class begin to see that the politics of science often get in the way of the pure quest for knowledge and that the quest for knowledge has dramatic political implications. This debate looks beyond "good vs. bad" and explores scientific justifications and social implications. Side one will argue that the risk of famine outweighs any ethical consideration. Side three will attack the safety of these crops and criticize the multinational corporations that have patented crop genes. Side two will attempt to create a middle ground arguing that regulation can solve both problems.

Debate Number Two: Environmental Racism. Environmental racism is a catchphrase used to describe the unequal distribution of toxic waste based on race. Arguing that significantly more toxic waste sites occur in communities of color, many activists and scientists have documented the devastating impacts these sites have on surrounding populations. A debate about environmental racism confronts the ethical responsibilities of scientists and the difficulties in solving environmental problems.

In a public forum event where the topic is "What can be done about environmental racism?" students can explore a variety of scientific and political solutions to this problem. Students might argue that the government should be responsible for cleaning up existing hazardous waste sites. Others might argue that new regulations should prevent unequal distribution of wastes in the future. Other students might criticize these approaches, arguing that pressure on waste industries will only encourage them to ship toxic waste to other countries or that communities of color will lose their jobs. Students may also call for various scientific approaches: bioremediation or the use of microbes to eat toxic waste, new cleaning technologies or the use of brownfields, recycled industrial areas that are to be used again for new industries. This debate can help students to see the complicated issues that environmental scientists must help to resolve. They can start to think through the potential ramifications of their own work and consider the meaning of their actions.

Conclusion
Through these discussions new ideas emerge and the potential power of science to help solve some of the devastating inequality comes

out. More important, through these debates, students recognize the power and importance of science and the responsibility of scientists to be self-critical about their own work and ideas. Science does not exist in a vacuum and debate can bring about this realization in your students.

Foreign Languages

The reason to debate in a foreign language class is obvious: students experience a new language by using it in a special and rigorous way. The debate process as outlined in Chapter 2 is the same one that students will need when they are trying to live in a foreign country and do business in a second language.

Foreign Languages and Debate

Debates can take place in any language that the participants understand. Much can be learned even from a debate in a language we cannot fully understand. At the World Debate Institute, a considerable amount of international debating now takes place in English because it is the world's most popular second language, but we believe promoting debate in a broad range of languages is vital.

Debate can be useful and educational in any language, as the main argument of this book indicates, but it can be especially useful for students who want to learn a second or third language in this spontaneous and logical format.

Why Debate Is Valuable to Foreign Language Classes

Debate has been shown to be an outstandingly productive exercise for language acquisition. In the United States, debate has been extremely successful in reaching out to non–English-speaking students and enabling them to achieve considerable language facility. Worldwide, debating is a valued technique for learning English. Debaters in Japan pioneered this practice and met with great success, often with English-speaking clubs sponsoring debates as a tool for language acquisition. Today the practice has spread globally through the International

Debate Education Association in cooperation with governments, schools, and private foundations. However, this technique is currently underutilized in classes designed to teach English speakers or anyone a new language.

Debates put students in situations where they will have to "think" in a different language. Memorization by beginning language students equips them with an array of words and phrases they can use to communicate. However, living and operating in a different culture involves problem solving and critical processes that require the manipulation of logical concepts, just as debating requires students to critically analyze their own arguments and those of others. In this way debate training can be exceedingly valuable to the intermediate and advanced language student.

Debate is a mechanism for enhancing cultural and social learning related to the language being studied. Language operates within the context of a culture and a society and cannot be well understood when studied in isolation. Debate topics can be framed around these cultural and social features. These topics can also be framed in a way that gives students lots of latitude in presenting their ideas, which reduces the anxiety of learning new vocabulary words. The topics do not have to be "serious" to facilitate a friendly and beneficial debate in a second language.

Sample Debate Topics for Foreign Language Classes

- Country X should have a national language.
- Country X should debate in its own language.
- Country X should debate only in English.
- Switzerland has a better form of government than X.
- No foreign language should be taught in our public schools.
- Foreign language instruction should be increased in our schools.
- The study of Latin and Greek is a needless waste of time.
- The system of government in X is preferable to that of Y.
- Vienna is a German city. [Variations suggested.]

- Spain is more culturally sophisticated than Hispanic America.
- French/German/Italian food is superior to French/German/ Italian food.
- The French language should avoid the inclusion of non- French words.
- The Spanish language should be globally standardized.
- The English language should be globally standardized.
- It is better to vacation in X than in Y.

Sample Debate Formats for Foreign Language Classes

Students will most likely find simple, one-on-one short debates to be the most useful format. This format allows many students to participate in a short amount of time and with a minimum of preparation. The less "serious" topics are probably best. The focus here is on basic language skills and not necessarily on elaborate new vocabulary. Because these debates are short and simple, strategies are advised for keeping the audience involved as much as possible within the format's time constraints.

Team debates are more useful at a higher level of language proficiency. These debates should feature more "serious" topics that involve more preparation. The focus should be on formal language use in a public situation. These debates should have the audience involved either as judges or speech givers. Pre-debate disclosure is very useful here to enhance the quality of the interaction. Make sure such disclosure takes place well in advance and in sufficient detail.

A public assembly debate is useful at various levels of language proficiency. Topics should be distributed either in advance for beginning speakers or more spontaneously for more advanced students. Some simple or complex topic is proposed, and each student has to make a brief speech (one or two minutes) in support of or opposition to the topic. If you'd like, students can be allowed to speak more than once given time constraints. A vote of the "house" can take place at the end of the speaking period. This activity is spontaneous and interactive and does not take up too much time.

Cross-examination can be a useful addition to any debate format being used for language instruction. It is interactive but at the same time far more formal than conversation training. Highly spontaneous, it reveals a student's language level. Students also find it to be very entertaining to watch.

Conclusion

Debating can add considerably to any foreign language classroom because it involves students in a level of critical thinking that transcends sheer translation or conversation as a way to learn a language. Considerable experience globally has established this fact; it is one of the most important contributions of debate to society—the ability to speak and reason with each other in more languages.

Geography

Geography is the stage on which the human drama is played out. Learning about and understanding the place and setting of events and conditions is vitally important for students. Debate can assist in this process.

Why Debate Is Valuable to Geography Classes

Debating is a useful way to look at important geographical issues, such as land use, political divisions among nations, and ecological transformations. Unlike the rhetoric of the political forum, which looks at these issues in terms of what is expedient, debating examines them in depth. While our immediate topographical features may remain steady within a human perspective, the ways those features are used and covered are changing. Debating is an excellent way to examine "possible futures" that may play out on a given topography.

Sample Debate Topics for Geography Classes

Many of the conflicts of the 20th and 21st centuries were and are caused by colonial powers creating borders without a good knowledge of topographical and human geography.

- Because of its geography, global warming would benefit country X.
- Satellite mapping of natural resources has allowed rich nations to take unfair advantage of poor nations.
- Secondary schools should increase the amount of time devoted to studying geography.
- The map is not the territory/the map is the territory.
- Throughout history, we see that geography is destiny.
- Large-scale human geographical engineering is currently too dangerous.
- South Korea should not move its national capital.
- Even after recent expansion, the European Union is not too geographically diverse.
- Greenland's population is too small and its surface area is too large to be an independent nation.
- The terms *Far East*, *Middle East*, and *Near East* should be retired.
- The global map should be standardized for official use as an X projection.
- Mapping is the ultimate tool of control.
- Mapping is the root of the Middle East crisis.
- The border between country X and country Y should be substantially redrawn.
- Satellite mapping information should be free.
- The GPS is a tool of liberation.
- Pakistan should never have been created.
- Every people deserve their own land.

Sample Debate Formats for Geography Classes

You can hold a public forum or a public debate about the need for study and mastery of geography. Secondary school students in a required geography course could debate topics such as, "Extensive instruction in geography is not necessary because of readily available reference material." Likewise, secondary students might debate topics such as, "Geography is not a wise career choice." Both of these topics use debate to teach the importance of geography.

First, you could stage a historical reenactment role-playing debate about the way colonial governments created borders. One side could represent the people in a given area (such as the Middle East after World War I) who call for new borders based on geographical features and human populations. The other side could advocate from the viewpoint of the colonial power. This could be planned during the semester and then be held as a public debate at the end of the course.

Second, a human geography class might look at the way in which new capitals, such as Brasilia, have been created and located. You could also use historical examples such as St. Petersburg, Ravenna, and Washington, D.C. Because different issues were involved in the creation of each of these cities, these debates would deal with a large number of geographical issues in a very specific way.

Third, you could hold a public debate or a public forum about the geographical nature of new and changing nations. For example, "Because it is too large and too underpopulated, Greenland should not become an independent state," might raise a variety of geographical issues in a very real way. You should give students advance notice of this event and supply some articles on the topic.

Conclusion

Geography is often seen as dry and boring, but students who debate geographic issues find the subject enlightening and exciting.

History

Debate has certainly made history, from the forums of ancient times to the international conferences of today. Debate is also a useful way to understand history, making the issues students confront "come alive" as the process calls on them to be personally responsible for critical communications about the subjects they are studying.

Why Debate Is Valuable to History Classes

Debate encourages students of history to find connections and useful lessons by engaging them in the understanding of where we have come from and where we are going. Debates are valuable to history students in the following ways:

First, the very nature of history is debatable. There is no one perfect history of any event; instead, many competing interpretations of historical facts, causes, and consequences are available. Students can examine the work of historians and compare them in critical exercises or argue issues of cause and effect in history, all within an organized critical communication format that can be adapted to a specific class. It is easy to come up with relevant topics for debate within almost any area of historical study.

Second, history is a process of storytelling at its most grand. Many students are enchanted by study of places and times that are exotic and different. Yet, competing stories exist at each level of historical exploration. The process of debating about history can, in some ways, be thought of as an exercise in competitive storytelling, where each side paints its own picture of events and possible futures while reinterpreting the stories of the other side. Students can learn about the ways in which the broader flows of history can be interpreted and understood.

Third, as we debate about history we rebuild the past. Debating within specific time and place restrictions puts students into situations in a very active and immediate way. Through representing individuals and groups from history, debates offer a better understanding of the historical texts and perhaps even the historical realities. In their arguments and presentations, students can attempt to rebuild the ideas and logical connections of the past. Certainly this process can never be fully accomplished, but the effort—the attempt to understand other peoples and other times—is an extremely important exercise for the students.

Fourth, debating allows students to take different perspectives on important issues. Many of the issues that come up in the study of history are related to how individuals construct other people—whether they denigrate or elevate them. We are rarely called on to consider who we are and assume, just for a moment, that we might be that other person. Through debate activities, students can develop an ability to operate "inside" the historical perspectives of other people and other groups. While a simple debate cannot fully train us to see things as others see them, it is a useful beginning to that process and something students seem to enjoy and appreciate.

Sample Debate Topics for History Classes

You can debate many of these topics from a contemporary perspective as well as from the perspective of the specific period.

- History is not to be trusted because the winners write it.
- America is an ahistorical society.
- The only thing we learn from history is that we learn nothing from history.
- History explains but cannot predict.
- Hollywood has destroyed more history than it has enshrined.
- History textbooks in public schools need major revisions.
- Oral history is more accurate than written history.
- Women should not be denied suffrage.
- We should repudiate history.
- Nationalism is a virtue.
- History is not her story.
- The advancement of civil liberty is more indebted to intellectual culture than to force of arms.
- The cotton gin is a greater invention than the electric telegraph.
- The United States should have entered World War I in 1914.
- The United States should not have renamed Washington National Airport after Ronald Reagan.
- The United States should have entered the League of Nations.
- The Volstead Act should be modified to permit the manufacture and sale of light wines and beer.

- The United States should have agreed to the cancellation of the Allied debts following World War I.
- The Allies should have agreed to the cancellation of the Axis debts after World War II.
- The United States should follow a policy of strict economic and military isolation toward all nations outside the Western Hemisphere engaged in armed international or civil conflict.
- A federal world government should be established.
- The further development of nuclear weapons should be prohibited by international agreement.
- The United States should have substantially reduced its military commitments to South Vietnam in the early 1970s.
- There should be an educational test as a qualification for voting.
- Daniel Webster was superior in intelligence to Stephen A. Douglas.
- Oliver Cromwell was a greater man than Napoleon Bonaparte.
- Toussaint L'Ouverture was the equal of George Washington as a soldier and statesman.
- Richard III was a worse monarch than Charles II.
- Athens was superior to Sparta as a political entity.
- Egypt was the cradle of European civilizations.
- Historically the Chinese civilization has been more advanced than the European.
- The Aztec and Inca civilizations were more sophisticated than the Spanish civilization that conquered them.
- We use history less to guide our actions now than previously.
- Politicians use history to justify the courses of action they prefer; they do not choose courses of action that are justified by history.

Sample Debate Formats for History Classes

Class subject matter will dictate topics, but most debate formats are appropriate for almost any history class. One-on-one, two-on-two, or public assembly formats can be very useful for debating issues. Almost any format can provide insight when used in the following ways. Debates can be held about the uses of history. The objectivity, or need for objectivity, can be a subject for debate. The way in which history is used or ignored to help frame decisions can be fruitful grounds for a debate. These kinds of debates can help students in an introductory class or even in a class for new majors in history. A high school class might have a debate about the need to study history and whether to reduce or expand history requirements.

Debates about whether to rewrite portions of history are illuminating. Significant criticisms have been voiced of accepted historical accounts that some claim need substantial revision. A debate might also be held about the need to revise history textbooks in school systems. This subject helps students understand the nature of historical accounts and requires them to investigate particular historical periods and accounts.

Students can engage in "what if?" debates, also called "historical re-creation" debates. In these debates, students imagine what would happen if something in history were different. Students might debate about what life would be like if the Axis powers had won World War II. Or they might explore what life would be like if President John Kennedy had not been assassinated. These debates emphasize imagination and exploration—looking to new ideas and stretching students' sense of reality.

Debates can be held in specific eras or with specific historical figures or groups. Great debates have occurred at various points in history over such issues as prohibition of alcohol, abolition of slavery, the granting of independence to colonies, the right of women to vote, and the creation of the League of Nations. One caution: Students might not feel confident being Napoleon or Ramses II. One technique is to require them to act as an agent for that person in the debate.

These kinds of debates can be useful ways to study history at many different levels. Debates often make history "come alive" for students as they act out the issues and the key players.

Conclusion

Debaters often use historical examples and lessons as proof for their arguments. Policy debates use history as a basis for future decisions. Value topics allow the exploration of changing ethical and moral standards. The integration of debating into the history classroom allows a deeper level of learning to be achieved.

International Relations

The study of international relations is vital to understanding the world. International relations theorists help to outline ways to map and chart the ebb and flow of international politics. Issues as varied as the independence of nongovernmental organizations and the value of economic sanctions as a tactic are the province of international relations.

Teaching international relations involves more than providing information about the treaties that govern the oceans; teaching is so often about the methods and philosophies of study, learning about other peoples' and nations' worldviews, and, often times, exploring the darkest part of our civilizations—wars. The introduction and use of classroom debates can help you reach some of your education goals for your international relations classes.

Why Debate Is Valuable to International Relations Classes

Students are attracted to international relations because of the allure of foreign places, the suggestion of power and importance, the perception (and reality) that history is made through international relations, and for other reasons. However, students attracted to the field might be surprised at the amount of difficult work and preparation necessary to master it. Knowledge of history, geography, economics, cultures, and negotiations are important components of training in international relations, but communication is the most important skill. Accordingly, debate is invaluable to this training because:

First, those involved with international relations need to be familiar with and skilled in oral advocacy. Communication skills of any kind can be difficult to develop, but those working with individuals from other societies face even more difficulties, especially when the interests of the parties may diverge. Open and publicly accountable debate is excellent training for such situations. The use of debating in the classroom can enhance an already exciting subject.

Second, both international affairs and debate are speculative. The scholar of international relations asks the question "what if . . ." about the past, present, and future. Like a debater speculating about what effects a particular policy proposal would have on other areas, the discipline of international relations invites participants to speculate about what could be. Debate forces students to "think ahead" about the impact of any given proposal—valuable training for future diplomats.

Third, both debate and international relations involve decisions about verbal expression that allow us to process issues cognitively and come to a conclusion. The international relations field offers various perspectives, including realism, balance of power, feminist international relations, nonviolent action, and others, that are used to make decisions. The debater is also concerned not just with the issues but how the issues will be balanced and decided.

Fourth, debate and international relations demand the use of perspective—seeing an issue through the eyes of another. Critical and important communication must proceed with some level of mutual understanding. Value hierarchies may be quite different among different international actors, thus making an understanding of the other parties involved essential. Debate can put students in situations where they will have to take the perspective of another party and make decisions based on that perspective. By engaging in this process while representing themselves in a personal way, students can begin to develop this critical skill.

Sample Debate Topics for International Relations Classes
- The United States should withdraw all its ground combat forces from bases located outside the Western Hemisphere.
- A unilateral freeze by the United States on the production and development of nuclear weapons would be desirable.

- The European Community ought/ought not to expand now.
- The poverty of the Third World is the fault of the First World.
- A global marketplace is good for us.
- The United States should be less involved in world affairs.
- The Western nations should reduce their commitment to Israel.
- Foreign policy significantly directed toward the furtherance of human rights is desirable.
- We should open the gates to immigrants.
- Realism is an inadequate framework for international relations.
- We should increase the international importance of nongovernmental organizations.
- We should actively pursue a world government.
- Major treaty X from the Cold War era should be abandoned.
- The United Nations should do less, not more.
- Nation X has a valid territorial claim against Nation Y.
- Nation X should pay reparations to Nation Y.
- Leader X's policy toward Nation Y was a failure.
- The Western Hemisphere should develop a free trade area.
- International organization X should be abolished.
- Stage a debate between the sides in a selected treaty negotiation.
- Stage a "what if" debate changing who won a major war.

Sample Debate Formats for International Relations Classes

The specific area of international relations study usually dictates the formats and uses of debating. However, the teacher should feel free to choose or design formats and topics that fit with the subject matter and his or her personal style. Debates are very flexible and retain most of their beneficial characteristics no matter how they are organized.

First, introductory classes should consider holding a debate to establish the importance of this area of study. Topics can be gathered from current events or from history but should attempt to show that international relations is a vital field. A public assembly format can be used or the class can be divided into different factions.

Second, debates about the "meta-issues" of international relations can be staged. In such events, teams of several students can either challenge prevailing wisdom or introduce an alternative perspective, such as feminist international relations or postmodern approaches. These kinds of debates get at the deeper issues and provide insight into "why" certain decisions are made in international relations. They also force students to question their own approaches to the field and reevaluate the way they make decisions.

Third, debates can be held about specific case studies. Two sides in a case study can be assigned that no student is actually identified with. The teams would then represent those sides in a debate. For example, issues about the future of Jerusalem, with students assigned as Israeli or Palestinian delegates, could be interesting for the entire class and educational for the students involved. Case studies can be drawn from the past, the present, or an imaginary future. The instructor should make sure that sufficient information is available to the students.

Fourth, debates can be held about specific policies. These debates can be about specific proposals and between two teams of two or three students. A 50-minute debate on a specific policy proposal can be very illuminating, and students especially enjoy the lively cross-examination periods. Any major policy proposal in the area of foreign affairs can be used here, assuming that it has both supporters and detractors so that students can research both sides. Students in the audience can either vote for the better debater or for the policy they most agree with. If the latter is chosen, have a pre-debate vote to compare to the post-debate vote.

Fifth, historical settings can be used. Students can stage a debate about a conference or negotiation they are studying, taking on the roles of the players in the event. This format requires some historical study, which may already be part of the curriculum. Those class members not represented as delegates can act as members of the press or other interested parties, offering their interpretation of the proceedings after the sides have made their presentations.

Sixth, "what if?" debates can be staged. In these short debates, participants can speculate on historical events, such as "What if the Axis

Powers had won World War II?" The first team would then present their interpretation of what the world would be like. A second team would then present their criticisms of the ideas of the first team, and then present their alternatives. It is advisable to have the first team disclose their points to the second team so that the debate will go quickly. The event can be concluded with a question period or comments from the rest of the class. The class might then vote for the team that had the best answers to the "what if?" question.

Conclusion

In competitive academic debate, international relations issues offer the opportunity for some of the most lively and enjoyable contests because of their importance and because citizens need to be broadly informed. There is every reason to bring the excitement of debating these issues into the classroom.

Law

In no field is there a more closely established relationship with debating than in law. Many students take up debating because they anticipate careers in the law, where many debates arise out of legal situations. Law schools strongly suggest debating as an activity and value it in making admissions decisions. The lawyer needs to have the skills of a debater.

This section is not aimed at those in law school, but to general secondary school and university students who are investigating legal subjects and their teachers. This approach does not assume a high degree of legal knowledge, but does presuppose some basic interest in the law and a desire to learn more.

Why Debate Is Valuable to Law Classes

Many connections exist between classes in law-related themes and the practice of debating:

First, debating and critical decision making is the method of law. The roles of the legal practitioner and debater are reasonably coterminous. Each one gathers the facts and engages in research, each formulates arguments for his or her side of the case, each presents those arguments orally to those making the decision, each looks for critical holes in the presentation of the other, and then each waits for the decision to be made. The preparation received from being involved in debate is directly relevant to the skills needed in the legal arena.

Second, both debating and law emphasize the use of oral argument. While legal briefs are filed and are important, the oral argument component of both law and debate is essential. The judge and jury must be persuaded and the presentation must be of a quality that will aid in the transmission of vital arguments and evidence. Many lawyers and many students lack sufficient training in oral communication skills; making debate a part of a law-related class addresses this problem. Even the seemingly disconnected formats like SPAR debates and public forums encourage the development and use of these skills.

Third, research is an essential part of both practices. When debating, there is no substitute for knowing your subject. The good lawyer faces the same need to learn the facts of the case and the existing relevant law in order to perform adequately. Debaters and lawyers need to learn to research in a targeted and efficient way to quickly gain needed information. A good grasp of bibliographic, electronic, and field research skills is very important. Research to prepare for a debate on a legal issue is direct training for the kinds of research needed in the legal field.

Fourth, both activities emphasize the need for properly briefing arguments. Arguments must be developed, then presented in a logical, organized, and appropriate format. The transition between the research phase to the briefing stage is key, as data become arguments and eventually a case. Both debaters and lawyers learn to anticipate the arguments of the other side, taking them into account in their original arguments by preempting them. A judge once told us that she could tell which of the lawyers had debate experience because the debaters tended to preempt and answer the other side's arguments in their initial presentation or brief, putting themselves one step ahead of the opposition.

Fifth, the topics that law classrooms cover are exciting topics for anyone to debate. Almost all crises that face our world today can be productively explored through a legal lens; thus, to consider the issue of genocide, a debate about the legal processes that are responding to the atrocities in Rwanda can get at the issues in a meaningful way. Almost every current topic of debate has a legal angle, and debates that focus on the ways that the law can respond and contribute to the solution of a problem are valuable.

Sample Debate Topics for Law Classes

- The decision in Case X should be reversed.
- The state should/should not seek the death penalty in capital cases involving persons under the age of 18.
- The legal system favors the rich.
- Judges should be elected, not appointed.
- Determining facts is more important than following legal procedure.
- People have lost faith in the legal system.
- Statutes of limitation in criminal/civil cases should be increased.
- The tort liability system damages our economy.
- We use legal means to resolve our differences more than we should.
- Punishment should be de-emphasized in the interests of rehabilitation.
- Released sex offenders should be identified for the community in which they live.
- The rights of the accused have been expanded to the detriment of the rights of the victim.
- The public's low opinion of lawyers is unjustified.
- There are too many lawyers.
- Military personnel should have all the legal rights of civilians.
- Gay marriages should be allowed.
- Prisons should be abolished for all except for the most dangerous offenders.

- Professional legal groups should be prohibited from political lobbying or from making campaign contributions.
- Restitution of damages is more important than punishment.
- We should eliminate capital punishment.
- "Victimless crimes" should be legalized.
- It is a citizen's duty to follow the law.
- Anarchy is a viable alternative to the rule of law.
- Legal protection of accused persons in country X unnecessarily hinders law enforcement agencies.
- Regulations requiring employees to be tested for controlled substances are an unwarranted invasion of privacy.
- The adversarial legal system should be replaced by a system devoted to making the correct decisions.
- Increased restrictions on the civilian possession of handguns in the United States would be justified.
- The separation of church and state is no longer necessary.
- The right to privacy is more important than the freedom of the press.
- Significant government restrictions on coverage by the media of terrorist activity are justified.
- One or more presently existing restrictions on the freedoms of press and/or speech should be curtailed or prohibited.

Sample Debate Formats for Law Classes

The nature of the precise legal subject matter will suggest appropriate formats for any given class. Here are a few basic suggestions:

First, begin an introductory class with a debate about the nature of law. Very basic issues often set the stage for later explorations and early debates can get students acquainted with each other and comfortable with the class setting. Issues such as our obligation to follow laws, our need for laws, the type of process for establishing laws that commands our respect, and other basic questions from the topic list all make excellent open debates. The public assemblies format or the division of the class into two teams is appropriate for this kind of general and introductory exercise.

Second, organize very simple single-issue debates. They might deal with narrow topics so that students can have a quick one-on-one debate about the issue. These quick debates can be scheduled on a few class days or one short debate can be scheduled in each class period or in each week.

Third, engage students in written brief debates. Assign some legal question on which students can present their arguments in writing. Keep the length of the briefs short. Encourage your students to make a number of clear arguments and not spend too much time on too few issues. One option is to assign them one of the other side's briefs to answer in writing. This exercise will encourage good composition and issue discovery.

Fourth, assign issue discovery exercises. Provide students with a legal question and have them draw up a list of issues in writing. Then have a public assembly-style meeting where students present their issues. Keep a record of these issues. You should have a list of the issues already prepared so you can see what the students have missed.

Fifth, develop cross-examination techniques. Students can be positioned on opposite sides of an issue and then cross-examine each other for three or four minutes. This exercise can be useful in training students to take depositions from witnesses. Many students can participate in a single class session.

Sixth, stage a mock trial, one of the most popular debate methods used in law classrooms. While the mock trial format is useful in many fields, it is most relevant in the legal field. Such events need adequate preparation by the students and a considerable amount of class time, but are well worth the effort. Assign students not arguing the case to the jury box or as members of the press (who can question the major players at the end of each session) or as witnesses and family members. The instructor can serve as the presiding judge or appoint a skilled student to fill this role.

Seventh, use legal debates to teach the application of legal knowledge to pending controversies. Rather than having a contest of advocacy based on the criteria of cost-benefit analysis or of morality, students can debate controversies and use the laws of the land as their framework. Students then become familiar with the basic laws surrounding a controversy (the question of an illegal search of an automobile during a drug arrest) and then have a debate about how a particular case will be resolved. This exercise teaches the students the basics of the law and encourages them to use their knowledge and envision its value. It is worthwhile to review the formats we suggest in Chapter 4 and apply them to each class and subject matter area.

Conclusion

Debate is an excellent method for any class dealing with legal issues. Because debate and law share so many characteristics, the subject matter is the method. The future of legal regimes will depend on the open public argument they use.

Literature

The stories we have told each other since the beginning of time have educated, enlightened, and elevated us. Those great stories of our past and present stand as bodies of literature that we now study and teach. Each story is heard differently by each individual, who interprets it using his or her own unique perspective. Part of the great educational potential of literature comes when we share with each other our interpretations of these works. Debate can be extremely valuable in the literature classroom to extend these interpretations.

Why Debate Is Valuable to Literature Classes

We have many ways to share and learn from great works of literature. Debate is one useful way that teachers should consider. Here are four reasons to recommend this integration of debate and literature:

First, debate can add an active element to an often-passive activity. While the mind is active when it is reading, the action is mostly cognitive, not behavioral. When students debate issues of literature, they take what they have cognitively processed and then present it and defend it before an audience. Literature becomes more personally relevant when students engage the work in this way.

Second, literature and debate both have substantial narrative and meta-narrative elements. Literature is usually narrative; debate can be narrative as well. The debater tells a story about how things are and how they might be. The debater also retells the story of the opponent's narrative, rephrasing it in ways that cast a different, and often less flattering light, on them. The debate process heightens the level of narrative exchange and reinterpretation.

Third, debates encourage people to share their literary experiences and learn from that process. Many people find "book groups" (where members read the same book, then meet once a month to discuss it) useful; the debate process, when focused on literature, can provide a similar experience. We are constantly struck by how others can read the same piece of literature and have a unique and valuable perspective to share. The illuminating and edifying results of literature can be heightened through such sharing, and debate is no exception.

Fourth, integrating debates into the literature classroom can make stories more personally relevant to the students. Often we read great works from long ago that seem a bit colorless to some students because of their language or unfamiliar period detail. By taking works of literature and staging a debate about them, debate students assume behaviors that heighten their personal involvement. Literature has much to teach all of us, and debate opens the door of personal relevance to students who are then able to incorporate its lessons.

Sample Debate Topics for Literature Classes

- Drama is a more powerful art form than the novel.
- Science fiction is an immature literary form.
- Fiction is inferior to nonfiction.
- Western literature has been overemphasized.
- The genre of X is inferior to the genre of Y.
- Author X is a better writer than Author Y.
- Novel X is a better work of literature than Novel Y.
- Play X is a better work of drama than Play Y.
- Character X is really the hero in work Y.

- Character X is really the villain in work Y.
- Work X is an attempt to explain the social situation of Y.
- Character X in work Y is guilty of crime Z. [Trial.]

Sample Debate Formats for Literature Classes

A number of debate formats work well in the literature class. A look at our topic list reveals some of them. Debates are fairly easy to organize if the students have read the work closely. Unlike debates that occur in a specific time in history that need extensive background information, a work of literature can often stand alone as a resource for students to create a productive debate. Below are suggestions for debates in literature classes.

First, put specific characters or institutions in a work of literature on trial. Is Hamlet guilty of murder? Is the coyote really the cause of the problem? Was Moll Flanders guilty of immorality? Students can be assigned as prosecutors, defense counsels, judge, jury, character witnesses, the accused, and other roles. With a bit of cooperation, a trial spanning several class periods can be staged. Teachers have told us that this is an extremely useful format.

Second, debate the nature of a work's characters. The better the work, the harder it is to determine who is wearing the hero's white hat or the villain's black hat. In many works, good arguments can be made either way for many different characters. This ambiguity allows students to dig deep to analyze characters and not take appearances for the fictional reality.

Third, use debates to compare two different works, either two works by the same author or two different authors writing about similar themes. There is no right answer, but such a debate forces students to develop standards for evaluating literature and then apply them to specific examples.

Fourth, use debates to compare two different writers. Granted that no two writers are really the same, a debate can be generated that makes the case for and against each author. This exercise forces students to develop standards for what a literary artist is trying to accomplish in his or her career and whether the artist succeeds or not.

Fifth, use debates to compare or evaluate different genres. Some literature is thought of as "high brow," some considered "mass market." Some critics view science fiction and mystery stories as immature genres because the forms are too restricted to be truly revealing, while others strongly disagree. Individual genres can be critiqued, or two genres compared, as appropriate for the class's discussion and lesson material.

Sixth, stage a debate that pits author against critic. Here, one debater plays the critic, providing criticism of the work of the author, and another debater represents the author defending her work. This format can lead to a lively and entertaining debate that is both instructive and interesting. Encourage students to represent authors they enjoy and challenge authors they do not, thus adding a personal element to the proceedings. This kind of debate explores the fertile territory of literary theory and criticism. It also teaches literature students the essential skill of criticism—to be able to judge and evaluate literary artifacts using a particular lens.

Conclusion

While debate is not often used to study literature, it is a powerful tool to consider. Interesting discussions can turn into dynamic and revealing exercises as students personally confront great literature in a public forum.

Mathematics

Despite the perception that mathematics is a field whose intricacies are best worked out on a blackboard, debate can be used to explore many aspects of the field. Issues ranging from the philosophy of mathematics to the ethical responsibility of mathematicians pose questions that have importance to all people. Debate contributes to the workings of mathematics classes and helps to analyze the subject's intricacies. While not a dominant teaching method for mathematics, debate can be an exciting supplement to your normal teaching methods.

Why Debate Is Valuable to Mathematics Classes

Debate can add to the mathematics classroom in three ways. First, it can encourage your students to become involved in the discipline's seemingly abstract elements. Second, debates can enable you to bring the historical contexts of mathematical theory to life in your classroom. Third, debates can explore the ethical responsibilities of mathematicians regarding their work.

Getting students involved in the study of mathematics can be very difficult. The astrophysicist Neil deGrasse Tyson lamented the inability of the general public to give astrophysicists their due in museums.

> The public hardly ever hears about the role of spectra in cosmic discovery because the concepts are just too far removed from the objects themselves to be explained efficiently. When creating exhibits of natural history museums or for any museum where real things matter, what designers typically seek are objects and artifacts suitable for display—rocks, bones, tools, fossils, memorabilia, and so forth. (34)

Similarly, the study of mathematics lacks obvious artifacts with which to spark a controversy for a debate. However, this lack is the very reason debate is so valuable to teachers, for it provides the contexts and the background to overcome these difficulties in teaching seemingly insignificant ideas. Imagine having a role-playing debate about the Copernican revolution. With students having carefully researched the roles of Ptolemy and Copernicus, the heated dialogue can help them understand the stakes involved in this debate. Debates about other mathematical discoveries can also help students understand that old paradigms of thought were successful because the theories worked in the context of the old world, not because people of that day were ignorant. Through debates students can envision how these mathematical changes affected the rest of the world. Debate can help raise the level of meaning in the study of a subject and can excite your students.

Largely because of the perception that mathematics involves the analysis and re-analysis of numbers, debate might not seem like a valuable format for mathematical pedagogy. Perhaps in the fields of geometry or algebra, students might take time to rework a historical theorem, but, in general, the study of mathematics is perceived to be deeply reliant on numbers. Nevertheless, many of the changes in mathematics occur through heated dialogue between mathematicians. The philosophic changes in mathematics can point your classroom to several heated debates. Consider debates about relativity, quark theory, dimensional mathematics, numbers theory, ideas about sound waves, set theory, string theory, and any number of radical theories such as Xeno's infamous assertion that halving the distance traveled means you never reach your goal. Debates on issues like these make the seemingly positivist mathematical studies seem almost postmodern. Debate can help make theories and ideas connect to implications, one of the core values of debate in the mathematics classroom.

Consider the areas of controversial study whose foundation is mathematics—biology, genetic engineering, code breaking, physics, computer science, and chemistry (to name a few). Rising mathematicians must be familiar with the ethical and power-related implications of their work. Debates can help to bring out the ramifications of mathematical exploration, pointing to the impact that mathematical advances can have on the world.

Sample Debate Topics for Mathematics Classes

- Does mathematics have metaphysical meaning?
- Does formalism represent all mathematical theory?
- Mathematics is an art form.
- Ptolemy was framed.
- Mathematics represents absolute truth.
- More advanced mathematics courses should be required in our schools.
- Calculators should not be allowed in the mathematics classroom.
- Mathematicians should be held responsible for the evil that is done because of their advances.

Sample Debate Formats for Mathematics Classes

Consider a debate on the topic "Should mathematicians be held responsible for evil that is done because of their advances?" Consider the role of advanced mathematicians at IBM, the American computer giant. Their successful creation of the computer was fundamental to the ability of the Nazi regime to round up and exterminate innocent people during the Holocaust. Or the example of the American scientists who created atomic bombs whose horrific implications still hang over our heads. This debate centers on the question of responsibility—and examples abound. The other side of this debate might be presented as whether mathematicians should be given credit for the positive work that they do. Should Einstein get credit for his discoveries? Another approach might be to argue that the use of mathematics should be carefully distinguished from the theoretical exploration of mathematical ideas. That no mathematician should be held responsible for the ideas that flow from his or her brain—that this freedom to create ideas unfettered is at the root of new mathematical discovery.

The kind of debate that works most effectively is a parliamentary debate with lots of audience involvement, perhaps with three people on each side and a long period of audience questions. It might also be possible to have a three-sided debate on this topic, with one side arguing that mathematicians should have no responsibility for what happens because of their discoveries, a second side arguing that mathematicians should be held responsible for evil that they perceive might happen, and a third side holding that mathematicians should be held responsible for any evil that emerges from their work.

Conclusion

As with every other discipline, mathematics teachers can use the flexible nature of debates as an important part of their curriculum. Using SPAR debates to encourage participation and to pique interest on the first days of class or some form of debate as final projects to involve students in research about famous mathematical theorems, teachers must fit debate to classroom needs. This section is only a brief introduction to the possibilities of debate in the mathematics classroom, but we urge you to consider and explore debate's many possibilities.

Media Studies

Media studies are an increasingly popular area in both secondary schools and universities. The social reality of the 21st century and the importance of media in it are the driving forces behind this increase in popularity. The media barrage from print, radio, television, Internet, cable, satellite connections, and wireless devices bathe us in a constant pulse of information. These messages have purposeful and directed agendas that require every citizen to be a more critical listener. As media outlets proliferate, individuals become overwhelmed and find it easier *not* to participate in online meetings or to become a broadcaster on a global stage. Every citizen needs to learn how to become an advocate. These challenges reinforce the importance of media studies in the curriculum, but they are also the forces that most call for debate instruction to sharpen critical listening and advocacy skills.

Why Debate Is Valuable to Media Studies Classes

Media studies and debating have important methods and goals in common, which suggest that integrating the two in the classroom could be quite productive. We describe the value of debate in the classroom below.

First, debate and media studies promote active criticism by individuals. Citizens need to be able to decode media messages to find flaws and weaknesses. In a debate students must decode the messages of the opposing team and do just that—locate weaknesses and areas of counterargument. Debaters must be able to listen not just to determine what the message is, but be able to state what's wrong about that message.

Robert McChesney, a professor in the Institute of Communications Research at the University of Illinois at Urbana-Champaign, in his book *Rich Media, Poor Democracy*, outlined the stakes to a society that allows media to remain an unquestioned variable.

At present, however, and for generations, the control and structure of the media industries has been decidedly off-limits as a subject in U.S. political debate. So long as that holds true, it is difficult to imagine any permanent qualitative change for the better in the U.S. media system. And without media reform, the prospects for making the United States a more egalitarian, self-governing, and humane society seem to dim to the point of nonexistence. (281)

Second, debate is an excellent forum for discussing media issues. Media studies issues offer very few policy or value absolutes—quite often, strong positions are defensible on several sides of an issue. Enduring issues such as freedom of expression, responsibility for mass communication, access to communications opportunities, institutional control of communications, and the standards of content evaluation are as old as communication itself yet are still vibrant today, with their significance magnified by the pervasive nature of media content delivery. These issues can be framed as topics for students to debate; the issues related to the specific subject matter can also be used to frame the topics. We urge teachers to draft their own topics, using the ones we provide as guidelines.

Third, debating is often an exercise in the evaluation of sources. The speakers in the debate act as sources, but they often use material and testimony from other sources. The debater quickly learns to analyze the source of critical evidence in any debate and evaluate its credibility based on the argument being made and the issues being discussed. Just as students learn to evaluate the credibility of power company executives in testimony about the environmental effects of their activities, so a student also learns to apply this process to media use, whether he or she is evaluating a product testimonial or questioning why a given "talking head" on television is considered credible. Debate helps students resolve conflicts of experts, which are often what they see in the media.

Sample Debate Topics for Media Studies Classes
- Modern television has sacrificed quality for entertainment.
- Television is more significant than the computer.

- Censorship of the news media can be justified.
- Art censorship should never be allowed.
- Censorship is unacceptable.
- Media domination by large corporations is undesirable.
- Lack of Internet access threatens to create a "digital divide" between rich and poor.
- Lack of Internet access threatens to create a "digital divide" between North and South.
- Privacy protection for media celebrities should be increased.
- Media violence contributes to violence in society.
- Television is dead.
- The media should provide equal time for opposing ideas.
- Public access television is a failed experiment.
- Reading is more productive than television viewing.
- Modern media are what brought down communism.
- Too much time on the Internet creates passivity.
- Television is guilty of creating a commodity culture.
- The merger of children's products and television programs is unfortunate.
- Media portrayal of minority groups has been harmful.
- Televised religious programming has caused a decline in personal religious event attendance.
- All electronic media should be nationalized and noncommercial.

Sample Debate Formats for Media Studies Classes

Debate can be used in a variety of ways in the media studies classroom. Because this is a new and vibrant field, many teachers are now developing an approach of their own to present this material, and we encourage you to consider integrating debates into your pedagogy. Here are some ways to accomplish this:

First, have the class create formal debates on enduring media issues. Free expression, aesthetics, content controls, and other issues can be brought to life in a team format for a 40- to 50-minute debate to illustrate these issues. Various topics that illustrate the course work can be staged throughout the term, with each student participating at least once.

Second, hold debates about the proposals of various media critics. It is easy to find fault with media institutions and affairs, but far more difficult to suggest specific proposals. Major media critics are often making proposals, such as abolishing television, nationalizing the electronic media, or ending media advertising. These proposals offer areas for a fruitful discussion about media issues present and future. Because there is usually a problem but the solution is less than perfect, the process is likely to reveal to students that policy goals are often difficult to achieve.

Third, debate about competing media. Each medium brings a different set of strengths and weaknesses, and a debate comparing them can be very useful, especially at an introductory level. For example, much is made of the benefits of reading as opposed to watching television, yet they have different strengths and weaknesses. These debates can be spontaneous and do not require considerable preparation, although some warning and ground rules might be useful. Contrast news sources from newspapers, radio, television, and the Internet. Contrast entertainment sources from reading, radio, television, videotape, and the Internet.

Fourth, stage programs to better understand how media news programming works. Choose a format found in the media that seems appropriate for analysis and have students reenact that program format using a different issue. Then, have the participants and the audience talk about the "rules" they learned by modeling that format. This exercise allows students to better understand how programming concepts directly influence content.

Conclusion

Media studies are a rewarding area to work with because of its relevance and vibrancy, and also because we are often familiar with how the media work. Debating is a way to add excitement to the field.

Through personal and critical engagement, debates help students better learn about the concepts in this field.

Multiculturalism

Although "multicultural" is an inexact category, it represents a useful grouping of a number of different courses that might be addressed in this section. These courses would include secondary school classes in comparative and world cultures, and related titles, as well as college-level courses in race and culture, cultural diversity, and introduction to multicultural studies. Many universities now require all students to take courses or seminars about the basic issues of multiculturalism. In many instances, these courses are an attempt to diversify curricula and move away from older and less global concepts. In this case, debate as a classroom tool can be extremely useful and exciting.

Why Debate Is Valuable to Multiculturalism Classes

Debate is useful both as a learning method and as a channel for discussion of multicultural issues. The multicultural classroom encompasses specific aspects that make debating easy, relevant, and enjoyable.

First, multicultural issues such as self-determination, civil rights, ethnic conflicts, immigration, refugee movements, discrimination, and economic justice form the core of issues that are today's major topics of discussion. In a vast number of debates, multicultural training will be essential to a strong performance.

Second, debating allows students to take different perspectives. Many of the issues that come up in the study of multiculturalism are related to how individuals construct the "other," a position we are rarely called on to assume. Through debate activities students can develop an ability to operate "inside" the perspectives of other peoples and other groups. Many of the ethnic conflicts students read about or hear about do not make sense until they are understood from the perspectives of those involved. While a simple debate cannot fully train anyone in how things are seen by others, it is a useful beginning to that process that students seem to enjoy and appreciate.

Third, debating trains students to be advocates. Multicultural issues are extremely important, and too often it seems responsible advocates are in short supply. We have found debate to be extremely empowering for people who have previously felt they lacked a "voice" to express their hopes, feelings, and ideas. Met on an empathic common ground of argument, people find it is possible to build bridges to one another through communication. Debaters are better able to become advocates, opinion leaders, and consciousness raisers. Perhaps more important, many students who are in positions of privilege find themselves engaging the ideas of multiculturalism on a much deeper level when they are debating; formerly, they may have seen such ideas and their discussion as irrelevant.

Fourth, debate allows students to make a balanced judgment about multicultural issues. In many instances, discussions of multicultural issues are too one way, either in presenting material to those who already agree with it or mocking the prospect of productive multiculturalism to those already opposed to it. Debate forces at least two sides of the issues to be dealt with in an open, public, and logical forum. Students must find the best issues to raise for each side of the topics developed and then compare them. Debate brings a more balanced discussion of issues than is found in many forums for multicultural issues.

Sample Debate Topics for Multiculturalism Classes

- Students who do not speak the dominant language should be offered bilingual education.
- Immigration regulations in our country need to be tightened.
- Our nation should have one official national language.
- The concept of race is an outdated social construction.
- The United States should offer reparations to Native Americans.
- Western nations should offer reparations to Africans for slavery.
- Class is more important than race.
- Some moral values transcend culture.
- In 1850 United States: Slavery should be abolished.

- Palestinians vs. Israelis: Jerusalem should be the capital of a new Palestinian nation.
- The emerging "clash of civilizations" will be a dark moment for human beings.
- We should oppose the practice of female genital mutilation in Africa.
- We should increase protections against racial discrimination in the workplace.
- We should avoid the use of racial categories whenever possible.
- Recent ethnic violence in Africa is a legacy of colonialism.
- University curricula need to be changed significantly to reflect a multicultural global reality.

Also: See many of the topics listed in the "Religion" section below.

Sample Debate Formats for Multiculturalism Classes

A number of debate formats can be used to fit multicultural classroom goals and subject matter.

First, ask students to debate why the study of multiculturalism is necessary. In many high schools, colleges, and universities, it is a required class and issues may need to be confronted early in the term. We suggest a public assembly format or dividing the class into two different groups and then staging a lively discussion about whether the class should be mandatory.

Second, engage students in a debate between two ethnic groups in conflict. Assign teams to represent sides that they normally would not speak for (such as ethnic groups they do not belong to) and then hold a debate about one of the central issues in their conflict. The group that seems to have the upper hand in the conflict could be given the negative side, so that the less dominant group can frame the debate through the presentation of their affirmative case. Students will need an opportunity to research the background for this conflict and learn about those they will represent. Remember that they are not "play acting" as members of that ethnic group but should work to represent the group's interests.

Third, ask students to debate the "clash of civilizations." Following along the theme of Samuel Huntington's essays and books surrounding "The Clash of Civilizations," the debate would be about whether we should take an optimistic or pessimistic view of the global interactions of major cultures. The affirmative could argue that such exchanges would go very poorly, with increased ethnic tensions, oppression, and intolerance. The negative could argue the opposite— that we will overcome difficulties and learn to create a more tolerant and peaceful world. Other important authors who might point toward exciting debate topics are postcolonialist theorists like Edward Said and Guyatri Spivak. Both argue that our current conceptions of culture are framed to permit violence against and to justify oppression of other nations. There is, of course, no one certain right answer in this debate, but it is an excellent vehicle for exploring multicultural issues and our perspectives on the subject.

Fourth, stage a debate about a current multicultural issue. Students would not play roles but would be themselves. Such debates could be one-on-one or team events of any length. Students should be assigned their topic and side well in advance so they can prepare. You could have different topics or one fairly broad topic that would be debated repeatedly, with each debate exploring a somewhat different issue.

Fifth, stage a debate set in a specific place and time. Provide students with historical background materials and biographies of the major figures to take part in the debate and then have them act out the disagreement in their own way. A debate set in 1850 United States about the abolition of slavery, a debate set in the early 20th century United Kingdom about voting rights for women, a debate set in post–World War II Saudi Arabia about driving or voting rights for women, or a debate set in 1950s Africa about independence for European colonies would be interesting and revealing. Students can use such debates as a way to understand how multicultural issues were considered in history.

Conclusion

We believe that the problems and misunderstandings of society need to be subjected to a respectful, logical, and open discussion through debating. The method and the subject matter seem well matched to provide deeper understanding of the issues.

Philosophy

The historical connections between debate and philosophy are long-standing. Ancient Greek and Roman philosophers are the historical antecedents for the methods of debate. Confucius and other Chinese philosophers wrote famous treatises that point to debate as a valuable method of learning. The very clash of ideas has its roots in philosophy. Thinkers ask the tough questions: Who are we?, Why are we here?, and What is the nature of our existence?—all vital areas for debate. The connection between this method and this discipline is natural.

Why Debate Is Valuable to Philosophy Classes

One essential reason for including debate in the philosophy class is pedagogical. Philosophy is difficult to teach! Like many of the most important areas of study, it is hard to get students excited about philosophy. Marshall Gregory, a professor of education and pedagogy at Marshall University, reminds us of the difficulty in conveying excitement about difficult texts.

> It is important for teachers to remember that great texts, fine art, and liberating topics are not automatically or transparently great, fine, and liberating to most students. (In all honesty, this goes for most teachers as well.) Just like our students now, merely coming into the presence of great art or great books or lofty topics did not fire most of our own interests when we were students. More likely than not, our interests were fired by the example of a teacher who seemed filled, somehow, with a special kind of life because of his or her love of a particular subject or discipline. As I look back, I realize that one commonality shared by all my favorite teachers is the way they seemed filled and animated by presences; by Jane Austen's power of language, by [Immanuel] Kant's depth of thought, by [Mary] Wollstonecraft's powerful arguments about the educa-

tion of women, by the spirit of [Johann Sebastian] Bach's music, by whatever. In addition, I found that the larger life these presences gave my teachers was in itself compelling to me. I was drawn to this larger life the way iron filings are drawn to a magnet. Once there, I found myself delightfully attracted, pleasurably bonded. (70)

As Marshall points out, teachers have difficulty getting students excited about topics that seem extraneous to their lives. Yet through debate, we can excite them to see the value in studying seemingly insignificant topics. The pursuit of knowledge can be thrilling, the spark that Marshall points to can flow through your classroom because students will be engaged with the subject matter. Rather than a lecture that seems irrelevant, student participation in the actualizing of knowledge will create new expectations, as students will be driven to listen and to be engaged with the subject matter.

Another important reason debate is valuable to the philosophy class is that its activities mesh well with the topics of the class. The study of being, of time, of how we know, and how we understand, the explorations of consciousness, metaphysics, and the nature of ethics and nature are all topics that lend themselves to a dialogue between informed advocates. Debate between philosophers creates major changes in the perceptions of the world. Debates about philosophy can teach students about the subjects of the class, show your students knowledge, and introduce these topics.

Sample Debate Topics for Philosophy Classes
- Knowledge must come before action.
- Nature is more important than nurture.
- Nietzsche was the last metaphysician.
- Postmodernism is bankrupt.
- The state of being is in flux.
- God is dead.
- Religion is real philosophy.
- "I think, therefore I am" (Descartes).
- We should abandon logical positivism.

- We should embrace the philosophy of X.
- Power is fluid.
- Morality is in the eye of the beholder.
- "Ethics are first philosophy" (Levinas).

Sample Debate Formats for Philosophy Classes

Because philosophy instruction comes in so many varieties, it is difficult to point to a single debate format that benefits students. Instead, we believe that the format and teaching method must be flexible and fit into your curriculum. The example given in this section is specific to a particular class and topic.

Imagine that you are teaching a Western philosophy class, tracing the roots of traditional philosophy from the Egyptians to John Dewey. During a section about the German philosopher Friedrich Nietzsche, your students are having difficulty understanding his core arguments because they cannot imagine a situation where common sense morality might be questionable. Therefore, you decide to have a public forum debate about this question and assign one half of the class to think of justifiable moral stances and the other side to consider examples of moral stances whose utility is crippled by inflexibility.

The students begin the debate with simple issues of stealing and being hungry, quickly moving to examples of abortion and euthanasia. While the examples being raised are excellent, and the class is getting excited about the topic, the skills of the debater show through when your students begin not only to provide their own examples to support their side, but also to attack their opponent's examples. One student might take issue with the supposedly "rock solid" moral stance "thou shalt not kill," arguing that in certain situations killing might be justified (euthanasia, during war, to save the greater good, etc.).

Through this format, students can begin to see the flexible nature of morality, one of the roots of Nietzsche's criticism. Some pieces of morality might be seen as examples of judgment applied unequally (e.g., moral opposition to nudity in pornography and in high art). Students might explore Nietzsche's ideas that morality is self-serving, used to justify particular preferences that are presented as absolutes.

You might need to make these connections in a postdebate dialogue, but using debates, students will begin to envision how arguments and ideas work and are created. Through this process new knowledge emerges.

Conclusion

Whether it is a heated spontaneous debate about the meaning of postmodernism or a well-researched role-playing debate about the Copernican revolution, debates provide a method of teaching philosophy that encourages students to become involved in the subject matter and better convey information about the discipline.

Religion

At first religion and debate may seem to be an odd pairing. Usually debating with people about their religious beliefs is nonproductive, even though evangelism of various sorts has been going on as long as human civilization. Religious opinions are firmly rooted in the cognitive processes of individuals, framing the way in which they see their lives. Religion deals with spiritual matters, often seen as incompatible with logic. Issues of "faith" can transcend issues of "logic" for religious persons. However, religion and spirituality are of extreme importance to many, many people. We do not intend to provide guidelines for how debate can be used to change the religious beliefs of individuals; rather, how debate can be used to help individuals learn about religion and religious issues.

Why Debate Is Valuable to Religion Classes

Debate can play a meaningful and productive role in religion classes, because religion is often a topic of argument and debate. Debate can also help individuals understand various religious beliefs, especially those they do not hold, for the following reasons:

First, religion is a common topic of informal debate and a common topic of discussion among students as they leave a home environment. At school they come into contact with students from different religious backgrounds. Many a late night dormitory discussion has centered on religious issues and disagreements about them. Students are curious about how other people can have different religious beliefs when their own seem so obviously correct. Debate in the religion classroom can use this already established reality to improve instruction about religion.

Second, various religions have many traditions of debate. The Jewish faith promotes scholarly study of sacred texts and debate about their interpretation as a rich part of its intellectual tradition. Tibetan Buddhism also stresses the practice of debate as essential for devotees.

Consider the introduction to the book *Torah Studies* (1992) by Rabbi Menachem M. Schneerson, the Lubavitcher rabbi. Famous for his extensive and intense talks, Schneerson produced a text filled with complicated debates about interpretation and meaning of the Torah. The translator, Jonathan Sacks, identifies the relation to debate in his introduction:

> To hear or read a talk of the Lubavitcher rebbe is to undertake a journey. We are challenged and forced to move: where we stand at the end is not where we were at the beginning. Time and again a sicha will be set in motion by a seemingly microscopic tension—a question on a comment by Rashi, perhaps, or a problem in understanding a halakhah, a practical provision of Jewish law. Once in motion, however, the argument leads us into fresh perspectives, provisional answers and new questions, until we climb rung by rung to the most elevated of vantage points. From here, as we survey the ground beneath us in its widest of contexts, the initial question is not only resolved but also revealed as the starting point of a major spiritual search. (iv)

Tibetan Buddhism has a practice of offering arguments and debating about them as both an educational and meditative practice. In America many college debating societies in the 18th and 19th centuries grew out of the need to more fully prepare students for careers in the Christian ministries. In ancient China and India some mysteries of the Buddha are regularly used as topics for debate. In modern America many strongly Christian universities emphasize debating because they believe such skills are an important part of their ultimate evangelical mission. These rich traditions can be explored within the religion classroom.

Third, debate gives insight into religion by comparing different modes of decision making. Kenneth Burke's concept of gaining perspective on something through the examination of incongruities is relevant here. We understand more about the concept of life by better understanding death, for example. In the case of religion, a logical discussion of issues regularly assigned to the realm of nonlogical faith can be highly illuminating. Students can learn about faith by applying logic to it, just as they can learn about logic by understanding the role of faith in human thinking.

Fourth, students can learn about religion through debate by assuming a certain set of religious beliefs. As with many debate experiences, we learn about our own convictions by examining contrasting and disagreeing convictions. When we "walk a mile" in the shoes of another, we better understand the other's situation and perspective. By asking a Christian and a Buddhist to reverse roles and engage in a debate of Christianity vs. Buddhism, we create real learning opportunities. William E. Paden, a professor of religion at the University of Vermont, argued that the recognition of a relative view of another person's idea of faith is a fundamental move of acknowledgment of that person's humanity (132–33). Debate can help bring out respectful criticism and exploration, as well as a new understanding to the study of religion.

Sample Debate Topics for Religion Classes

- Ecumenical movements that attempt to bring religions together are ill-advised.
- God does not exist and never has.
- The institution of religion has, throughout history, done more harm than good.
- The similarity in many religions suggests a common religious reality.

- X person is guilty of violating the tenets of Y religion (Galileo vs. Catholicism, Salman Rushdi vs. Iranian Islam, Darwin vs. fundamentalist Christianity, etc.).
- Human beings create religions to meet their own needs.
- The right to religious practice is more important than other rights (e.g., Santeria animal sacrifice vs. animal rights, Rastafarian ganja smoking vs. antidrug laws, wine at Christian communion vs. anti-alcohol laws, polygamy vs. bigamy laws, Native American Church use of peyote vs. antidrug laws, Native American beliefs in not disturbing burial grounds vs. archeological scientific explorations).
- Science is more important now than religion.
- Science and technology have become our new religion.
- Religion is the opiate of the people.
- Emile Durkheim was right.
- Rudolph Otto was right.
- Religion should be individual, not institutional.
- God can prevent evil, but doesn't.
- The right to die is the ultimate personal freedom.
- Activism in politics by religious groups harms the political process.
- Divorce is compatible with Christianity.
- Morality is separable from religion.
- The inebriate is not accountable to God for the crimes he commits while intoxicated.
- There is no confusion between the findings of geology and the Holy Bible.
- We would all be better off if we were atheists.

Sample Debate Formats for Religion Classes

Debate can be used in many ways in the religion classroom. The topics listed above refer to themes that can be adapted to a specific subject being studied. Formats can be modified so that debating fits well within the time constraints of the class, the subject matter, and the students' interests.

As with all debates, take special care to assure that students are not offended by the debates or asked to do anything objectionable to them. All religious beliefs must be treated with respect, even when they are being rigorously criticized. The teacher may encourage students to meet with her if they feel uncomfortable about the subject they are debating. In fact, some students may hold religious beliefs that do not allow them to take part in some of the proposed debate formats.

First, encourage students to debate about the advisability of studying religion, a useful exercise for an introductory class. Stage the debate using a public assembly format or between the class divided into two different sides. This format can help students understand the role and importance that religion plays in human existence. It can also help them understand the issues of individual and social responsibility, which are often a part of many different religions.

Second, engage students in debates about the meta-issues that surround religion, such as the existence of God, the need to bring religions together into a common spiritual belief, and the institutional vs. personal orientation of religions. These topics can be used to explore broad issues that transcend many major religions and can be staged as ongoing debates, or through a number of different debates on related topics. This process will involve students as well as offer them a broader perspective on religion than they would usually get in a classroom.

Third, recreate important historical religious trials by providing students with the facts of a given case, a biography of the accused, and background on the religious tradition raising the charge. This event might be staged over several class periods so that the subject is covered in proper detail. Students also need time for preparation and research. Ask class members to serve as jury, judge, defense, prosecution, and witnesses. Witnesses and other actors would be asked to play the role assigned to them. Students will learn about the historical era and religion's role by getting inside that particular faith and understanding the arguments and ideas used to support the charges and those used in defense.

Fourth, stage debates between different religions, particularly relevant to comparative religion classes. Ask the debaters to make arguments to support their assigned religious belief and indict the opposing religious belief. Related religious belief can be contrasted this way as well, such as Catholic vs. Orthodox, Sunni vs. Shi'a, Indian vs. Japanese Buddhism, and others. Students can use these debates as a way to demonstrate their mastery of the material or as a term project. Be sure to emphasize that these debates are not designed to arrive at a verdict of which religion is better; rather, they are vehicles to explore these religions. You may choose not to have judges or the audience vote for a winner, but simply assign quality ratings to the debaters based on their performance.

Conclusion

Although religion can be a matter of strong personal conviction, debate can offer a method for understanding the subject and issues that create controversy. The religion classroom is a good setting for the open exploration of issues relating to specific religions or religious experience in general. When it is used with sensitivity and an open mind, debating in the religion classroom can illuminate similarities and differences of religious faith.

Science

Science would not develop or mature without debate. New information jostles old theories, new theories are conceived and critiqued, accepted or disproved, and then the process begins again. Each experiment is a logical attempt to demonstrate or disprove a given hypothesis. That proof may not always be obtained, but the learning process continues throughout.

At first glance, you might think that debate and science have so little in common that this section would be fairly brief. We believe the opposite to be the case. Science as method and study merges well with debate and open critical discourse, inviting us to make a decision.

Why Debate Is Valuable to Science Classes

Debate is compatible with the study of science for many reasons. The brief list below describes the successful use of debating in the science classroom.

First, both science and debate are conducted in public. The scientific process calls for public exchange of information and open scholarly communication. When new scientific ideas challenge old ones, the process rarely takes place in private or confidential circles, but in journals, symposia, and even scholarly staged debates. Although the public may not have a high level of specific scientific knowledge, they are nevertheless extremely interested in the issues and applications of science, thus empowering the media to bring scientific issues to their attention. This publicity empowers the public to ask questions of the scientific community.

Second, science and debate are investigative. The process of debate invites people to investigate a field to discover the issues and develop proofs not unlike science. The process of investigation, discovery, and proof is similar. Students who wish to become either scientists or debaters need to learn the skills of information acquisition, issue discovery, and decision making based on the data and the issues.

Third, science and debate are critical exercises. Just as the debater asks critical questions of opposing advocates to develop arguments against them, the scientist is constantly asking critical questions in an attempt to make new discoveries. Theories, explanations, and findings are acceptable only if they survive strict critical scrutiny. Social and personal associations have, again and again, been irrelevant to a critical search for what might be accepted as scientific truth. Debaters are eager to be critical because that is how they gain distinction, just as scientists are eager to be critical because that allows them to gain both new insights and distinction. Debate is also an important tool for questioning scientists about their own power and position in society. Debate can help to foster the self-awareness that provides increased ethical dialogue about the power and nature of science.

Fourth, science and debate are exercises of repetition. Experiments are replicated to verify results as well as to clarify issues. Some experiments support existing findings, some do not. Experiments are replicated because the results might be different; in debate this repetition and replication are equally important for the way students learn and develop. A debate is a sort of argument laboratory in which ideas and logic are tested and tested again. Often the results are different, but learning still takes place, just as a study that fails to replicate a result always tells us something important about either the study or the hypothesis.

Debate and science have so much in common that a cross-fertilization of them in the classroom is always productive.

Sample Debate Topics for Science Classes

- Scientists have moral responsibility for their discoveries.
- The theory "X" should be rejected.
- This proposed experiment should be approved.
- There has been too much reliance on the scientific method.
- Our character will be insufficient for managing our scientific discoveries.
- This field of scientific study should not be required in secondary schools.
- The viewpoints of "X critic of the field" should be taken seriously.
- Science has triumphed over religion.
- A free market best promotes scientific advances.
- Scientific advances create as many losers as winners.
- The scientific discovery of X was regrettable.
- Animal experimentation is scientifically unreliable.
- Animal experimentation is ethically bankrupt.
- Human cloning is ethically unacceptable.
- Genetically engineered crops should be unregulated.
- We should label genetically engineered food.
- Country X has the greatest scientific legacy.
- Science should not be held responsible for Nazi scientific discoveries.

- The process of institutional review should be abandoned.
- Gaining consent from test subjects is unnecessary.

Sample Debate Formats for Science Classes

The use of debates within the science classroom will, of course, depend on the specific area and level of study as well as the class's goals. Teachers should use debates to assist students in reaching those goals. Within these constraints, debate can be used in a science classroom in a number of ways.

First, ask students to debate about whether any field of science is worthy of their study. Many students are first introduced to scientific study in a "required" class. Too often students view science study as an unnecessarily challenging exercise in mastering discrete data that they do not consider directly relevant to them. In this example, introductory students would be encouraged to debate with the instructor or each other to come up with reasons why this class should not be required as well as justifications for its requirement. You could use a public assembly format or divide the class into two teams for this exercise. This simple introductory technique involves students actively in saying what many of them are thinking, and frames the reasons to study this particular subject. This exercise sets the stage for the students' active involvement in science, not the passive memorization that many areas of scientific instruction require.

Second, ask to debate specific scientific theories. Have the affirmative present and defend a theory against a negative team, or an affirmative team might present a case against a popular theory. Whether it is the theory of evolution or the theory of continental drift, the theory behind the extinction of the dinosaurs or any other scientific theory that can be challenged, a theory can be usefully examined within a debate format.

Third, hold debates to frame the "big issues" found in any field of scientific discovery. These big issues can be thought of as enduring or current areas of controversy in a field. Usually the affirmative provides the minority viewpoint on any of these big issues and sets the stage for the debate by making a case against the majority viewpoint.

Fourth, hold debates to evaluate specific experimental designs. Quite often students are asked to design their own experiments. They can present their proposal for an experiment in some detail and then have other students or the instructor to criticize their proposal. The experiment's designers would have to respond to such criticism, either with a defense or an adjustment of their methods. This kind of debate requires prior disclosure by proponents of the experiment so that the criticism offered is substantive and useful. Prior disclosure need not be a lengthy process. All can participate either as proponents or critics, or both. The result will be a much better sense of how to construct experiments and prepare for future criticisms.

Fifth, use debates to follow newsworthy scientific issues. Most newsworthy areas of scientific concern are controversial and have different perspectives and viewpoints. The areas selected for debate are assigned to students as debate topics, which can include human bioengineering, climate manipulation, the fight against illness and disease, recent scientific discoveries about the past, or DNA markers as criminal evidence. This practice not only familiarizes students with these controversial areas but also indicates to them the relevance and immediacy of science as part of our world.

Sixth, ask students to debate about the minority voices found in science. Each field has qualified and published scientists who tend to see things a bit differently from the majority in the field. Their views can be very useful to explore, not because they are correct, but because we need to understand the arguments against what we believe to fully understand what and why we hold the beliefs we do. Students can read one of these minority theorists, and then develop a debate based on that perspective. This practice demonstrates to students that, even in the sciences, knowledge is a dynamic and changing, not something set in stone.

Seventh, engage students in debates about issues of science set in a specific historical period or involving historical figures. For example, hold a debate about Darwin's theory of evolution as staged in the late 19th century. The affirmative team forwards Darwin's approach, while the negative team uses the arguments offered by Darwin's contemporary critics. Likewise, hold a debate between Copernicus and Ptolemy about the basic design of the solar system. Such a solar system debate might also be staged in the time of Galileo and involve Galileo on one side and the Roman Catholic church on the other. Enact these debates not as if they were taking place now, but as if they were taking place in a given historical period. You'll need to provide appropriate background materials as well as biographies of any persons represented in these debates. Such debates help people understand the historical context of science and give them a better understanding of how scientific disputes are carried on today.

Eighth, scrutinize the scientific method itself. The scientific method has contributed much to our current world, but it is not unassailable. As the basis for social and personal action, it has been strongly criticized by postmodern theorists as well as by feminist and majority world critics. In this debate the affirmative, in the role of these theorists, could present a critique of the scientific method that states it is overemphasized. This exercise helps bring to the surface the most basic assumptions of the scientific method and allows students to explore them. As we noted, debate is a method for students to explore and develop new issues and ideas; this exercise will certainly provide that opportunity.

Ninth, ask students to debate the ethical status of science in our society. The very power that scientific announcements have in forming the public consciousness suggests that we should take a careful look at the making of science. By examining the language, ideas, and meaning of science in society, students can become more ethical and self-reflexive scientists, aware of the meaning of their pronouncements and arguments. More important, ethical issues of research, and experimentation ranging from that done on animals to issues of human consent, can be debated. These debates provide the reasons why an ethical eye always needs to be cast upon scientific exploration.

Conclusion

Too often the science classroom is seen as boring, passive, and irrelevant. Through the use of one or more of these debate techniques, science instruction better achieves the goal of imparting information and dispelling these stereotypes by showing students that scientific activity is vibrant, alive, accessible, and personally relevant. Just as students often love the experiments and lab work associated with science study, so they will come to love debates as a part of science study as well.

Social Services

The social services encompass a huge and growing field, the focus of which is to improve the quality of life for specific individuals, often individuals in need of assistance. This field's critical processes for success include communication, problem solving, and the resolution of disagreements. Debating these areas provides students with useful experience.

Why Debate Is Valuable to Social Services Classes

Social services students can build many skills through their involvement in debate. While debate's general critical-thinking skills are useful to all students, including those in the social services, debating and the social services merge productively in several areas.

First, communication skills are an important part of effective work in social services. Social services providers need to engage in critical and problem-solving communication sessions with a variety of clients who have varying communication styles. These events often involve information gathering, analysis of situations and information, problem solving, and planning for future action. Social services providers also engage in active communication with their peers about the appropriate course of action for clients and programs. Social services providers are also required to give formal presentations for administrative or public relations reasons. Debating can sharpen the skills necessary in all these communication settings.

Second, social services work can involve the resolution of disagreements. Social services providers may disagree with clients about policies, practices, or behaviors. Disagreement may also take place among social services providers acting as a team. These providers also need to interact with administrators, funding organizations, or government officials to justify and analyze policies and behaviors. In all of these instances, the judgment, evaluation, and presentation skills promoted by debating can be extremely useful.

Third, social services providers need to understand the differing perspectives of those involved. Clients have distinct and often unique perspectives on the social services transaction. Members of the public, social services organization administrators, and related government bodies also have unique perspectives that the social services provider needs to understand. Debating allows social services providers to assume these roles in critical communication events and begin to comprehend more of what it is like to be a client, an administrator, a government official, or a concerned member of the public. Debating allows the student to assume these roles in critical communication incidents to better empathize with those with whom they will be working.

Fourth, social services providers engage in many examples of case building. Individual cases need to be researched, documented, and understood. The information and history of these cases must be organized logically to permit analysis. Quite often such cases provide examples of problems that need to be addressed. Likewise, social services providers are often called on to "make a case" for the course of action and procedures followed. Social services providers may also be asked to make a case for their programs as they exist or as planned for change and reform. In all of these instances, the skills students learn from debating and building their own logical "cases" will assist them later as social services providers.

Sample Debate Topics for Social Services Classes

- Basic medical care is a privilege, not a right.
- Would-be parents should be licensed before having children.
- We should listen to the leading critics of our field.
- "Helping" relationships often end up being relationships of social control.

- All social service interventions in our field must be preceded by the permission of the client.
- Social services should be broadly deinstitutionalized.
- The use of behavior modifying drugs should be severely limited.
- Radical reforms should be implemented in our field.
- All social services interventions should be guided by a team approach.
- Social services bureaucracy should be streamlined to improve client services.
- Reforms should be adopted to improve the job satisfaction of social services providers.
- Certification standards for social services providers should be strengthened.
- The professionalization of social services has gone too far.
- Clients have a right to eccentric individuality unless it threatens their physical safety.
- Mental health professionals do more harm than good.
- The current service regimen for client X should be changed.
- The social services provider in case X has acted negligently.

Sample Debate Formats for Social Services Classes

A wide variety of formats can be used for debates in social services classes. You may wish to consider a number of thematic approaches within these topics and formats.

First, introduce role-playing into the debate formats. Place students into any number of debate situations but in roles they would normally not occupy. Students can represent clients, a specific client, administrators, public service agencies, or citizens investigating the provision of social services. Making arguments and critically analyzing positions from the perspective of another person assists students in understanding and empathizing with those they will be working with. Such roles might include a client who opposes receiving certain kinds of services or treatments, a social services provider peer who disagrees with the decisions of other social services providers, an administrator who seeks to improve or economize on service delivery, or citizens demanding more and better services for less money. Provide students with descriptions of the roles they will be playing, including a short biography of the person they are impersonating.

Second, model debates after real adversarial situations likely to arise in a social services context. Design debates to allow students to explore these situations long before they ever arise in real casework. Several different adversarial situations might arise in providing social services, such as conflicts about what is to be done between the state and the client or the client and the social services provider, among social services providers who favor different approaches, between social services providers and administrators or peer review organizations that challenge decisions, between competing advocates of different models of social services provision, or between social services providers and bureaucratic systems. All of these situations can be modeled in a debate so students can prepare for adversarial situations that will arise. The debates can be one-on-one and rather short for client vs. provider debates, a bit longer for debates between services providers, and fairly substantial when defending provider decisions and evaluating programs.

Third, focus debates on the nature and pitfalls of "helping" relationships. At the foundation of social services is the concept that professionals in the field can give substantial "help" to those who are in "need." This role can often create a sense of hierarchy and superiority, where the provider knows far more than the person who needs services and enacts a top-down model of communication and makes decisions that can be detrimental. In some situations the needs of the provider can overshadow the needs of the client, creating working services bureaucracies but not providing the best assistance to clients. "Helping" can also be seen as a form of "control" in some situations. Questions of individual autonomy vs. individual well-being and social productivity are often at issue here. Debates can help students explore when "help" becomes "control" and when the services provide help to the service program itself and to society, but not necessarily to the individual client. Consider a debate about the implications of labeling various individuals who need help. Students might argue that this kind of labeling can cause negative outcomes. The role of social services providers as "professionals" can also complicate this situation. Debates about the nature of helping, as well as client control, autonomy, and responsibility to the community, can help clarify these issues and better prepare students for a more productive professional life.

Fourth, focus debates on the ideas and proposals of leading critics of a particular social services area. Understanding the arguments of critics of a given field can help students better understand that field and the issues at stake there. For example, some critics (Thomas Szaz) question the role of modern mental health services, arguing that they create dependency and violate personal autonomy. Other critics (Michel Foucault) identify increasing levels of "social service" with increasing levels of "social control." Still other critics (Ivan Illich) believe that providing social services through professional and state-run networks has undermined individual, family, and community support for those in need of services and has been, on balance, detrimental. If these perspectives are appropriate for a given class, they can be assigned as debates. These debates then highlight many important aspects of social services that the student may not have yet explored. Debates thus provide students with a deeper insight and understanding of their efforts to become professionals in this field.

Many other approaches can be used in the social services classroom. Your own issues and concerns can easily be translated into a debate topic and a debate format.

Conclusion

Social services require cooperation and compromise within a framework of decision making and disagreement. Often the way in which social services succeed or fail is based on how these factors mesh as well as the use of skilled communication. Debating the many important issues surrounding social services can assist students in both their preparation and their performance in the field.

Sociology

The field of sociology studies the intricate relationships of humans and how they frame and create societies. These issues are extremely well suited for exploration in a debate setting, in part because the students are familiar with the workings of society. As human beings, they have opinions about our social structures that they can express through debate.

Why Debate Is Valuable to Sociology Classes

Humankind is diverse. People hold a wide variety of values, attitudes, and beliefs. The debate process, which has participants comparing and contrasting various ideas and perspectives, helps students appreciate and better understand diversity. Understanding how societies are structured often entails deep investigation into morally ambiguous concepts such as "good" and "nature"—these are topics well suited to a debate environment.

Most debate topics have a sociological component. Whether we are debating street crime, corporate behavior, family life and practices, or the problems of peace and war, we are dealing with issues that have a profound sociological relevance. Debating sociological issues can be a valuable and productive way to understand crucial concepts.

Sample Debate Topics for Sociology Classes

- Crime is best explained by social/individual causes.
- Ageism is as evil as sexism.
- Poverty is the cause of most juvenile crime.
- True social change is better achieved through social movements than through government mandates.
- Music is an accurate documentation of social change.
- Deviant behavior is most often in the eye of the beholder.
- Strict social norms are the enemies of individual freedom.
- Mental health services should be mostly delivered outside of residential institutions.
- A guaranteed annual income would be a good way to reduce poverty.

- Society gets the corporations it deserves.
- Society gets the politicians it deserves.
- Sociological phenomenon X is best understood through theory Y.
- Sociological phenomenon X is best investigated through methodology Y.
- Tradition dictates the role of the elderly in our society.
- Childhood is a relatively recent invention.
- Citizens today are less able to deal with the concept of death.

Sample Debate Formats for Sociology Classes

You can use a large number of formats and arrangements for debating in a sociology class. Here are just a few possibilities:

First, hold a public forum on whether sociology should be a required subject in schools, or you could have students debate the desirability of increasing the number of required sociology courses. Debating these topics could help beginning students understand the importance of sociology as well as review the possible areas they might study.

Second, stage a public debate about research methodologies. The topic could be that one research methodology (such as quantitative research) is more valuable than another method (such as qualitative research). Such a topic would enable students to consider the strengths and weaknesses of each method. Too often students emerge from a course of advanced sociological study with an understanding of and preference for one methodology. A debate contrasting methodologies would encourage students to investigate other perspectives.

Third, stage a debate about the causes of various sociological phenomena such as crime or deviant behavior. This will encourage students to look and evaluate a wide variety of factors. If you develop a variety of narrow topics, you could stage a series of debates that involve all students.

Fourth, integrate a number of extemporaneous debates into the course based on topics covered in the syllabus or taught during a particular class. You can stage one during each class with a few minutes warning. Inform the participants of their topic and excuse them from the room for five minutes before asking them to return for a very short SPAR debate. This type of debate enables you to involve many students in a minimum amount of time.

Fifth, involve advanced students in debates about their research or study plans by asking them to defend their plans against one or two critics. Have the student give a written copy of his or her research plan to the critics for their review and preparation. The debate would consist of the student offering a short presentation of the research plan, criticisms by one critic followed by a defense, criticisms by a second critic followed by a defense, then questions from the audience. This could be a very useful way to train advanced students in designing and evaluating research proposals and preparing for doctoral defenses.

Sixth, because many sociological phenomena are the target of government action, you could stage a debate about the advisability of specific government policies. These debates could either feature an evaluation of specific policies (mandatory sex education classes in elementary schools) or could be more open ended in their structure (government should act to reduce the spread of sexually transmitted diseases). These debates could be large (such as a public forum or a public debate) or could be smaller and be staged at various times during the term. Because these would be prepared debates, you should assign topics and sides, and develop a schedule of debates. You can use different topics for each debate, or, if the topic is fairly broad and open ended, you can use it in a series of debates.

Seventh, you might craft the entire course to reflect the goals of the role play. Bruce Luske, a professor of sociology at Marist College, runs a course on social inequality in which students are given different levels of work. On the first day of the course, students are assigned to a socioeconomic class—a few get to be upper-class wealthy citizens, many become poor and destitute, with a few middle-class citizens. Throughout the course, the amount of work the students have to do is tied to the socioeconomic class they were assigned. Students are called on to debate at each session.

Conclusion

Sociologists attempt to understand issues such as social inequality, patterns of behavior, forces for social change and resistance, and how social systems work. Debate is useful in helping students understand these topics.

Sports and Recreation

Debating has much in common with sport. It is a game in which individuals cooperate in order to compete against other individuals. Debate has "sides," as well as teams, matches, judges, rules, tournaments, leagues, and all the rest. Because debate has so much of sport, it is an ideal method for use in classes that address sports and recreation issues and training. Important issues, practices, and skills can be developed through the use of debating in the classroom.

Why Debate Is Valuable to Sports and Recreation Classes

Because debate is a process of learning and evaluating, it is a broadly applicable tool for pedagogy. The specifics of the study of sports and recreation lend themselves well to the use of debating for several reasons.

First, debating allows students to directly experience and experiment with competition in a new and different way. While most competition in sports is based on physical action and skill (although certainly a significant mental element is involved in almost all sports), debate is more about the individual's intellect and communication skills. It is very different to lose at pool or other recreational game than it is to lose at debate. The debate loss and win call into question basic values of self-worth, such as ability to express oneself and the ability to think critically about ideas. Those heavily involved with sports have discovered that debating brings them a much better understanding of competition. In addition to competition, debating allows much the same experience of the cooperation and teamwork called for in sports. With proper guidance, students can learn not just about the topic being debated, but also about competition and cooperation, issues that will be important to them as they apply their knowledge about sports and recreation.

Second, debating allows for exploration of the social implications of sports and recreation. Sports and recreation exist in society because they fulfill basic human needs, social and individual, physical and mental. Often these important foundation issues relating to sports and recreation do not get sufficient attention. Debating is an ideal way to explore these issues, as the topics below suggest.

Third, debating mixes logic with fun. Some games stimulate, some games educate, some games demonstrate skill, some games involve logical problem solving, and some games provide thrills. The game of debate adds the logical problem-solving element to the experience of those who normally use games to demonstrate skills. While many games have an intellectual aspect to them, the game of debate features the intellect as a primary component. Students who are familiar with the use and practice of games in sports and recreation (skill and thrill) can now experience these features in the classroom, giving learning a familiar and welcome context. Debates can inject enjoyment into the classroom.

Sample Debate Topics for Sports and Recreation Classes

- The role of leisure in modern society has been overemphasized.
- Recreation should be designed to improve and educate the individual.
- Professional sports in modern society have been overemphasized.
- Team sports have been overemphasized.
- Competition is often a destructive force in sports and recreation.
- Recreation and leisure activities should be environmentally benign.
- There is too much work and not enough play.
- Protective equipment should be mandatory in all sports that require it at the professional level.

- Athletes with disabilities should be given compensatory advantages when in competition.
- The professionalization of officiating should be increased at all levels of sport.
- Physical education should be required study in college and university.
- Physical education in high school should be an elective.
- All sports should be coeducational.
- More unconventional sports should be a part of the Olympic Games.
- The Olympic Games should be discontinued.
- College athletes should be paid for their services.
- For the benefit of the national park system, human use should be decreased.
- Most amusement parks are a waste of time and money.
- Rock climbers should not climb on Native American sacred spaces.

Sample Debate Formats for Sports and Recreation Classes

Debate can be productively used in the sports and recreation classroom in a variety of ways. The formats chosen should mirror the content of the class and allow students to explore content in fruitful and interesting ways.

First, organize debates to explore the basic social issues that underlie sports and recreation. Organize team debates to explore many different issues or one major abstract issue. The use of sports and recreation to fill leisure time, the importance or lack of importance of leisure time, supposedly "productive" recreation (such as reading, acting, crafts, painting, activism, etc.) vs. supposedly "nonproductive" recreation (such as watching sporting events, viewing television, doing nothing), the role of recreation and sports in mental health, the role of recreation and sports in physical fitness, and other such issues are good debate subjects. While many classes teach the "what" and the "how" of sports and recreation, debate can help students understand the "why."

Second, use debates to explore competition and team-building issues. Debates can be "about" competition as a topic, but they can also help illustrate cooperation and competition as manipulated variables within the debate. For example, hold one debate as a cooperative discussion, where sides are not assigned and winners are decided on how they analyzed the issues. Students who produce the best cooperative discussion are rewarded in this exercise. Another example involves students speaking as individuals to state their position on an issue, after which students with similar positions form "teams" or "parties," and the debate proceeds from there, although students are allowed to defect from one group and join another during the arguments if their team's position begins to stray from their own personal position or as they admire the arguments made by other groups and decide to join them. Rather than just two groups, often three or four groups will emerge. Such exercises help students understand how groups form, mature, and change.

Third, use debates in contrasting sports and recreation to another major activity in all of our lives: work. We spend huge amounts of time at work, and often we justify the need for sports and recreation as a contrast to it. Students debate topics that allow them to explore what it is about work that necessitates sports and recreation, as well as how work itself can be made more like recreation to reduce this bifurcation. Some critics say there need be no firm distinctions between "play" and "work," and that tasks and roles can be redesigned so that we do not have to choose between them.

Fourth, use debates to emphasize their "play" elements. For example, pick an idea, and then have a person give one reason to support it, followed by another who gives a reason to oppose it. No student is allowed to repeat an argument and must give a new argument. A panel of student judges determines if an argument is a repeat or is so weak that it does not qualify, in which case they remove that person from the debate. This simple exercise is easy and fun, and as it quickly advances, students are amazed at the ideas people express. This activity is enjoyable and rewards creative thinking. Students can learn that "sport" involves not only the body but also features the mind.

Conclusion

Sports and recreation are growing fields as individuals have more time away from work and the means to enjoy themselves in active and organized ways. While not the primary teaching method in this subject area, debates can add significantly to classes as they explore themes relevant to the field. Students of sports and recreation usually prefer a classroom that is more active and less passive, thus debating could be a useful addition.

Technology and Society

Technology has traditionally had a substantial impact on society. The adoption of stable agriculture, the invention of gunpowder, the development and application of steam power, and the invention of the transistor had major impacts on social structure and the way people live their lives. All of these changes suggest areas that are ripe with debate possibilities.

Technological advances are some of the most powerful forces shaping global human society in the 21st century. In the past, major technological changes might have an important impact every few generations. Now they affect every generation.

The great controversies we face today are related to technology, such as its impact on military affairs, the economy, and education. Students familiar with these controversies can better understand them, as well as the overall role of technology in society, by debating these issues.

Why Debate Is Valuable to Technology and Society Classes

Debating can be a very valuable and productive way to engage students in a wide variety of issues. Technology is increasingly affecting the individual through issues such as invasion of privacy, government surveillance and database construction, the application of biotechnology and cybernetics to health care and genetic engineering, personal communication through enhanced wireless communication, and the use of the Internet for recreation.

Technology is increasingly affecting the environment through global warming, the use of genetically modified crops and animals, the production of industrial pollutants, the threat of ozone depletion, mechanized agriculture, and deforestation and the depletion of water resources by irrigation and pumping from ground water reserves.

Technology is increasingly affecting military affairs and operations though the development of new generations of nuclear weapons, the use of long-distance precision guided munitions, the development of "nonlethal" weapons to make military force easier to use, the militarization of space, the development of antimissile defense programs, the spread of weapons of mass destruction to national and subnational groups, and the ability of some nations to project military force on a global level to influence the actions of and events in nations not able to defend themselves.

Technology is increasingly affecting economic relations through automation of the workplace, the creation of information workers, the decline of manufacturing industries, the creation of an online workplace and marketplace, the emergence of a cashless economy, the need to change careers during a lifetime, and the decentralization and fragmentation of entertainment networks through the Internet and home viewing and recording.

Technology is increasingly affecting education through the use of the Internet for resources and distance learning, the creation of a "digital divide" between those receiving high-technology education and those who are not, the use of behavior modifying drugs to manage students, home schooling using technological resources, the impact on the knowledge base through the use of websites not editorially reviewed, the decline of the use of books, the creation of information appliances to substitute for memory, and the creation of a global educational culture and its marginalizing of other educational traditions.

Technology is well suited for debating in the classroom for other reasons. First, these discussions tend to be very future oriented, focused on difference new technology makes to lives and careers. As new technological advances are made, there is a constant need for debate about what they mean and how they should be implemented and controlled.

Second, since there is wide disagreement about these issues, many of the arguments that would be used in a debate are readily available to students. Students can find arguments and sources spanning a broad spectrum of beliefs about the benefits of technological change and application.

Third, issues relating to technology come up repeatedly during the life of any given student, thus debating about these issues prepares all students for the decisions about technology he or she will have to make in the future.

Sample Debate Topics for Technology and Society Classes

- The Internet poses a significant threat to individual privacy.
- The government should be restricted in its abilities to engage in surveillance of its citizens.
- Cloning of humans should not be allowed.
- Parents should be able to use bioengineering to select the attributes of their children.
- The Internet has decreased the quality of life.
- The internal combustion engine must be de-emphasized to prevent global warming.
- Genetically modified foods and animals should be excluded from commercial markets.
- The world would have been better off if the discovery of X had been delayed by 100 years.
- A sustainable agriculture model should broadly replace the current model of mechanized agriculture.
- Nation-states should emphasize the use of nonlethal weapons in military affairs.
- Space should never be militarized.
- No nation should deploy a national missile defense.
- Nuclear power should be de-emphasized as an energy source.
- A unilateral freeze by the United States on the production and development of nuclear weapons is desirable.

- Let the information superhighway be toll free.
- Space exploration and development should be an international priority.
- Computers are the answer.
- The Internet is the new opiate of the masses.
- Television is more significant than the computer.
- Scientists have moral responsibility for their discoveries.

Sample Debate Formats for Technology and Society Classes

An infinite number of approaches can be taken to debating technology issues in the classroom. Instructors should adapt debate formats and topics to match the specific subject matter of the class. Here are a few ideas for implementing debates in your classroom.

Students can engage in very short, one-on-one debates about the merits and problems of specific technological innovations. These debates can take place in 20 minutes or less and be staged throughout the term. Each student can engage in one or more such debates. These debates can have a fairly narrow focus, perhaps exploring the nature of specific technological innovations such as mobile telephones, the Internet, or cloning of farm animals.

Teams of two students could engage in longer debates about the social implications of various areas of technology. Here the focus is on an area of technology and whether it is beneficial for society. Often the contest will be between the substantive benefits of a specific area of technology vs. the social harms stemming from the application of technology to this area. For example, automation increases productivity but decreases employment. These topics can be changed for each debate or, if broad enough, could be repeated a number of times. Encourage discussion after the debates to involve students in these issues, and urge them to develop new issues and new lines of arguments in situations where the same topic will be debated several times.

Larger teams can engage in debates that focus on the value and ethical dimensions of the implementation of technology. Here the focus is on the deeper issues of equity, freedom, democracy, and individual autonomy. These topics do not include the practical benefits of technology, but may focus on a comparison of these practical benefits with the abstract values listed above. Issues of individual autonomy, the ability of people to adjust to change, and the identification of the winners and losers from technological applications should be pursued in these debates.

A major project could be to stage a trial, either of a particular technology or a scientist. Gunpowder could be put on trial in a classroom proceeding, as could nuclear power, biotechnology, or animal experimentation. A particular scientist or group of scientists could also be put on trial for not considering the implications of their discoveries, such as those working on the Manhattan Project to develop the first nuclear weapon, Christiaan Barnard for developing organ transplantation, or the US Agency for International Development for promoting high-technology chemical-dependent agriculture in the majority world during the 1960s and 1970s.

Conclusion
Technology and its impact on society is a rich area for debates in the classroom. By personalizing the experience of evaluating technologies and how they affect us all, students become more familiar with the basic issues involved. These issues emerge repeatedly during the life of students as citizens and can be recalled and reviewed when they make decisions both as individuals choosing lifestyles and as citizens choosing policy directions for societies.

Women's Studies
The importance of studying about gender and sexuality cannot be overstated. At almost every intersection of our lives, gender is a central variable. Workplace issues, family norms, societal controversies, and international politics are all analyzed in the field of women's studies.

Why Debate Is Valuable to Women's Studies Classes
Debate is a natural part of the discipline of women's studies—the kind of controversies presented offer themselves for vigorous dialogue.

Because women's studies classes cover a wide variety of issues that affect our daily lives, debating these topics can lead to change in key area of our lives.

Often when learning about a concept that has fallen out of favor (such as all-female communes), students have difficulty imagining what might justify such political decisions. Debates offer a chance for students to advocate and argue for just such policies.

Sample Debate Topics for Women's Studies Classes

- Nature vs. nurture.
- Women's work makes up the bulk of the economy.
- Transgender struggles are misguided.
- We should have proportional gender representation.
- Breasts are for breastfeeding.
- Menstruation is power.
- Women should separate from men for some organizing.
- Men can teach women's studies.
- The Michigan Womyn's Music Festival should allow transgender women to participate.
- Women are closer to nature than men.
- Women should hold 51% of the public offices.
- Women's sports should be equally funded.
- Single-sex schools are best for women.
- Advertising causes eating disorders.
- Men's studies should be equally funded.
- Women's stories are more important than CNN.

Sample Debate Formats for Women's Studies Classes

You can use debates to spark students' interest in an issue, encourage them to understand politics from a gender perspective, or simply to inform. Depending on how teachers frame the debates, classroom events can achieve a number of educational goals.

First, schedule a debate about the Michigan Womyn's Music Festival, a 20+-year institution that has been criticized for excluding transgender women. The topic "The festival should include transgender women" would be excellent because it encompasses several themes, including sexuality, gender, women-only spaces, and the question "Who is a woman?"

You could organize the session as a four-on-four debate with the rest of the class getting a 20-minute question-and-answer period. Each speaker would present arguments that centered on the question of transgendered women's exclusion. One side would present the arguments for Michigan Womyn's Music Festival to stay "women born, women only." These arguments might include the value of shared women's experience and the safety of women who have been sexually assaulted. The negative side would point out the discrimination that transgender individuals face and argue that men who become women offer a unique benefit to a women's festival.

Second, topics like "nature vs. nurture" are great for extended debates. Students might debate this topic from cultural, political, and then evolutionary biological perspectives.

Third, women's studies classes offer great opportunities for role-playing debates. In one of our classrooms we create a role-playing exercise asking students to debate the US Don't Ask Don't Tell policy of gays in the military. This offers a chance to look at issues of gender and sexuality in the context of a public policy. Students are given quotations from experts and asked to assume the arguments presented in those quotations. With experts from both sides of the debate about gays in the military represented, the class is put into the role of a think tank discussing the issue before presenting a report before Congress. With a subject that might be difficult to debate about (gay rights), the role-playing exercise gives students a chance to encounter and advocate for positions they might never otherwise encounter and they get a chance to debate the issue without having to worry about what people think about what they say—because they are role-playing. In this example, students get a chance to debate about mainstreaming gay culture, the risks to gays and lesbians and the opportunity for social change presented by the United States military. Other students get to role-play academic experts who present theories about gender and sexuality.

Conclusion

Women's studies classes are one of the most fruitful places for debates. The enduring controversies stand as wonderful debate topics. We encourage you to use debate as one method of instruction.

Appendixes

Tools for Debates

Appendix I: Evaluation Form

Student name: _____

Topic: _____

Criteria	Excellent = A	Good = B	Average = C	Below average = D
Knowledge in creation of arguments				
Knowledge in support for specific arguments				
Knowledge in refuting opposing arguments				
Knowledge in answering questions				
Knowledge in summarizing debate				
Other				
Total				

Appendix 2: Debate Ballot, Checklist Format

Student name:_____

Topic: _____

Evaluation of the subject matter

How effectively did the student use information from the class and the shared knowledge base of the students?

☐ Poor   ☐ Fair   ☐ Acceptable   ☐ Excellent   ☐ Fantastic

How recent is the research?

☐ Poor   ☐ Fair   ☐ Acceptable   ☐ Excellent   ☐ Fantastic

Is the research complete?

☐ Poor   ☐ Fair   ☐ Acceptable   ☐ Excellent   ☐ Fantastic

How biased is the evidence?

☐ Poor   ☐ Fair   ☐ Acceptable   ☐ Excellent   ☐ Fantastic

Evaluation of debate skills and preparation

How persuasive is the student?

☐ Poor   ☐ Fair   ☐ Acceptable   ☐ Excellent   ☐ Fantastic

How well organized is the student?

☐ Poor   ☐ Fair   ☐ Acceptable   ☐ Excellent   ☐ Fantastic

How effectively does the student focus on the central ideas of the debate?

☐ Poor   ☐ Fair   ☐ Acceptable   ☐ Excellent   ☐ Fantastic

Evaluation of arguments

Do the arguments presented relate to the rest of the arguments in the debate?

☐ Poor   ☐ Fair   ☐ Acceptable   ☐ Excellent   ☐ Fantastic

Do the arguments have assertions, reasons, and evidence?

☐ Poor   ☐ Fair   ☐ Acceptable   ☐ Excellent   ☐ Fantastic

Has the student explained the implications of the arguments?

☐ Poor   ☐ Fair   ☐ Acceptable   ☐ Excellent   ☐ Fantastic

Appendix 3: Sample Debate Formats

20-Minute Debate 1 on 1

First Affirmative Speech	4 minutes	Prove your case for the topic
First Negative Speech	4 minutes	Refute, introduce new issues
Second Affirmative Speech	3 minutes	Refute and summarize
Second Negative Speech	3 minutes	Refute and summarize

Each team has 3 minutes preparation time.

30-Minute Debate 1 on 1 with cross-examination

First Affirmative Speech	5 minutes	Prove your case for the topic
Cross-examination	3 minutes	
First Negative Speech	5 minutes	Refute, introduce new issues
Cross-examination	3 minutes	
Second Affirmative Speech	4 minutes	Refute and summarize
Second Negative Speech	4 minutes	Refute and summarize

Each team has 3 minutes preparation time.

30-Minute Debate 2 on 2

First Affirmative Speech	4 minutes	Prove your case for the topic
First Negative Speech	4 minutes	Refute, introduce new issues
Second Affirmative Speech	4 minutes	Refute
Second Negative Speech	4 minutes	Refute
Affirmative Rebuttal	2 minutes	Summarize
Negative Rebuttal	2 minutes	Summarize

Each team has 3 minutes preparation time.

40-Minute Debate 2 on 2 with cross-examination

First Affirmative Speech	5 minutes	Prove your case for the topic
Cross-examination	3 minutes	
First Negative Speech	5 minutes	Refute, introduce new issues
Cross-examination	3 minutes	
Second Affirmative Speech	5 minutes	Refute and summarize
Cross-examination	3 minutes	
Second Negative Speech	5 minutes	Refute and summarize
Cross-examination	3 minutes	
Affirmative Rebuttal	2 minutes	Summarize
Negative Rebuttal	2 minutes	Summarize

Each team has 3 minutes preparation time.

55-Minute Debate 3 on 3 with questions

First Affirmative Speech	4 minutes	Prove your case for the topic
Cross-examination	3 minutes	
First Negative Speech	4 minutes	Refute, introduce new issues
Cross-examination	3 minutes	
Second Affirmative Speech	5 minutes	Refute
Second Negative Speech	5 minutes	Refute
Questions from Audience	15 minutes	
Third Affirmative Speech	4 minutes	Summarize
Third Negative Speech	4 minutes	Summarize

Each team has 4 minutes preparation time.

60-Minute Debate 2 on 2 with cross-examination

First Affirmative Speech	5 minutes	Prove your case for the topic
Cross-examination	3 minutes	
First Negative Speech	5 minutes	Refute, introduce new issues
Cross-examination	3 minutes	
Second Affirmative Speech	6 minutes	Refute
Cross-examination	3 minutes	
Second Negative Speech	6 minutes	Refute
Cross-examination	3 minutes	
First Negative Rebuttal	3 minutes	Refute
First Affirmative Rebuttal	3 minutes	Refute
Second Negative Rebuttal	3 minutes	Summarize
Second Affirmative Rebuttal	3 minutes	Summarize

Each team has 7 minutes preparation time.

60-Minute Trial (may be held over two days)

Introduction of players	2 minutes
Read the charges	2 minutes
Case for the Prosecution	5 minutes
Prosecution witness #1	5 minutes
Defense questions	3 minutes
Prosecution witness #2	5 minutes
Case for the Defense	5 minutes
Defense witness #1	5 minutes
Prosecution questions	3 minutes
Defense witness #2	5 minutes
Prosecution questions	3 minutes
Prosecution summary	5 minutes
Defense summary	5 minutes
[Break to adjudicate]	
Read verdict	1 minute

Each side has 3 minutes preparation time.

Appendix 4: What Format is for You?

	Positive Elements	Negative Elements
The public forum debate	• Involves many students • Good for introducing subject matter • Encourages creativity • Little preparation needed • Mixes well with other formats • No research required	• Can reinforce student ideologies • Can be dominated by a few vocal students
The spontaneous debate	• Fun and engaging • Excellent way to work on delivery, organization, and language choices • Reduces stress about future debates • No research required	• Topics can fizzle
The policy debate	• Excellent for students to show mastery of a subject • In-depth analysis of a topic • Encourages research and preparation	• Jargon can create an entry barrier • Requires preparation and setup time
The parliamentary debate	• Encourages teamwork and creativity • Excellent for enhancing oratory skills	• Creative interpretation of topics can move debates in new directions • Research is optional
The role-playing debate	• Fits easily into many courses • Decreases speaker's anxiety because students aren't representing themselves	• Requires familiarity of all students involved
The mock trial	• Structured environment • Good for legal-oriented topics	• Can have a high entry barrier because of jargon
The model congress debate	• Available for many students • Topics are student driven	• Requires preparation

Inspiration for Debaters

Appendix 5: Aristotle on the Value of Debate

The Value of Debate

Debate is fascinating in its own right; intelligent people find it a demanding and stimulating sport. But what value besides pleasure will the debater find in this activity? How will it aid his personal development and further his career? Will debate help her contribute to the public good? For an answer to these questions, it might be interesting to turn first to the most famous of all authorities on the subject, Aristotle.

Aristotle on the Value of Debate

Writing in the fourth century BCE Aristotle listed four values accruing from the knowledge of rhetoric. These values are as valid in the modern world as they were in ancient Greece.

1. To prevent the triumph of fraud and injustice. The techniques which the debater learns in academic debate are invaluable later when [she or] he is called upon to speak out for what [she or] he believes, and to condemn what [she or] he considers wrong. Democracy depends on free criticism of those in power, and the more clearly reasoned and forcibly expressed the criticism is, the more valuable it can be in defending what is right.

2. To instruct when scientific instruction is of no avail. It often happens that, when one tries to induce other people to adopt a plan of action, it is not enough to be in a sound position; one must also be convincing. Simple fact does not always recommend itself. The trained debater will be able to combine clear reasoning with persuasive techniques in order to make [her or] his plan acceptable.

3. To make us argue out both sides of a case. Debating gives a person perspective, and frees [her or] him from prejudice. [She or] He learns to understand what can be said on the other side of a case, and that insight helps [her or] him to meet objections to [her or]

his position. [She or] He becomes more effective in [her or] his daily life because [she or] he is not caught unaware in making [her or] his decisions.

4. To help one defend oneself. In our daily life, we are all confronted with situations in which we must be able to ward off attack. We live in a competitive society in which someone else often wants what we have. In order to maintain our own position, we need the skills of debate to answer attacks, just and unjust, upon ourselves.

Source: Lionel Crocker, *Argumentation and Debate* (New York: American Institute of Banking, 1962), 11–12.

Appendix 6: John Stuart Mill on Debate in "On Liberty"

The process of debate raises certain fundamental questions about our opinions: How did we arrive at them? Why do we hold them? What alternative opinions exist and how do they compare with our own? The ability to pose and answer these questions has long been considered the hallmark of a truly educated person. In his essay *On Liberty* (1859), political philosopher John Stuart Mill (1806–1873) identified the ability and willingness to subject opinions to debate as a prerequisite for the attainment of wisdom and, ultimately, of liberty itself.

> In the case of any person whose judgment is really deserving of confidence, how has it become so? Because [she or] he has kept [her or] his mind open to criticism of [her or] his opinions and conduct. Because it has been [her or] his practice to listen to all that could be said against [her or] him; to profit by as much of it as was just, and expound to [her or] himself, and upon occasion to others, the fallacy of what was fallacious. Because [she or] he has felt, that the only way in which a human being can make some approach to knowing the whole of a subject, is by hearing what can be said about it by persons of every variety of opinion, and studying all modes in which it can be looked at by every character of mind. No wise [woman or] man ever acquired [her or] his wisdom in any mode but this; nor is it in the nature of human intellect to become wise in any other manner. (20)

Mill distinguished between "received opinion," uncritically accepted by an audience from some figure of authority, and an opinion formed through controversy and critical deliberation. It is only through the latter process, Mill argued, that the individual should be able to hold and express an opinion with genuine conviction. An untested opinion, he insisted, even if it happens to be true, "is but one superstition the more accidentally clinging to the words that enunciate a truth" (35).

There is the greatest difference between presuming an opinion to be true, because, with every opportunity for contesting it, it has not been refuted, and assuming its truth for the purpose of not permitting its refutation. Complete liberty of contradicting and disproving our opinion, is the very condition which justifies us in assuming its truth for purposes of action; and on no other terms can a being with human faculties have any rational assurance of being right (19).

For Mill, debate is a process by which firm convictions on important issues are formed. These convictions may not be the opinions that one took into the dispute, for these may be proven partly or completely wrong through the process of debate. Yet one may expect to emerge from the process of debate with a far more detailed and accurate understanding of the issues involved and with far greater confidence in the conclusions one has drawn from the dispute. "The steady habit of correcting and completing [her or] his own opinion by collating it with those of others," Mill insisted, "so far from causing doubt and hesitation in carrying it into practice, is the only stable foundation for a just reliance on it" (20).

Mill was himself a person of strong opinions tested through disputation. He debated many of the great issues of his day and some of the timeless issues of the human condition, such as the responsibilities of representative government, the nature of human freedom, and the dynamics of power and oppression in the subjugation of women. But Mill did not view the proper scope of debate as limited to political or legal questions or its proper forum as limited to the formal deliberations of organized bodies. He instead conceived of debate as a "habit of mind" that should be cultivated by individuals for application to all affairs, whether personal, religious, political, scientific, or those drawn from what he termed "the business of life." "On every subject on which difference of opinion is possible," Mill insisted, "the truth depends on a balance to be struck between two sets of conflicting reasons" (36). We should withhold our confident endorsement of opinions until they have withstood the test of reasoned disputation. We should, he advised, issue "a standing invitation to the whole world to prove them unfounded" and not be satisfied until that invitation has been accepted (21).

Willingness to subject one's opinions to disputation is a necessary but not sufficient condition for the achievement of true debate. For an opinion to be truly tested, it must first be given the strongest possible expression. The best available arguments for the opinion must be advanced, and supported by the most powerful evidence and reasoning that can be mustered. It is not enough to hold an opinion that turns out to be true; one must have come to that opinion for the best reasons. Furthermore, for an opinion to be truly tested, it must be confronted with the strongest possible counterarguments, also supported by the most persuasive evidence and reasoning that can be found.

The clash of varying opinions is best achieved through genuine debate, in which the conflicting positions are advocated by different parties who are committed to them. The presentation of different views by a single speaker is no substitute for real debate. Although it is possible for a single speaker to both support a given position and describe and refute contrary views, such a presentation is likely to produce a lesser challenge to the position being advocated than would an actual debate. In an ideal debate, Mill wrote, the opposing sides would be defended by knowledgeable persons who earnestly believe the positions they advocate in the dispute.

Mill recognized, however, that such disputants are often not available to discuss matters of immediate importance. In order to provide the best possible disputation of ideas in this common circumstance, Mill endorsed a form of academic debate familiar to modern students: a debate in which the participants skillfully defend positions that do not necessarily represent their own personal beliefs. "So essential is this discipline to a real understanding of moral and human subjects," he insisted, "that if opponents of all important truths do not exist, it is indispensable to imagine them, and supply them with the strongest arguments which the most skilful devil's advocate can conjure up" (37).

The abilities to identify the strongest positions and counterpositions on a given issue and to support and defend them in the best ways possible are precisely the skills of debate that this text aims to enhance. It is designed to familiarize students with the range of argumentative resources and strategies that are available to the skillful disputant and to describe the processes of reasoning and critical analysis through which these strategies may best be employed. This text is conceived as a practical guide to the persuasive and sound expression of one's own opinions and to the powerful refutation of the positions one may oppose.

Most of the skills, strategies, and purposes that guide today's debaters are ancient in origin. The importance Mill placed on the intellectual activity of debate was hardly novel. Indeed, it reflected a centuries-old understanding of debate in many cultures as a hallmark of civilization, social order, and knowledge.

Source: Robert James Branham, *Debate and Critical Analysis: The Harmony of Conflict* (Hillsdale, N.J.: Lawrence Erlbaum Associates, 1991), 2–4.

Appendix 7: Suggestions for a Successful Debater

Analysis
1. The debater should seek the most thorough knowledge of the topic and the most complete evidence to support her or his arguments.
2. The debater should choose arguments that are important enough to have a great deal of readily available evidence behind them.
3. The debater should not be afraid to use the "standard" case that many other teams are using. Often it can be refined or intensely developed during the season to become the best case. Non-thinking teams frequently are lulled into a false sense of security by what they think is a standard case but which is really capable of important refinements.

Organization
1. Choose the pattern of organization that best fits the analysis.
2. Carefully check the feedback of judges to see how effective the organization is.

Presentation of Arguments
1. Affirmative
   a. The affirmative should actively support its burden of proof.
   b. The affirmative should remain on the offensive.
   c. With few exceptions, the affirmative should narrow the range of arguments in the debate.
2. Negative
   a. The negative should actively support the presumption that goes with the present system.
   b. The negative should try to become the offensive team and put the affirmative team on the defensive.
   c. With a few exceptions, the negative should try to expand the range of arguments in the debate.

Refutation and Rebuttal
1. The debater should listen carefully to the opposition's arguments. It does little good to argue against an argument that has been misinterpreted.

2. The debater should state the argument [she or] he is attacking and indicate to the judge why [she or] he is attacking it.
3. The debater should state [her or] his counterargument.
4. The debater should present the evidence for [her or] his counterargument.
5. The debater should lend perspective to the development by showing how it affects the debate.
6. The debater should realize that it is possible for the opposition to tell the truth; [she or] he should not contest obviously valid arguments. Instead, [she or] he should analyze the relationship of the argument to the larger case or should move on to arguments that are contestable.

Delivery in Debate
1. The debater should realize that the debate takes place in the mind of the critic.
2. The debater should highlight important arguments by wording them in an interesting and memorable way.
3. The debater should forecast [her or] his attack.
4. The debater should erect signposts as [she or] he goes along to help the judge know where the speaker is in [her or] his case.
5. The debater should provide a brief summary and perspective at the end of the speech.
6. The debater should avoid all speaking mannerisms that detract from [her or] his delivery.
7. The debater should avoid debate clichés. [Her or] his language should be appropriate to the material and an expression of [her or] his own personality.
8. The debater should avoid sarcasm or other personal attacks on the opposition.
9. The debater should maintain poise throughout the debate. [She or] he should not talk or be rude during [her or] his opposition's turn at the speaker's stand.

Source: Roy V. Wood, *Strategic Debate*, 2nd ed. (Skokie, Ill.: National Textbook Co., 1974), 185.

Appendix 8: The Value of Debating—A Letter to a Student

Dear John,

So you are thinking of going out for debating and possibly taking part in discussion as well and want to know if this activity is worth the work involved? I wonder how you happened to think about it enough to write me. You may be one of the better students in your class, and appreciate the opportunity to add to your education. Possibly some teacher has suggested to you that the problem of the year is an excellent one to study to understand more about our world today. Perhaps you have thought only of the fun of trips, the thrill of public acclaim, the pleasure of winning, the pride in representing the school in a form of competition which depends on brains rather than brawn. Almost any motive may have given you the idea. I remember a high school debater who joined the squad to be near a red-haired girl, he did all right. But when you have debated a year or more I am sure you will find that debating has many solid values for you. When you have been out of school, you will look back and say, "I got more out of debating than I did out of any other course I took in school."

How do I know this? Debaters always demand proof, they want evidence, so I collected some facts. I sent out letters to the two hundred members of the Bates College Chapter of Delta Sigma Rho, one of the national honorary forensic societies, to inquire what success they had had in life, and whether they considered their training and experience in debating of any value to them in their careers. The response was so significant that the college published a bulletin containing excerpts from their replies. Most of them were students of mine and I could talk all night about them.

You don't have to wait till you start your career before you begin to get dividends from debating. A high school debate coach was one of the Delta Sigma Rho members who replied to my inquiry: "Although I have had only a few on my debate squad each year, it is apparent that the speech experience has been an important part of their personality development. A typical example is a brilliant lad who dissolved in pools of mortification every time he had to make the simplest response in class. In his sophomore year he was hopeless as a speaker but contributed a great deal to the arguments and evidence of the team. By the end of his senior year he had become a polished speaker and ranked among the top high school debaters for New England in all the tournaments in which he participated. The four debaters on that team applied to Harvard, Dartmouth, Bates, and the University of New Hampshire and were promptly accepted. All four institutions indicated that the high school experience in debating activity was a strong recommendation in their favor."

The Headmaster of a well-known college preparatory school wrote, "In my forty years of coaching debating in both public and private schools, it has been a source of satisfaction to me that in the schools with which I have been connected, the boys and girls with debate experience have been outstanding in the group of successful graduates. These youngsters have been the ones with the keenest interest in public affairs and the greatest facility in public speaking through their college and post-college years."

These dividends continue through college and graduate school. A student in a big graduate school wrote, "Preparing for my classes in graduate courses is like preparing for a practice debate." One of my former students got interested in science in the Army and, after working at Los Alamos, he attended Massachusetts Institute of Technology where he finished second in his class. Then he went on to complete his original plan to be a lawyer. He finished first in his class at Harvard Law School and was editor of the *Harvard Law Review*. He was later law clerk to Justice Frankfurter of the Supreme Court. He wrote, "Skill in organization obtained in debating is the most valuable asset to the student in law school." He went on to say that the skills best developed by the newer discussion methods are those most needed by a law clerk. [Those] who stood high in their classes at Cornell, Chicago, Columbia and Yale Law Schools gave the same sort of testimony

The dividends from debating get larger as one enters [her or] his chosen career. A Lieutenant Commander in the Navy had been a

New England champion before leaving college to enlist. After the war he returned to college and was again champion. He wrote, "You may sometimes think that the Navy is a highly illogical outfit, but I found that my training in logic in debating stood me in good stead in the Navy." The Chancellor of the University of California at Santa Barbara wrote, "If I were to choose any single activity in school which contributed most to my career, I would certainly choose debating." A college president replied, "My debating experiences have greatly influenced my writing and my public utterances."

A professor at Ohio Wesleyan University stated, "Any success I may have had as a classroom teacher comes from the fact that I constantly make use of what I learned from my debate experience." A prominent clergyman joined these other professional men with, "Debate training did more for me in the practical side of my ministry than any other preparation I received. It taught me to think more clearly, to speak more convincingly, and to ask myself many a time is it necessary? Is it expedient? Will it work?"

Of course, John, these [people] did not just sit back and let the debate coach make successes of them, they worked at it. And debate does take work. But this very work is one of the holdover values of the activity. Since the debater is so busy, [she or] he has to learn to make the best use of [her or] his time. As you will find, this is a very necessary habit for a successful college student. A former director of the state YMCA camp testified, "Debate started me on a pace that I still keep. The necessity of organizing time and energy to get done all the things I was doing at college still continues in my present work."

In fact, one of the most interesting replies from the field of business came from a [woman] who had been doing television research for one of the larger advertising companies and had been handling some of the better known programs. She said, "I got my job through my debate training. I was interviewed by the head of the department, a man with a steel-trap mind and disconcerting ability to put you on the defensive immediately. It was a harrowing hour, but something like one of our tougher debates—Keep your head, let the other fellow do a lot of talking—and then demolish his arguments." A somewhat similar reaction came from a male, former president of our debate council, as follows, "I have a new job with General Electric which I owe to my debate training. Two years ago, the head of this division of General Electric spoke to a group of us at our plant, and I was the only one who gave him any resistance. I told him his logic was perfect if one agreed with his premises, but as tactfully as possible I told him I did not agree with his major premise, and why. Instead of getting rid of me, two years later he remembered it and brought me to New York as his assistant."

A former governor of Maine, later a bigwig in the motion picture industry, wrote how much his debate training helped him in his seven political campaigns and on a trip to England where he had to get the British Motion Picture Producers to accept the American Production Code. He succeeded in this latter difficult job because of his debate training.

A later Governor of Maine, now Senator from that state, not only answered the questionnaire with favorable comments, but addressed the American Forensic Association on "The Influence of Debating on the Career of a Public Servant." You may read that address in "Vital Speeches" for October 15, 1957.

The head of the Department of Zoology at Columbia University wrote, "My experience in debating has been fully as valuable in my career as my scientific training." The public health consultant to the World Health Organization of the United Nations and professor emeritus at Massachusetts Institute of Technology told of the value of argumentation in presenting a health plan in Iran or Egypt. The editor of one of our greatest national newspapers wrote, "As deputy chief of the United States delegation to the United Nations Conference on Freedom of Information at Geneva in 1948, I had to debate day in and day out with delegates of many other countries. Particularly, I had to meet the arguments of the Soviet representatives and their satellites and help to convince our friends in the in between states of the validity of our defense of free speech."

Of course, these successful people who replied were college debaters, but most of them were high school debaters, too. I remember one of them when he was a senior in high school, and a member of the first State Championship high school debating team that I ever coached. A few years ago he was general counsel for the National Labor Relations Board and at one time had the responsibility of hiring more than five hundred lawyers for the federal government. He wrote, "I have for years given preference in employment and paid premium salaries to lawyers who, in addition to adequate professional background, have the advantage of debate training. They get all the facts. They analyze them accurately. They present them logically and clearly." This former high school debater is now Vice-President and General Counsel of Vultee Aircraft Corporation and recognizes the value of debate training in his own career.

Another state champion high school debater has been AP correspondent at Rome for many years, then at Buenos Aires, and now at Mexico City. I remember when he began debating in high school with my squad at the age of fifteen, and later when he made a trip around the world with the Bates Debating Team. He wrote, "Debate training has specific values as preparation for news reporting; it favors conciseness, the necessity of analyzing both sides of an issue, it encourages impartiality and objectivity. Its discipline in organizing material is invaluable preparation for marshalling facts in orderly news stories."

But it's not only the state champion debaters who praise their training, the alternate on the high school team to which the previous speaker belonged also reported. He did not make the team in high school but eventually did in college. He, too, made the debate trip around the world, and became a lawyer. He was solicitor for the Securities & Exchange Commission and is now special assistant to the Attorney General of the United States, assigned to the office of solicitor general and engaged in representing the government before the Supreme Court. He wrote, "The most important part of my work today—arguing a case in appellate court—is very much a form of debating. The chief element is the preparation and briefing; if the lawyer is dull and uninteresting [she or] he is likely to put the court to sleep and lose his case." (He confessed to me privately that a certain justice did fall asleep recently, and he was forced to get more pep into his delivery lest he lose the attention entirely of the famous jurist!)

Those boys came from Maine high schools. I have a picture in my scrapbook of a red-haired lad receiving the trophy for the high school championship of New Hampshire. As editor of the Encyclopedia Americana Annual, he wrote, "Debate training plays a part in every issue of the Americana Annual and in every article I write or edit." (He added a personal note that it was through debating on the high school level that he met the girl who was to become his wife and claimed that they do not spend their time together arguing, either. They must have been colleagues; you have to learn to get along with your colleagues to be a good debater, John!)

Through their publication in 1948 (first edition) I can take a little credit for helping some professional men by these letters which I am writing you. A lawyer engaged in representing the airlines before the Civil Aeronautics Commission was most flattering in writing, "To all of us who participated in debate, the training has affected our approach to problems ever since. In my own case, I have consciously adverted to some of the processes and practices which we used in formulating the initial argument on a given debate subject. [Sounds like a lawyer, doesn't he?] When it has been difficult to start a legal brief which must tie together a two or three thousand page transcript of testimony and many thousand pages of exhibits, I have consciously reached back to the approaches we used in debating as a starting point for outlining and drafting such an adversary argument. I am not ashamed to say that I have a very vivid recollection, in beginning the drafting of a brief directed to a rather complicated and difficult question, of referring to your manual for high schools which you called 'So You Want to Debate'."

During the 1960 Presidential campaign, "Freedom and Union" made a survey of many [women and] men in the political limelight, both presidential candidates, governors, senators, and congress[persons]. More than half of them had had experience in school debating. Of these, 89% recommended debating strongly to high school students with political ambitions. This included both Mr. Nixon and Mr. Kennedy. The replies were consistent in urging debaters to do adequate research, listen to both sides, be sincere, be logical, and be fair. These important people found that from their school debating they learned how to organize a speech, to gain self-assurance, and how to present a speech.

There you have it, John; in high school, college, graduate school and in business and professional careers, both men and women who have debated report on the experience as a valuable one. College presidents, teachers, sales[persons], clergy, business executives, lawyers, social workers, scientists, editors, and homemakers, all praise debate and discussion as paying big dividends for the time and effort expended. These leaders in business and professions mention among the values of debate study of the problems of the day, training for collecting and judging information, distinguishing between fact and sound reasoning, analyzing problems, selecting and meeting arguments, influencing audiences, and many more.

These testimonies have all come from former debaters of one small institution, but many distinguished Americans today were debaters in many other colleges and universities and began this training in high school, John, as you are thinking of doing.

Other studies besides this one of mine have shown the significance attached to debate training by former participants, and have furnished proof of the success of high school debaters. For example, the president of National Delta Sigma Rho, the debating fraternity, states that more than half of its members were also members of Phi Beta Kappa, the fraternity designed to honor high academic standing in college. Another study seems to indicate that more debaters than participants in any other extra-curricular school activity are found in Who's Who. Yes, John, I think you will always be glad you decided to go out for debating. It takes time and means work, but it pays off. It's fun, too. One of these who wrote regarding the values was William Metz, now a college professor. He says he will never forget when he was introduced as "Mr. Mess" and came near living up to his name! So, if you feel encouraged to try out, just let me know, and I'll write you more about the way debating and discussion are conducted

Yours for a valuable activity—debating.

Brooks Quimby

Source: Brooks Quimby, *So You Want to Discuss and Debate?* Rev. ed. (Portland, Maine: J. Weston Walch, 1962), 1–8.

Appendix 9: The Ten Principles of Debate

Decision by Debate reflects ten principles:

1. Debate as a method of decision provides for the rigorous examination and testing of pertinent data and inferences through the give-and-take of informed controversy. Hence, properly employed, it is a means for arriving at judgments that are reflective and decisions that are critical.

2. A debater is not a propagator who seeks to win unqualified acceptance for a predetermined point of view while defeating an opposing view. Rather, when [she or] he places [her or] himself in the highest tradition of debate, [she or] he is an investigator who co-operates with fellow investigators in searching out the truth or in selecting that course of common action which seems best for all concerned, debaters and public alike.

3. Debate is not limited to a particular type of subject matter, a particular sort of audience, or a particular mode of discourse. It is a generic species of deliberation, the principles and procedures of which are applicable to informed, responsible controversy however and wherever it may take place.

4. One learns about debate and becomes skilled in its use in three different but related ways: by the thoughtful observation and analysis of debates, past and present; by guided practice; and by gaining an understanding of the theory of debate, as embodied in the discipline of argumentation. No one of these methods of learning is less important than the others; all deserve equal attention from the student and equal emphasis by the teacher.

5. Research is an indispensable part of reflective decision-making. One does not become a debater at the moment [she or] he rises to speak or sits down to write. [She or] He becomes a debater long before—when [she or] he begins [her or] his study of the problem about which [she or] he will eventually propound judgments. Debate is a process that reaches from tentative explorations of subject matter to the final decision.

6. Traditional Aristotelian logic provides an imperfect description of how [women and] men actually reason today in argumentative controversies. A more accurate and useful logic for today may be

inferred from the formulations of the contemporary English logician Stephen Toulmin.

7. Personal and emotional proofs, no less than logical proofs, are relevant to critical decisions. An extension of Toulmin's analysis of argument provides a formula whereby personal, emotional, and logical proofs may be reduced to a common structure and made subject to comparable tests. The debater is thus able to bring all three modes of artistic proof within the framework of critical controversy.

8. While the ultimate goal of the philosopher may be to exhibit relationships among ideas per se, the ultimate goal of the debater is to use ideas as proofs for influencing the beliefs of listeners or readers. A knowledge of how belief functions is, therefore, an essential part of the debater's study.

9. The effective communication of arguments to others depends on adeptness in style and delivery. Clarity and attractiveness are the common criteria, and these criteria urge that debaters express each argument so that it will be given exactly the weight it deserves—no more and no less.

10. Practice debates in the classroom and in college forensics tournaments are not ends in themselves, but means of developing the skills and attitudes necessary for responsible participation in the debating situations of later life where free citizens determine public policy.

Source: Douglas Ehninger and Wayne Brockriede, *Decision by Debate* (New York: Dodd, Mead, 1963), vii–viii.

Bibliography

Abbot, Edwin A. *Flatland*. London: Penguin Books, 1987.

Barker, Roseanne. "Videography to Teach Debate." Paper presented at International Debate Education Association conference, Istanbul, Turkey, November 2004.

Blatner, Adam. "Role-playing in Education." 2002. Available at http://www.blatner.com/adam/pdntbk/rlplayedu.htm (accessed December 14, 2005).

Bonwell, Charles C., and James A. Eison. "Active Learning: Creating Excitement in the Classroom." Washington, D.C.: ERIC Clearinghouse on Higher Education and George Washington University, 1991. ERIC Identifier: ED340272.

Branham, Robert James. *Debate and Critical Analysis: The Harmony of Conflict*. Hillsdale, N.J.: Lawrence Erlbaum Associates, 1991.

Cialdini, Robert. "The Science of Persuasion." *Scientific American*, February 2001, 76–81.

Cotts, Cynthia. "Dateline: 43rd Street: How the 'Times' Straddles the Globalization Debate." *Village Voice*, August 21, 2001, 31.

Crocker, Lionel. *Argumentation and Debate*. New York: American Institute of Banking, 1962.

Dawson, Jodie. "Self-advocacy: A Valuable Skill for Your Teenager." SchwabLearning.org, 2004. Available at http://www.schwablearning.org/articles.asp?r=522 (accessed December 14, 2005).

Edelman, Murray. *From Art to Politics*. Chicago: University of Chicago Press, 1995.

Ehninger, Douglas, and Wayne Brockriede. *Decision by Debate*. New York: Dodd, Mead, 1963.

Foster, William Trufant. *Argumentation and Debating*. 2nd ed. Boston: Houghton Mifflin, 1945.

Freeley, Austin J. *Argumentation and Debate: Critical Thinking for Reasoned Decision Making*. 9th ed. Belmont, N.Y.: Wadsworth Publishing, 1996.

Giroux, Henry. Impure *Acts: The Practical Politics of Cultural Studies*. New York: Routledge, 2000.

———. *Schooling and the Struggle for Public Life: Critical Pedagogy in the Modern Age*. Minneapolis: University of Minnesota Press, 1988.

Gregory, Marshall. "Curriculum, Pedagogy, and Teacherly Ethos," *Pedagogy* 1, no. 1 (2001): 69–89.

Keedy, Bruce. "Hysteria." *Adbusters* 9, no. 5, September/October 2001, 46–47.

Knight, Christopher. "Art for School's Sake: Too Many Institutions Want Students to Conform to Criteria That Can Be Tested and Evaluated. The Result Is Pedagogy, Not Creativity." *Los Angeles Times,* July 8, 2001, C7.

Lunsford, Andrea, and John Ruszkiewicz. *Everything's an Argument*. Boston: Bedford/St. Martin's Press, 1999.

McBurney, James H., James M. O'Neill, and Glen E. Mills. *Argumentation and Debate: Techniques of a Free Society*. New York: Macmillan, 1951.

McChesney, Robert. *Rich Media, Poor Democracy: Communication Politics in Dubious Times*. New York: The New Press, 1999.

Meany, John, and Kate Shuster. *Art, Argument and Advocacy: Mastering Parliamentary Debate*. New York: International Debate Education Association, 2002.

———. *On That Point: An Introduction to Parliamentary Debate*. New York: International Debate Education Association, 2003.

Myers, D. G. *Social Psychology*. 4th ed. New York: McGraw Hill, 1996.

National Forensic League. "Student Congress Manual," 2004. Available at http://www.nflonline.org/AboutNFL/LeagueManuals (accessed December 14, 2005).

New York University School of Continuing and Professional Studies. "NYC Professionals Expect Three or More Careers During Lifetime." News release, September 23, 2004. Available at http://www.scps.nyu.edu/about/article.jsp?artId=10087 (accessed December 14, 2005).

Nietzsche, Friedrich. *Untimely Meditations*. Edited by Daniel Breazeale. Translated by R. J. Hollingdale. Cambridge: Cambridge University Press, 1997.

Paden, William E. *Interpreting the Sacred: Ways of Viewing Religion*. Boston, Beacon Press, 1992.

Paul, Richard, and Linda Elder. *The Miniature Guide to Critical Thinking: Concepts and Tools*. Dillon Beach, Calif.: Foundation for Critical Thinking, 2001.

"Psycho Design." *Adbusters* 9, no. 5 (September/October 2001): 57–58.

Quimby, Brooks. *So You Want to Discuss and Debate?* Rev. ed. Portland, Maine: J. Weston Walch, 1962.

Ross, M. Donna. "Cross Examination in Mock Trial." *The Rostrum*, February 1998. Available at http://debate.uvm.edu/NFL/rostrumlibmocktrial.html (accessed December 31, 2005).

———. "Mock Trial: An Open and Shut Case." *The Rostrum*, May 1997. Available at http://debate.uvm.edu/NFL/rostrumlibmocktrial.html (accessed December 31, 2005).

———. "Mock Trial: Get Going." *The Rostrum*, May 1997. Available at http://debate.uvm.edu/NFL/rostrumlibmocktrial.html (accessed December 31, 2005).

———. "Mock Trial: Who Goes Where?" *The Rostrum*, June 1997. Available at http://debate.uvm.edu/NFL/rostrumlibmocktrial.html (accessed December 31, 2005).

———. "Try Mock Trial." *The Rostrum*, April 1997. Available at http://debate.uvm.edu/NFL/rostrumlibmocktrial.html (accessed December 31, 2005).

Schank, Roger, and Chip Cleary. "Learning by Doing." Chapter 6 of *Engines for Education*, Institute for the Learning Sciences. Available at http://www.engines4ed.org/hyperbook/nodes/NODE-120-pg.html (accessed December 15, 2005).

———. "Learning Is Fun." Epilogue to *Engines for Education*, Institute for the Learning Sciences. Available at http://www.engines4ed.org/hyperbook/nodes/NODE-282-pg.html (accessed December 15, 2005).

Shuster, Kate. "Everything Is Everything Else: Argument Theory/Conspiracy Theory." Paper presented at International Debate Education Association conference, Istanbul, Turkey, November 2004.

Snider, Alfred. "Flashpoint: Revenge on Empty Television." Paper presented at International Debate Education Association conference, Istanbul, Turkey, November 2004.

Spencer-Notabartolo, Alexis. "The Roundtable Discussion: A Model for Debate and Argumentation Accessibility." Paper presented at International Debate Education Association conference, Istanbul, Turkey, November 2004.

Tannen, Deborah. *Argument Culture: Moving From Debate to Dialogue*. New York: Random House, 1998.

Tyson, Neil deGrasse. "Over the Rainbow: The Astrophysicist's Pot of Gold Lies Along the Entire Spectrum." *Natural History* 110, no. 7 (September 2001): 30–35.

Whang, Patricia A., and Gisele A. Waters. "Transformational Spaces in Teacher Education: Map(ping) a Pedagogy Linked to a Practice of Freedom." *Journal of Teacher Education* 52, no. 3 (May/June 2001): 197–210.

Willhoft, Waldo. *Modern Debate Practice*. New York: Prentice-Hall, 1929.

Windes, Russel R., and Robert M. O'Neil. *A Guide to Debate*. Portland Maine: J. Weston Walch, 1964.

Wood, Roy V. *Strategic Debate*. 2nd ed. Skokie, Ill.: National Textbook Co., 1974.

X, Malcolm. *The Autobiography of Malcolm X*. With Alex Haley. New York: Grove Press, 1964.

Index

Intellectual power, debates and, 14–15
Intellectual survival skills, 4
Interaction, 25–26, 38
International relations classroom debates, 217–221
Intimidation, 141
Introductory articles as research tools, 20
Introductory debates, formats for, 51–58
Investigation, 16–18
Issue discovery, 16–18, 95–98
Issues
  as elements, 96
  notes organized by, 24–25
  understanding complex, through debates, 193–4

Judging, 109–110, 143–144

Keedy, Jeffrey, 182
Keyword list, 19, 21, 112
Knight, Christopher, 179
Knowledge
  critical thinking and, 44
  debate topics and, 94
  evaluating, 153
  interdisciplinary, 47
  new patterns in, creating, 46–47
  shared ideas and, 10
  utilization of, 37–38

Language, 85, 207–210
Language education, developed use of, 13–15
Law classroom debates, 221–226
Layout, flow sheets, 104
Learning
  active and passive, 34–35
  enjoyable, 47–49
  interactive, 10, 16
  lifelong, 2
  process of and debates, 12, 14
  through interaction, 38
Legislation, debates in, 7
Letters, use in outlining, 98–99
Liberty, debate and, 285–288
Limited search pool, research, 18–19
Listening skills, 32–33, 289–290

Literature classroom debates, 226–229
Loaded terms, topics, 85
Logic, 4, 17, 105
Logos, rhetorical approach of, 17
Lunsford, Andrea, 36–37
Luske, Bruce, 262

Major points, 98
Malcom X. *see* X, Malcom
Mannerisms, delivery, 290
Mapping, public debates, 172
Mathematics classroom debates, 229–232
McChesney, Robert, 233–234
Media, 148–149
Media studies classroom debates, 233–236
Meikeljohn, Alexander, 1
Mill, John Stuart, debate and liberty, 285–288
Misconceptions, debates, 10–11
Mock trial debates, 68–71, 282
Model congress debate, 71–73, 282
Moral imperative, challenging, 121–122
Motivation, 35–36, 39, 291–297
Movement, speech delivery, 103
Multi-sided debate format, 75–77
Multiculturalism classroom debates, 237–241
Mutually eroding values, 119

National Forensic League website, 72
National identity, debates and, 183
Natural speech delivery principles, 102
Negated symbols, 105
Negative debating, 115–124, 289
Negative evidence, affirmative case building, 112
Neutral language, topics selection, 85
Newspapers, public debates and, 173–174
Nietzsche, Friedrich, 39–40

Notations, 98–99
Notes
  see also Flow sheets
  organization of, 24–25
  student audience and, 142–143
  taking while listening, 32
  teaching skills of, 103–106
Numbers, use in outlining, 98–99

Observers, inviting from outside, 134–135
Offensive topics, 85
O'Neil, Robert, 58–59
Online assistance. *see* Websites
Operationalizing issues of subject matter, 37–38
Opinions, 285, 287
Opposing sides, role in analysis, 6
Opposing viewpoints, critical evaluation of, 28–29
Oral communication skills, 30–32, 101–103
  see also Public speaking
Organization
  better debater, 289
  comprehension and, 97–98
  evaluating student, 155
  importance of, 94
  issues, 97
  major points, 98
  notes, 24–25
  signposting, 100
  speeches and, 97–101
  value of, 292

Paden, William E., 246
Panel of questioners format, 74–75
Paper, choice of for flowing, 104
Parameters, determining, 79–80
Parliamentary debate format, 282
Participants, variations of number, 73–74
Passive and active learning, 34–35
Pathos, rhetorical approaches, 17
Paul, Richard, 45
Pens, choice of for flowing, 104